They That
Be Wise

They That
Be Wise

A Novel

David D. Boggs

MOUNTAIN ARBOR
PRESS

MOUNTAIN ARBOR PRESS

Alpharetta, Georgia

ISBN: 978-1-6653-0899-1 - Paperback
eISBN: 978-1-6653-0900-4 - eBook

Library of Congress Control Number: 2024913172

♾This paper meets the requirements of ANSI/NISO Z39.48-1992 (Permanence of Paper)

070824

To my dear wife—thank you for trusting me!

*"And they that be wise shall shine as
the brightness of the firmament; and they that turn
many to righteousness as the stars for ever and ever."*

———————

Daniel 12:3

1

Summer 1980

It had been three days since Jesse Hunter received the message that his dad had died. The note stated that services would be on the following Saturday at the old graveyard.

When Jesse was little and months would stretch by without seeing his dad, he would sometimes pretend that his dad had died, just to see how he might feel. Most times it was sadness, occasionally a narrow nothingness, but in those times when loneliness would nearly swallow him whole, he couldn't hold back the tears. And now, years later, after it had finally come to pass, he didn't know what to feel. And that the news had come from his father's wife—a woman he hadn't known existed—only added to this uncertainty.

On his way to the services, aside from the occasional chitchat of his wife and three children, the drive was almost peaceful.

It had been years since he had been to Oakton, a little town in the north of the state, where his dad's claim to a place had mostly been just a post office box. Jesse wasn't even sure if he could remember the turn-off to the small, almost-hidden-from-itself farming town. Here, away from the crowded urban areas, where the land began to open, towns were few and sometimes marked out simply where two highways crossed, where a gas station, food market, feed store, and post office stood their ground from their respective corners.

But what anchored the land were the family ranches. Having lived here for generations, the people took their land for granted, but not in a thankless sense.

Out here, patchwork quilts of crops blanketed the land. Glass surfaces of the flooded rice fields, reflecting the lazy cumulus floating in the cerulean expanse above, blurred the boundaries. Alfalfa fields, plunging back from the roads, extended their sweet aroma to season the thick air. Only the sourness of the cattle pastures wounded the soft breezes. And in time, even that sharp odor would dissolve into the mildness of familiarity.

A grid of country roads, thick with dust, separated one's land from another's. Here, despite the frequent north wind's dryness and the summer's heat, walnut, prune, and almond (rhyming with salmon) trees bore their fruit.

Since hearing of his dad's death, Jesse had sifted through the memories he had held onto over the years, searching for just one that he could pocket for comfort. But like the dog that chases its tail, he gradually realized that which could not be caught must be given up.

Whenever Jesse thought of people, they appeared in a place, or grounded in a location. With his mother, it was primping in front of her vanity, imagining herself a movie star. And his mother-in-law presided over her polished dining table with her grand-children on one side and her daughters on the other, "holding court" during the formal dinners she insisted upon. And the rare times he allowed himself to think of his grandfather, the outline of his profile naturally blended with the ranch. But try as he might, he could not picture his dad in a home. Though, on those rare occasions when his dad did come to mind, his image suddenly materialized like a warning sign on a country road, illuminated by a passing car.

In math class, Jesse learned about angles—acute, obtuse, reflexive, and right. One day, as his teacher scratched out an acute angle on the chalkboard, it hit him; with lines joined together at the beginning, but growing farther apart as they extended into infinity, she was diagramming their relationship. But as different as Jessie and his dad were, they did share the sense of not belonging—their binding link.

This sense of not belonging had always been with him and dogged him even into marriage. Jesse loved his wife and children and appreciated his home and job. And that wasn't the issue anyway. It was just that he had never known what it felt like to belong anywhere. Most times he felt like a stranger in a strange land— the terrain and the language were familiar, but the customs were not. Though he knew his native land must exist, he wasn't sure how to ask anyone the way there.

. . .

"Who'll be at the funeral?" Alix asked, staring out the window, her needlepoint in a roll on her lap. "Anyone you've told me about?"

Tapping the brake to warn a tailgater, he answered, "Honestly, I don't know. Everyone's either died or moved away or I've lost touch with them."

Close to the road stood a vacant farmhouse. Gaping holes stared blankly where windows had once been. A cow munched some weeds at the steps of a leaning porch. "I guess Dad was about the last one."

Alix unrolled her needlepoint and measured out a length of yarn. "I hope you'll be all right up here." She attempted a few stabs to thread the needle, and then gave up, fishing through her purse for her glasses.

He knew he was a source of worry for her, and it had gotten to the point where he was even beginning to concern himself. He knew he was withdrawing more into himself; into a world that existed more in his head. It was in this place that he hoped worry and anxiety would not find him. When he and Alix were first married, he shared easily. But lately with the kids and other demands, he began to feel he kept shutting the doors.

In the city, where he worked, Jesse was the perpetual observer. Most times he felt invisible, and often he could convince himself that no one could see him unless he willed it. But this game only reinforced the nagging feeling that he didn't belong. In his work as a financial manager, he felt he was merely pantomiming the actions, giving his boss the reports he expected—handing in the analysis because it needed to be done, not because he enjoyed doing it. He felt as indistinguishable as one column of numbers from another on those reports.

He often found himself drifting off, daydreaming about a life without responsibilities. Lately, he felt as though he was acting in the wrong movie—and a bad actor at that. Feeling sorry for Alix and the kids, he wondered if she should have married someone else.

He knew his anxiety was catching up to him and something needed to be done. During the past several months, he frequently had the same nightmare. It would start off behind the wheel of an expensive car he couldn't afford, on a narrow road climbing a mountainside. But that didn't seem to worry him; he knew he was a good driver. But, stealing a glimpse over the side, he realized— one wrong move and the car would fly off the road and crash below.

Then in the next scene, he felt the road growing narrower while he fought hard to keep the car to the inside edge. As the tires would begin spinning away at the soft shoulder, and feeling the car slip over the edge, he would wake up in a cold sweat, where he would discover Alix tenderly stroking his head.

Though awake and safe from the nightmare, he knew deep down he was in danger. He knew it wasn't the car that was heading towards destruction; it was him recklessly moving towards a nervous breakdown.

One night, the nightmare included Alix and the children in the car with him. It had taken Alix longer than usual to calm him, but just as he drifted back to sleep, she asked if she could call her counselor friend for help.

He ignored her. It wasn't that he didn't want to share his fears; it was just that he didn't know where to start.

"You know, Jesse," Alix broke through his reverie, "Dr. Laurel says—"

"Who's Dr. Laurel?"

"You know! The psychologist on the radio." She pretended not to notice when he rolled his eyes. "Anyway, she says that sometimes when people have had a difficult childhood, it affects them more when they have children."

He watched her begin playing with her hair as she always did when she was uncertain.

"Not sure what you mean?" He stared straight ahead, grinding his teeth.

Alix leaned in towards him. "Dr. Laurel says as children approach each age, this often opens the doors of their parents' childhood. And if the parents had a tough growing-up, they tend to always trip over this until it's resolved." She cleared her throat. "And though you barely say much about yours anymore, it's becoming more apparent it's affecting you."

"You mean when we first married, I was all fun and games, not a care in the world. But now with children I'm no fun and a bore! I'm losing it?"

"Not exactly." She glanced over her shoulder at the three who were playing a game. "But you have to admit you've been acting differently."

"Come on, Alix …"

"What, Jesse? I'm worried."

"Hey, did I ever tell you … did you hear about the parrot that spent five minutes in the freezer as a punishment for saying a four-letter word and when he was let out wanted to know what the chicken had done? See, I can be light."

"Make jokes if you want but it's getting worse." She punched the needle through the canvas but pulled it out, noticing it was the wrong color.

"You don't enjoy the children's activities. You always have some excuse when it comes time to play catch with Tyler or when I asked you to take him to baseball tryouts."

Jesse gripped the steering wheel, watching the color disappear from his knuckles.

"Remember the time during Jordan's parent-teacher conference you sat in a daze and said nothing? Or the time you had an anxiety attack and had to leave in the middle of Claire's dance recital? And ..." She took a deep breath and ran her fingers through her hair. "How about the nights at the dinner table, when you sit and stare off?"

"Come on, give me a break. I told you I grew up with a son of a bitch of a stepfather who wouldn't allow anyone to talk at the table. That's where most of the fighting started. I can't tell you how many times I had to pick my dinner plate up off the floor where Jack had thrown it. You'd feel the same—"

"I know, honey. But still, you're not there with us."

"Not true! I'm there. You're not giving me enough credit. In fact, I'm there a lot. Now ... take my dad. He was never—"

"Ah. That's it. We're not talking about your dad. And you are there, but not all of you. Jesse, we need more of you. When the children are sharing with you, they need to know you're listening with your heart, not your ears. They need to know that you're not fighting each moment you're with them, gritting your teeth and looking like a racehorse, ready to bolt at any second. You know kids are very intuitive. They know when they have half your attention."

God! How he hated talking about this, especially knowing she was right. Usually when the conversation wasn't going his way, he'd head out and jump in his car, pursuing some errand.

"Dammit!" he said under his breath when he slammed on his brakes, avoiding a car intent on making a U-turn across the median. "Hell. You know I love you and the kids."

"We know. But where are you when you're quiet and staring off?"

"Look. Do we have to talk about this now? We're on our way to a funeral!"

2

Of the places he had created to escape, the ranch's garden was Jesse's favorite. He liked to picture himself under the warm sun, his hands working the dark cool earth, preparing it for the seedlings that he would watch grow to mark his days.

The garden was square with a fountain in the middle where the two gravel walkways intersected. The fountain's soothing bubbling and the mourning doves balancing on the edge always seemed to mend his frayed nerves. To the south stood a square house surrounded by a porch. And on the north side, a walnut tree shaded a latticed summerhouse; there he imagined Alix, a subtle breeze playing with her hair, as she would read letters to him from their grown children, describing how happy and safe they were. This imaginary scene always calmed him.

"Jesse?" Alix nudged him.

"Yeah? Sorry."

"Where are you?"

"I don't know."

"Jess. Come on."

"I don't know how to explain. I do disappear at times. I admit it. Like my mind is somewhere else."

"Where?"

"I don't know, exactly … a place where problems don't exist. A world of my own making. No stress, no fear … where I belong."

"Well, then you're not too far away."

"Why do you say that?"

"Because you belong here with us. We love you very much. You just must believe it. Trust it!" She poked him in the ribs. "And besides, when you find the place where problems don't exist, you'll …"

"I'll what?" He glanced over.

"You'll have your own radio program." She smiled at her cleverness.

He felt relieved she was pleased.

"Didn't you say your grandfather taught you a lot?"

"Yeah. But he didn't teach me about being a good husband and father."

"Really? Are you sure? Maybe it wasn't in the specifics."

"Specifics?"

"You know, an artist is taught about composition, color, texture—the techniques. Then he goes on to apply them to his own creation. Kind of like this needlepoint. Someone drew out the design, but it's up to me to complete it."

"So? What has that to do with Gramps?" Funny she should speak about the artist, he thought. His grandfather had explained to him and his three cousins the same thing that summer, years ago, when they had planted walnut trees on the Three Sisters' Place.

"Just that … when I first met you, you used to speak of your grandfather, your eyes would light up, you'd become more animated. You seemed to … I don't know … breathe differently."

"Really? You could see that?"

"Uh-huh."

"He was wonderful!" he blurted out, surprising himself. "He helped me get through."

The memories of his grandfather were precious treasures, like photographs, hidden deep in a vault safe from a corrosive world. Only when no one was around could they be taken out and studied.

"He must have been very wise and giving to have done that. You complain about not having a dad to ask advice from. Well, maybe your grandfather is the one that can help you."

"But how? He's dead."

"Think back to what he taught you."

"It's been too many years." He shook his head slowly. "I've tried. It's like I can't get to it."

"What do you mean you can't get to it?"

"It's like I'm in a labyrinth at times. I can go forward, or I can go backward, but I'm not sure I'm moving in the right direction. I know what he taught me is somewhere there; I just can't figure out how to get to it."

"Haven't you asked yourself why you drove up here?"

"To pay my respects to a dad who was never there?" He slowed the station wagon down. "You think I shouldn't have come up?"

"No. I mean this was where your grandfather lived. Maybe you really came up here to connect with that. Your dad's funeral was just a reason."

"But I did want to say goodbye."

He remembered the last time he had said goodbye to his dad. Driving the massive diesel tractor, Jesse had watched him from the side of a fence. When he tried to shout goodbye, the tractor's deafening noise had swallowed up his words. He hadn't thought of that in years.

"I'm sure that's part of it." She checked the needlepoint for any missed stitches.

"Maybe you're right. It wasn't really for the funeral—I mean, for my dad. Hell, I'm sure he wouldn't have come to mine. He never responded to our wedding announcement or the kid's birth announcements."

"Being with your grandfather was a good time for you, wasn't it?"

Strange how the years seemed to crowd out what he had learned from the old man. He had grown tired of fighting. And yet, now at this moment, maybe he was being given a chance to get back to what his grandfather had taught him.

At the county line, he was amazed how tangible the feelings of his grandfather had suddenly become. He wondered why. Was it the smell of freshly mown alfalfa drifting from the fields? Or the way the sun shone through the orchards leaving jigsaw shadows on the ground? Or was it the oak trees with their outstretched branches, beckoning to him while shading the farmhouses beneath?

"We love you, Jesse." Alix patted his leg.

"I'm not sure I deserve it."

"Don't ever say that. You're a good person. You deserve—"

"Daddy, how much longer?" Claire, his eldest daughter, squirmed in her seat. "I'm tired of sitting here. Can't we stop for something to eat?"

Her sister, Jordan, looked up from her sports magazine. She always wore her baseball hat backwards. "Yeah, come on, Dad. I'm thirsty."

The rear-view mirror framed the two pleading faces.

Then from the last seat, five-year-old Tyler turned from the game he played with the passing cars, winning points for each driver who returned his wave. "Daddy, will I get to see your daddy?"

Claire rolled her eyes. "No, Tyler. Daddy's father's dead. We're going to the funeral."

Tyler, with a shrug of his shoulders, resumed waving at passing cars.

A few minutes later, they passed a weathered sign that read,

"Welcome to Oakton County
The best kept secret"

Nearly twenty years had passed since Jesse had been here, but suddenly it all was familiar. As a rule, small farming towns don't change much. It wasn't so much on the surface that he detected the change; it was something deeper. A feeling that they were waiting for him, that he was supposed to be here.

Coming up on the right was an exit that drew him off the freeway.

Alix surveyed the area. "Are we close?"

"Are we there yet?" Claire chimed in.

"Almost." He pointed to the east. "See the hills?"

"There, Dad?" Jordan pointed.

"That's it."

"What are they called?"

"The Buttes. The smallest mountain range in the world. And to their west is the town. See that continuous line of trees? They're cottonwoods, and between them is the river. And a little further north, not far from that is Hunter's Bluff."

"What's Hunter's Bluff?" Claire asked.

"The place on my grandfather's ranch where the riverboat would dock."

Just before town, he saw a speed limit sign that was used for target practice. He tapped his brake. And farther down, partially tucked behind a Duck Club sign, a mud-spattered patrol car sat. He tapped the brake again.

"There above the trees ..." He pointed.

"What? Above what trees?" Claire scanned the horizon.

"The steeple. That's the church in the graveyard.

"Yes, we're almost there." He took a deep breath. "Not much longer." His middle daughter stared back at the pair of eyes in the mirror. "I promise."

One after another, down the road in single file, they came—pickups, so thick with dirt, their original color had long ago been forgotten. He knew he stuck out like a sore thumb in the recently washed station wagon.

At the edge of town, the golden dome of the courthouse protruded above a cloud of cottonwoods.

It was all coming back to him, much like discovering one's childhood drawings tucked safely in the pages of a book on a top shelf. Jesse scanned the rice fields where the green shoots poked through the water's placid surface and farmhouses floated, stranded like islands in archipelagoes.

"It's been so long, so long," he said mostly to himself. Poking his head out the window, he let the air thick with fragrances pound against his face. *Gramps?* He sent the words silently into the wind. *Are you there?*

Stashing her book away in her backpack, Claire glanced out the window. "Daddy, what was it like here? Did you like it?"

"Yes. I loved being here."

"But I thought you missed your mom while you were here."

"Yeah. But I had some special times up here."

"What kind of special times?" Jordan piped up.

Jesse hesitated for a moment for the picture to come to him, a little grateful to Alix for her prodding. "My grandfather was a wise old man, and one summer we spent together … well, what he shared opened up a whole new world to me."

Harvesting the scene with his eyes, gathering it all in, not willing to miss a grain, he knew now why the drive was feeling different. He could feel the memories of his grandfather guide their way to fill his thoughts. This was where his grandfather had lived—still lived in a sense. The old man was waiting for him.

Alix pointed out a farmhouse.

"That reminds me," Jesse said, "of the house my grandfather built on the ranch."

"What was it like?" Claire asked.

"Well, I can see it as plain as day. There was a huge oak tree that shaded the house. The house was perfectly square and two stories. I remember the yard had lots of flowers and shrubs. Gramps loved flowers. Oh yeah. It had a picket fence to keep the chickens out."

"Why?" Claire asked.

"Because chickens will destroy flowers. And green-and-white

striped canvas awnings hung above the windows upstairs to block the sun. Downstairs, a covered porch encircled the house—keeping the downstairs rooms cooler. A fruit orchard blocked the house from the road. Gave it a little privacy."

"What kind of fruit trees?" Alix asked.

"Oranges, lemons, figs, pomegranates ... but the one we all loved was the bloody-orange tree." Will's tree—he hadn't thought about that in years.

"A bloody what?" Claire made a face.

"A bloody orange, at least that's what we called it. Inside, it's a deep red. The fruit is very sweet. It was special because we hadn't seen one."

Driving into Oakton, Alix and the children fell silent as they entered a place they had scarcely heard about but one that they sensed had affected Jesse in a profound way.

Oversized two-story homes, built with the money that the Southern founding fathers brought with them after the Civil War, lined both sides of 10th Street.

Just before the river, he made a right onto Market Street, where he searched for the train tracks that were no longer there.

Market Street, once bustling with businesses, was nearly deserted. But the old courthouse stood proud, like an old Southern gentleman, ignoring the changes nipping at his ankles.

The end of the street gave way to a narrow, graveled road that led to an oasis-like plot of property dotted with ancient oaks shading a neatly mown lawn. A white clapboard church anchored the corner of the graveyard as it had done for as long as anyone's memory.

Navigating through the fieldstone posts, he drove around the remains of a rusty gate that someone had dragged to the side. The crunching of the gravel from the tires announced their arrival to the deaf old graveyard. Near the main road in the older section stood monuments, many of sculptured marble angels with outstretched wings, perched as though ready for flight, but kept back by years of weathering. In the back, in the newer section, grass bordered the smaller monuments set in the ground.

Back there, someone had set up a blue awning. Underneath, two rows of chairs faced each other, but no one was around.

Jesse had barely stopped the car before the children spilled out and ran towards the stones. Grabbing his tie and jacket, he trailed Alix to the awning. On the ground, amidst the chairs, bouquets of flowers barely hid a mound of fresh dirt. Twenty yards away, an old man trimmed a rosebush.

Waving to get the man's attention, he shouted, "I've come from out of town for a funeral. Do you know where the services would be?"

The man eyed the children who darted close to his newly pruned roses. "Well, don't know of anymore, except the one you're standing at, a few hours ago."

Following the man's gaze, Jesse confronted the mound of flowers.

A little bit away, the children dashed from one stone to another. Discovering a row of stones with their family name chiseled deep, they whooped and hollered, yelling out the names. With each name the children called out, an image began to drift his way.

Right now, he wanted more than anything to be alone. Having driven all the way up anticipating this funeral, and discovering it had all happened without him, he didn't know now what to think or do. The tension building had stiffened his shoulder and neck muscles, the telltale beginnings of one of his migraines. Jesse searched for a place where he could rest and noticed a stone bench nearby, beckoning.

Alix snuck up behind him and massaged a knot in his neck. "Are you going to be okay?"

"Yeah. I'll be all right."

"I'm sorry."

"You know, it's not any different now." He wondered who had attended the services and who had left the flowers. "This was the way it always was. He would never talk to me. It was always like there was six feet of plexiglass between us. Now it's six feet of earth."

Coming around, she cupped his face in her hands. "I love you."

"Alix, I'll try to be bet—"

She put her finger to his lips. "Shhh … don't worry about that. You need to say goodbye now." She turned to catch up to the children and laughed as she joined them in their adventure of seeking unknown relations in the stones.

Soon, a breeze washed over him. Lying back on the bench, he closed his eyes, and strangely, the throbbing in his head began to disappear. It was as though the porous stone bench was absorbing the stress.

He shuddered to think where he would've been without that summer he spent with his grandfather. How had his life changed because of this place? That summer of his fifteenth year, he had come here, after so many years of being beaten down by his step-father Jack, convinced he was worthless and belonged to no one. But then miraculously, at that summer's end, he returned home bearing his grandfather's gift.

The gentle cooing of a mourning dove, beckoning to her mate nearby, was the declaration that the key had turned, and the door was now opening wide for him. Somehow, he realized this was the only place that could take all his anxieties away. The irony was not lost when he considered how strange it was to be reborn here, in this place where they laid the dead.

Though the cemetery was empty, he was not alone; everyone was here, after all. Without any effort, he found himself falling back rapidly.

3

Summer 1960

I n the kitchen, Jesse's mother sat motionless as a statue, waiting for one of Jack's tirades to end. Down the hall, with a pillow over his head, Jesse lay captive in one of his frequent nightmares.

Jack yelled that she was a cretin because she had forgotten to pick up his dry cleaning! She was a moron because she hadn't remembered that he was to try an important case the next day! She was stupid because he wouldn't be able to wear his favorite suit because she hadn't thought to pick it up at the laundry!

Knowing Lynn was working hard not to react, which always made him angrier, he grabbed a plate from the cupboard and sent it flying across the room, where it shattered at her feet in pieces, before sending another. But still, she willed herself not to move.

After the last plate came the frightening silence. Exchanging one nightmare for another, Jesse, now fully awake, every muscle tensed, stared at the door waiting for the all too familiar next scene.

"What the hell!" Jack fumbled with the knob. "Goddammit! I told you never to lock this door!"

Two powerful kicks split the door in two. One half crashed to the floor while the other half stubbornly clung to its hinges. Once again, Jack would have more to complain about when he'd fix it later, after he'd calmed down.

Standing in the middle of the room now was a little man whose anger convulsed his little frame of a body. His eyes bulged, and the muscles of his neck throbbed. A protruding artery on his neck looked like it was ready to burst. Though Lynn's feeble protests traveled down the hall, she knew better than to follow.

"What are you still doing in bed?" he growled. "You little asshole!" His thin, nicotine-stained lips, tightly wrapped around the butt of a cigarette bobbing up and down, accentuated each word.

Over the years, Jesse would force himself to make up funny things to think about when Jack was like this. It was the only way he could duck from his fear and sidestep the sourness beginning to rise from his stomach. Sometimes, when Jack would come home bragging about how great a day he had in court, Jesse would picture him dressed in a Tarzan loincloth, beating his chest. Other times, during Jack's more violent outbursts, Jesse envisioned a runt of a yappy dog that peed when it was overly excited. Whenever he conjured up these images, an unconscious smile materialized that had unintentional effects, like adding oxygen to a spark; Jack's anger would burst into a full flame. When he was in a fit like this, it was best to try to be invisible. But there was nowhere to hide.

"What d'ya ...what d'ya think this is, a resort?" Jack spewed. Though he lost interest in every project he began, as seen by the unfinished jobs around the house, he possessed a talent for not letting up until his victims had felt the full brunt of his wrath.

"By the time I get back, you ..." He caught sight of Jesse's duffle bag over in the corner, and a crooked grin appeared on his contorted face. "You better have your lazy ass outta this house." Turning on his heel, Jack kicked the splintered half door out of his way before stomping down the hall and storming outside, slamming the front door so hard the house shook. Whenever Jack left, it was as though Jesse and his mother gasped for air until the house could refill with oxygen.

In the silence that followed these outbursts, his mother would typically appear at his side. When Jesse was little, he believed she came to comfort, but as he grew older, he realized it was she who sought solace.

But today was different. There was no time for that. A few days ago, school had let out for summer vacation. Soon his mother would drop him off at the train station, and then after a two-hour journey he would be safely at his grandfather's ranch. And it was there he was to spend the summer with his father, Daniel Samuel Hunter.

Jesse looked forward to the summer visits with his grand-father, but his dad puzzled him. When his dad would ask him questions, they seemed forced. And then when Jesse would try to answer, Dan seemed more interested in his latest hunting mag-azine.

Though the ranch was Dan's home, Jesse's grandfather, Samuel Orion Hunter, had given up on keeping track of him. Over the years, Sam grew accustomed to his eldest son seldom being home at night. When the upstairs bedroom grew unbearably hot, Dan would often throw a sleeping bag in the back of his pickup where he would sleep out on the side of a deserted road under the stars. A loner and a drifter, showing no concern for things and less for comfort, he seemed to exist in a perpetual state of denial. A few women who had dared to get to know him couldn't tell after the encounter if he was really a deep thinker or just angry.

Dan was a rugged man. Jet-black hair crowning a chiseled face caused many heads in town to turn. Sky-blue eyes topped an aq-uiline nose, with full lips and a defined cleft chin below. Though he kept to himself much of the time, what kept people at bay was Dan's uneasy silence. When Jesse wanted to conjure up his dad, the image that materialized was a man leaning against a fence, a cigarette dangling from his bottom lip, his sinewy arms tightly crossed over his chest. In a perpetual squint, he seemed to stare through his cigarette's cloud of smoke with a look of defiance.

Jesse had memories from the time he was about five or six, when his dad was more there than not. Many times, on their walks, he would entertain Jesse with a funny story. Most stories revolved around the farmyard animals getting into predicaments based on their own personality quirks. He also had a knack to end each story in a way that made the animals funny to picture, making Jesse laugh out loud. And with each laugh, Dan's eyes would sparkle.

It was during this period that Jesse felt his dad's existence was more like a power than a person. Like the power Jesse felt as a youngster when his dad picked him up one day to toss him over an irrigation canal so that he wouldn't have to walk all the way around to the bridge. For a split second, sailing over the canal, he felt as though he was weightless and free. And the thrill came from knowing that he was sailing through the air because of his father's strength. He felt proud and safe to know that it was his own dad who was this strong.

But as Jesse grew older, in proportion as his dad's power seemed to fade, his dad's distance grew more apparent. Left behind was just a form. A form that was disappearing into a shadow, which was always away, "working up north."

Now, Jesse crawled out of bed, stepping around the remnants of the splintered door. Searching through his jeans pocket, he pulled out the train schedule; the train wouldn't leave for another hour. He felt torn about leaving. Though he would miss his mother and worry about her, he couldn't help counting the days before he could escape.

Lately, he had the impression that he was there for a specific purpose—his mother's purpose. As Jack grew increasingly more violent, it dawned on Jesse that his mother relied on him differently now. He grew convinced his sole purpose was to protect her. He began to hate Jack for how he treated his mother. And as Jack grew more aware of Jesse's hatred for him, the more his wrath spread from Lynn to him.

In letters to his grandfather, Jesse was tempted to write the old man what his life was like. But he knew he couldn't—not exactly anyway. Lynn warned that if the old man ever discovered what their lives were like, she would forbid Jesse his trips to the ranch. She feared Sam would go to court and take Jesse away from her. And if this were to get out, Jack would be sure to lose his position at the law firm and her life would be even more miserable. After time, Jesse had convinced himself that she needed his protection, because without him she would fear for her life.

Dragging his duffle bag down the hall, he found his mother where Jack had left her, hunched over the kitchen table, surrounded by a half-circle of broken dishes, staring at the front door.

"I'm sorry." She sniveled and tried to get to her feet. Grinding her cigarette into a pile of last night's dried dinner, she turned to him. "I know what you think, but it's not his fault. Not this time, anyway. He's under a lot of pressure. He has a big case coming up."

Jesse had learned these were the familiar, empty words that were really for herself. "Mom! Look at me! Look at this place! How much longer—"

"Stop!" She doubled over and fell back in her chair. Jesse guessed her ulcer must be acting up again.

She searched her robe pockets for matches and lit another cigarette. "And this your last morning here before you leave."

"Mom?" Their eyes played cat and mouse. "Maybe I shouldn't go—"

"Of course, you'll go." She exhaled a sphere of gray smoke that surrounded her. As she pushed her hair back, Jesse saw a fresh bruise above her eye. Again, her eyes filled with tears. "I'll ... miss you ... terribly. But it'll be okay. Honest. I'll be all right."

Suddenly the clock over the stove captured her interest, and she quickly checked the one on the wall. Then she examined her wristwatch.

"They're wrong! They're all wrong!" she cried out, as though she had just awakened from a stupor.

Disappearing down the hallway, she cried out, "You can't miss the train. I can't have your grandfather thinking something might be wrong."

. . .

As the train pulled out of the station, Lynn sat in her convertible in the parking lot waving. Jesse waved back though he wanted to turn away. But he knew this would cause more tears. The ranch was supposed to be a place of escape, and he couldn't make a clean break with a picture of his crying mother trailing him.

Gathering speed, while the train click-clacked, click-clacked down the track, he took deep breaths and tried to settle in, praying for the calm that usually came if he was patient.

The city buildings quickly gave way to tracts of houses, and then to farmhouses surrounded by open fields. This train ride was a necessary part of the transition needed to leave his mother and Jack behind.

Through the countryside, the train picking up full speed pulled him further from his mother. He felt like a giant rubber band—part of him stretched out toward the ranch while the other part latched onto his mother. If only he were strong enough, he would pull her with him onto the ranch. But, before he knew it, like a rubber band stretched beyond its limit—snapping, they would both fly in opposite directions.

The first landmark Jesse always looked for when the train crossed the county line was the outline of the small mountain range that lay to the east, not far from his grandfather's ranch. The sight of these twin peaks acted as a beacon of safety, ensuring he was far from Jack. And not until the water tower at the river's edge in Oakton appeared would he be convinced that this world and Jack's would never overlap.

Rumbling slowly down the middle of Market Street, the train came to a halt at the foot of the courthouse steps. Jesse grabbed his duffle bag and checked for his dad, but he was nowhere in sight. The conductor threw a stool out to the street for Jesse to step down on.

From the middle of the street, he scoured the sidewalks but saw no one. Seconds later, the train's whistle cut through the air, announcing its departure.

The town seemed deserted and too quiet—it gave him a creepy feeling. If it were all in black and white, it would have reminded him of the beginning of a *Twilight Zone* episode. But the sweet smell of alfalfa drifting from fields across the river calmed him a bit. Thinking he might have to wait for his dad, he headed towards a shady place near one of the marble statues on the courthouse stairs. As he reached the steps, a familiar voice broke the silence.

"Hey. Nephew! I'm over here." Jesse caught sight of a man bounding around the corner. "How the hell are you?"

"Hey, Uncle." Jesse peered around the big man. "Where's Dad?"

"Oh. Your dad. Um, I think he's working up north. He should be back down in a few days … he's … well … um … How the hell are you?" Colton grabbed Jesse's hand and shook it up and down quickly as though he were priming a pump.

It was strange how different Colton Pearson Hunter was from his older brother. If Dan had been the only son, then with Colton not around, Dan's coldness might not be so obvious. But Colton was the light side of the moon to Dan's dark side. When Dan entered a room, people marked the exits, but when Colton followed, it was as though he had thrown open all the windows, allowing everyone to exhale.

Laugh lines in the shape of a sunburst accentuated Colton's light blue eyes. So proud was he of his thick blond hair, he refused to wear a cowboy hat. Once he admitted to his wife, Lil, that he knew he was good-looking, but he assured her he would always be faithful. Though barrel-chested and robust, he was not over-weight, just solid. He loved flexing his biceps for his three daughters, who squealed with laughter while Lil rolled her eyes in mock exasperation.

Colton always had a joke or funny story ready and was con-stantly winking and poking someone in the side at the punch line. But all that paled in comparison to what impressed Jesse the most about his uncle: He was the kindest man Jesse had ever known.

"Come on. It's hotter than hell out here." Colton scooped up the duffle bag and disappeared around the corner, with Jesse try-ing to keep up. "Let's get you out to your grandpa's. Been talking about nothing more all week long."

Shoving a stack of hunting and fishing magazines off the seat, Jesse climbed into the pickup. "How's Gramps?"

"Fine, fine. Slowing down a little. But that's to be expected. Not as young as he would like you to believe."

At the end of Main Street, he made a left onto Bridge Street, which led out of town. But the middle section of the bridge had turned to allow a barge to pass by.

Colton cut the engine and sank back in the seat before fishing a cigarette from a pack wedged in the sun visor. "D'ya smoke?" he said as he lit it.

Jesse stared.

"Don't worry. I wouldn't tell the old man if you did."

Jesse shook his head.

"Just as well. They'll do you in, eventually. Haw, haw, haw!" Colton reached over to poke him in the side, but Jesse dodged him.

"Hey. Everything okay?"

"Sorry, Uncle. I was just wondering why Dad didn't come."

"Well. Jesse, he's busy right now. I know he was sorry he couldn't pick you up. But he told me that he'll be around in the next few days." He took a drag from his cigarette and concentrated on blowing perfectly formed smoke rings out the window.

"But, hey, the old man is anxious for you to come. He's got your area in the garden ready to plant, and he's got the chores all set out for you to..." Colton eyed Jesse, who didn't seem to be listening, staring at the slow-moving barge. "How's your mother and ... um ... hell, what's his name again? I always—"

"You mean Jack?" Why did his uncle have to ask about him? The whole point of the train trip was to put Jack out of his mind. The air currents here should never bear the sound of his name. In this country, Jack was nothing—having no weight, no substance, no existence.

"Mom is fine. And Jack's Jack."

His uncle seemed to make a face like he got a whiff of something decaying at the river's edge. "Gonna ask me about the cousins?"

Jesse sat up, glad the subject was changing. "When will I get to see Leeney?" Leeney was all tomboy, and because she and Jesse were born within days of each other, the family referred to them as the "twins." Leeney was the youngest of the girls, Steph was a year older, and Shay, a year older than her.

"Leeney'll be around shortly. But you won't see your Aunt Lil or Steph or Shay for another month."

"Why not?"

"They're traveling."

"Why didn't Leeney or you go?"

"At this time of year?" Colton cast Jesse a look as though he asked where they could buy a Christmas tree. "This is the busiest time. Lil knows I can't take off now. And you know Leeney, she won't leave my side. The other two insisted on going with their mother. Frankly, between us girls ... haw, haw, haw ... being cooped up in a henhouse is not all it's made out to be."

By this time, the bridge had completed its turn back towards the road.

"Where'd they go?"

"St. Louis."

"What for?"

Colton turned the ignition and threw the pickup into gear. "Something they're pursuing. They've got it in their head that ... well. It has nothing to do with anything." He cleared his throat and spat out the window. "Hey. How's school going? Going out for football this fall?"

Ah. Questions about sports at school. He was always the last one chosen for team sports, and it was humiliating to watch the team captains exchange looks as to who would get stuck with him. It wasn't that he didn't have athletic ability. He was a good athlete on his own. He was a strong runner in track and not bad in tennis. But he couldn't connect in team sports. Whatever the sport, when the ball came in his direction and all eyes were on him, the knot in his stomach got tighter until he threw the ball to someone else.

"No. No football this year." Before his uncle continued down the list of sports, he asked, "How are the horses? Any new ones? Gramps wrote something about Bella ready to foal soon. When's she gonna have it?"

"The next few weeks, for sure." He winked at Jesse. "Might be a little surprise there for you."

"Surprise? What d'ya mean?"

"Never mind. I've said too much already." He flicked the cigarette out the window. "And your grandfather just took another horse for trade—Mad Hatter Max, I call him."

"Can I ride him?"

Colton shook his head. "I'm not sure. The old man thinks he's too unstable. Mistreated or something. I'm not too worried about him. But just the same, I told him I'd try to work it out of him. He just needs to know who's in charge, that's all. In fact, I think he's a damn fine horse. A Tennessee Walker, he is. The Walkers are friendly. So, I don't know what's got into this one. But he'll be okay. If you're lucky, we'll get him so you can ride him before you head home."

The land on the other side of the bridge was known as the Eastside. Several miles up the road, at Sam's ranch, the road made a sharp left, drawing close to the river's edge at the Bluff, the ranch's western border. And opposite, to the east, the land extended back hundreds of acres toward the gentle rise of the Buttes.

The first ranch after the bridge was called the Three Sisters' Place. Though his grandfather had bought it years ago, to the older folks, a place never gave up the original family's name. The land had been lately plowed, and the roadside frontage had neat rows of holes newly drilled.

"What's going on there?" Jesse pointed.

"The old man's going to plant some walnuts on the front section. Get ready for some hard work."

That reminded him of a picnic his grandfather's housekeeper, Stanza, and her husband had prepared there near the river before he left for home last summer.

"Uncle. How's Stanza and Hank?"

"Ah. They're both fine. They're visiting with Stanza's pack of relatives in Mexico. But they should be back soon. She wouldn't leave your grandfather for too long." He chuckled. "He won't admit it, but he's gotten so used to having her around, he couldn't get along without her. And Hank keeps up on the yard."

Black walnut trees bordered the road, casting a little shade on their drive. Mailboxes at the edge of the road marked where the gravel paths led to houses hidden deep in the orchards.

Within a few minutes, Colton approached the home place. Slowing down, he maneuvered between the stone gates into the graveled yard. From somewhere deep in the walnut orchard, the old man's dogs raced towards the pickup.

"Well. Here we are. Listen, I'm going to let you greet the old man yourself. I've got a thousand things to do. But I'll see you soon. I'll bring Leeney down soon, and you both can catch up. Okay?"

4

L ater that evening, a gentle breeze from the west stirred the leaves to shimmer in the twilight. Above the horizon, where the edge of the hills looked as though they had been torn from paper, layers of orange, yellow, and blue shone luminescence. But then with each degree of the sun's decline, the oranges and yellows conceded to the deeper reds before finally surrendering to the deepest of blues.

Oblivious of the display above, Jesse trudged along the dusty road returning from his hike from the back field. His grandfather had been out when he'd arrived that afternoon, and he'd gotten tired of waiting around the house. As he walked, the dogs pestered him, dropping sticks at his feet. He tossed one as far as he could and watched the dogs scramble for it.

A mourning dove sang her way from a nearby tree, and he imagined how her nest, high above, protected her nestlings from all that would try to invade their safety. He wished his mother could feel the peace here that they never would feel at home.

Walking on, kicking at the dirt clods in the road to watch them explode into dust, suddenly, a strong baritone voice rang out through the orchard. "Yo, Jesse! Dinner's ready."

With that, the dogs made a beeline to the house, and Jesse joined their race.

Underneath the trumpet vine at the outdoor sink, he splashed cold water on his face. On the porch, the dogs paced in anxious circles, as they did every night at supper time. Hopping up the porch stairs and remembering his discovery that afternoon, Jesse leaned over the railing to get another glimpse of the cellar's stairwell.

Stepping into the kitchen, he was almost overcome with the heat. But the smell of his grandfather's cooking made his stomach grumble with hunger, seeming to make the heat a fair price to pay. Jesse hung his hat next to his grandfather's on the rack near the mirror.

Catching a glimpse of himself in the glass, he brushed his blond hair out of his eyes. That afternoon, when his grandfather had returned from the Giffen place down the road, the first thing he'd said was that Jesse could use a haircut. He ran his fingers through the unruly mess. His skin, though now pale white, in a few weeks would be a chestnut brown like his grandfather's. At summer's end when Lynn would meet him at the station, she would remark how her son had changed into a gypsy.

Brushing his hand across his chin, he wanted to shave, but you couldn't waste a razor on "peach fuzz." He wished he was better looking. At least the kind of looks that made the girls' heads turn. He knew he wasn't awful looking, but he always felt awkward and clumsy. Once after pestering his mother whether he looked like his dad, she had told him he had his father's blue eyes, then walked away seeming pleased that the resemblance ended there. He wished his nose wasn't so broad, but his mother had assured him he would "grow into it." Puffing himself up a little, he inspected his chest and arms. Noticing how the girls looked at the guys in the weight room at school, he had begun to do push-ups every morning.

"Jesse Samuel Hunter!" The old man held out a plate full of fried chicken smothered in milk gravy, fried okra, and buttermilk biscuits. "Here, this is yours. And if you can break away from admiring the lad in the mirror, get us some tea!"

He slid his plate onto the table and then grabbed two mason jars from the sideboard.

"Hope you're hungry," Gramps commented more to himself than to Jesse. "I'm sure I've cooked more than we can possibly eat. Not used to cooking for a bunch of people anymore," he added under his breath.

As if the heat outside wasn't enough, the wood stove made the kitchen as hot as Nebuchadnezzar's fire. The old man brushed beads of sweat from his face with his sleeve. Arm garters held up the long sleeves of his blue work shirt. His blue jeans were new, but his laced-up work boots had been seasoned decades before. From the back pocket of his jeans, a faded blue bandana corner stuck out. The tightly cinched brown belt held everything together, seeming to show that the old man was always in control. Though he hunched over just a bit, which subtracted from his former six feet, he was still solid.

In the living room, resting on the mantel in a silver frame was a sepia-toned photograph of his grandfather taken some time in his late teens. Sometimes, Jesse would sneak into the living room and stare at the likeness, wishing he could have known his grandfather then. The picture captured him with hair falling over the clean lines of his forehead, with a strong jaw and nose and deep-set eyes. Broad-shouldered, he stood with arms crossed over his chest, staring back at the camera with a wide, toothy grin.

Jesse slid into a chair at the table. A noisy old fan on the sideboard stirred the air faintly. Unlike the rest of the large farmhouse, the kitchen was bare of any decoration. On the ranch, everything had a purpose and was deliberately placed, where it was readily available. This carried over to the kitchen.

Jesse relished how different this kitchen was from his mother's, which had sleek chrome fixtures and matching plastic upholstered chairs surrounding a red Formica table. Her dishes, always being replaced, were hidden behind cabinet doors. But here, in this eating area, worn and shiny from many years of use, rested an old table with a half-dozen mismatched chairs surrounding it. Next to the table was an antique pine sideboard, now bereft of paint, stacked full of dishes on its open shelves with a dozen mason jars lined up—the only drinking glasses.

At home, his mother kept the windows shut in the summer with the air conditioner perpetually on, which caused Jack to yell about the utility bill. But here, across from the stove, two open windows above the sink allowed the scent of the farmyard to slip into the room. On the windowsill, a radio, permanently tuned to the news and weather station, seemingly provided the only direct link to the outside world.

To the left of the counter, a door led into a large pantry. Stored in this dark cool room were neatly stacked and labeled fruit preserves and pickled vegetables that his aunt Lil put up, gleaned from the garden's harvest. When Stanza would start up with how the old man needed an air conditioner, his grandfather would escape to the cool pantry to sip his iced tea in peace for as long as he liked.

With dinner on the table, Sam took the seat across from his grandson and immediately bowed his head and clasped his hands.

"Dear Lord," the old man began.

Jesse studied his grandfather.

"We thank you ..."

Noticing the many lines that lay on his face, Jesse could see, like Colton's, the familiar, short starburst lines radiating from the corners of his eyes.

"... for the good You've provided."

Unlike others his age, the old man's vision had remained crystal clear over the years. *What have these eyes seen in their lifetime?* Jesse wondered. *What happiness created these laugh lines around his eyes?*

"We ask for Your guidance for those that look to us for protection."

His thinning hair, like a well-earned crown, lay gently on his head. An indented line, made from his hat, encircled his head. Because he never left the house without his hat, his forehead was lily white.

"We thank you, Lord, for your protection, bounty, and grace."

His cheeks, nose, and chin, however, did not escape the summer sun. This unprotected part of his face was weathered a dark brown.

"Amen!"

The old man reached for the salt and pepper. As Jesse made no move, he asked, "Not hungry?" and then shook the pepper shaker until his food was covered in a gray blanket. "When we were youngsters, my mother and daddy never allowed us to leave the table until our plates were shiny clean." He winked.

Jesse smiled back. For the first time, he sensed how old his grandfather was. The years of their lives overlapped so briefly. Once again, he began to wonder about all his grandfather must have done in his lifetime.

Looking up from his plate, the old man caught his grandson staring at him. "Well, my boy, what did you do while you were waiting for me?"

"Gramps, I followed one of the cats this afternoon down the cellar steps. I found a board down there with something on it. 'Built in the year of our Lord, 1914—'"

"For Grace with much love," his grandfather finished.

He seemed to look straight through Jesse, searching the pages of his long life, laboring to focus on some obscure object. And when he had located the object of the search, a hint of a smile came to his lips, and his eyes began to sparkle.

"Your grandmother's name was Grace, and 1914 was the year I built this house."

No one had ever bothered to tell Jesse his grandmother's name, and he had never thought to ask.

The old man studied Jesse's face, which seemed to reveal many unanswered questions. He recalled his growing concern lately about the boy's obvious problems at home. When each of Jesse's letters came, he left them open on the table for Dan. Though the boy seemed very careful never to write about exactly what happened at home, it didn't take a detective to see he was in danger. One day, the old man surprised Dan reading one. When Sam took the opportunity to explain his concern for Jesse, Dan spat back that he'd do best to mind his own business and then stormed out.

During the last few years, the old man had discovered in some ways he was gradually separating himself from his familiar world. Many times, while riding his horse or walking in the yard, he found himself exploring the incidents of his past. Often this contemplation was like reading an illustrated book of his life. Thumbing through certain chapters brought old memories to the surface. Some events that were once vastly important, he discovered, now lay for years forgotten. While others, unimportant at the time, rang with immediate attention in his attempt to understand why they had occurred and his reactions to them.

Now, Sam found himself alone, faced with deciding if he should help. But his life had grown serene, he argued. Besides, it was too late to make amends for any mistakes.

Sitting across from this troubled teenager, he wasn't sure what to do. The length of years had made his many decisions easier to live with—ensuring a safe distance from each. How many years had he spent worrying about Dan with nothing to show for his heartache? All his efforts had amounted to nothing in trying to change Dan after Grace's death. And what could he possibly do about ensuring that his grandson would be safe, knowing that the boy's mother and father had essentially done nothing? No, he tried to convince himself, his place was to finish out his life enjoying what little remained in the comfort of his ranch.

And yet, when he was younger, working the ranch, he was content and believed he lacked nothing. Then, one night, like one who studies the sky and is suddenly jarred by a shooting star—so it was when Grace burst into his life. And if he had stubbornly ignored her, like ignoring a shooting star, how empty his life would have been.

The days and years, like the many pages of a book, flashed before him, bringing him to this exact moment sitting across from his grandson.

"Gramps. What was she like?"

Did he, Samuel Hunter, the boy's only hope, think he could turn away from this? Had he ever stepped aside from any of his responsibilities? No. And he wasn't going to start now.

"My lad. I have an idea. How about during the summer I'll tell you about your grandmother, the ranch, and what life was like when I was younger." He piled his biscuit high with Lil's strawberry preserves and stuffed half in his mouth.

Jesse's eyes brightened.

"Let's see, where to begin?" The old man licked the preserves from his fingers. "Where to ... sometimes it's necessary to dig deep. I mean really deep. Below the surface of something to find its true meaning and purpose."

Jesse knitted his brow.

"Kind of like the oak tree in the yard." The old man worked to explain. "To stand that many years, that old oak has deep roots even though we can't see them. The roots grab deep, keeping it secure through the storms and winds."

Jesse blinked.

"Seems to me," the old man continued, "most people go through life not asking any questions. While others judge by the little they see on the surface. You know, to really understand a person, you've got to jump into their skin to understand how they feel or why they do what they do."

Jesse listened intently but looked a little puzzled.

The old man thought maybe he was too old and too tired to tell the story. "Let's see, um ... My boy, do you know, everyone comes into this world with one desire? To know that they belong."

"Gramps. Do you mean—"

"What I mean is, life's much more than what meets the eye. Life has so much beauty and depth. Those that can't see this are just sleepwalking!"

Wondering if he was connecting to the lad, he decided he'd said enough for the night. "Let's have dessert out on the porch, my boy."

The old man dropped their dinner plates on the porch where the dogs could growl over the few remaining scraps.

A few minutes later, balancing two plates of apple pie a-la-mode, Jesse made his way out to the front porch. He handed a plate to his grandfather and then took a seat next to him.

The frogs and crickets began the strains of the night music they played every summer evening.

His grandfather said everyone had the same desire—to belong, Jesse thought. Everyone was searching for the same thing—to belong? At home, he was no better than a worthless mutt forced to sit under the table, waiting to be kicked by Jack whenever his stepfather took the notion. He didn't belong there, that was for sure.

Sitting side by side, now revived by the cooler air drifting from the river, Jesse and his grandfather settled in to enjoy their dessert and the summer music.

5

At four-thirty every morning without fail, Sam's eyes would pop open. The old saying on the Eastside was that the sun wouldn't peek over the Buttes without checking to make sure Sam was up first. Never did this vary except for that spring, years ago, when Grace had become ill. After sitting up with her most of the night, he would permit himself to sleep a little later but still be up before his boys.

To Jesse, here for nearly a week, climbing out of a soft bed to stumble around in the dark searching for his clothes was not fun. And then to greet the smell of bacon, eggs, hotcakes, potatoes, fruit, and whatever else his grandfather thought necessary to stuff a stomach for a full day's work was just plain brutal. But once his stomach was full and he was out and about, he felt better and realized the early start wasn't so bad. While most people at home were slumbering through the first moments of a new day, the country up here was far ahead.

After breakfast, he and Gramps made their way to the barn to begin the day's chores. Jesse loved the familiar soundtrack in the old man's yard. The crunch of gravel under his feet, a crow's cawing from the cottonwoods, finches and sparrows sending their songs from the oak, and a woodpecker beating on a tree nearby.

Long shadows gliding across the yard suggested a parade of sorts. Gramps was in the lead; next came Jesse, followed by the two dogs, two cats, and several noisy ducks. These creatures anticipated this daily routine when the old man scattered morning treats.

At the barn, the participants broke formation and gathered around the old man. The arrival of the entourage garnered the curiosity of the horses nearby. Nair, the old man's palomino mare, and Dan's horse, Nilam, poked their heads over the Dutch doors. A few stalls farther down, another one, snorting and jerking, eyes wide open, made the other horses nervous.

"Gramps. Is that Max?"

Jesse was fascinated that his uncle wouldn't think twice about taming such a horse. What a gulf existed between his uncle and Jack. Many nights, it seemed that Jack could barely wait before bursting through the front door, to brag about some juvenile delinquent he had thrown in the slammer and how "the poor goddamn jerk wouldn't forget Mr. Jack Tappan very soon because Mr. Jack Tappan was a goddamn shrewd lawyer."

He imagined how Jack would approach Max. First, he'd strut around bragging he was just the person to break the creature in. He'd tell anyone who would listen how he would do it and why. Finally, he'd announce loudly that he'd "break every goddamn bone in this sorry ass of a creature, by the time he was through! By God, the horse wouldn't forget Jack Tappan after that!"

Then, it would end with Jack's crumpled body in the corner of the stable, where "the sorry ass of a creature" had kicked him into the wall. Though Jesse felt a tad guilty in the pleasure of this picture, he thought he'd almost give up one of his days on the ranch just to see it. He began to think Max might not be so bad, after all.

The old man glanced over his shoulder. "What's so funny?"

"Nothing, Gramps." Though he tried not to think of Jack up here, this was too funny.

"And, yes, that is Max." Opening his fist, Sam let the ducks fight for the grain. "Reminds me. I don't want you going near him."

"Uncle said he was pretty wild." Jesse tried petting one of the cats but backed off after it scratched his finger. "What's he like?"

"Took him in trade from Monte. Usually the Walkers are docile, but I don't have a good feeling about this one."

"Why?" Jesse sucked his bloodied finger.

"Monte took him in trade from a man he didn't know. Been mistreated or neglected. Not sure. Monte thought I could do something with him. Anyway, until I can see if he'll come around, best you steer clear.

"Have you seen Bella yet?" The old man winked. Bella was a newer edition to the stables.

"No."

"Well. She's with foal."

Ah, the surprise his uncle had not meant to spoil. He was going to have a horse of his own! "When will she have it?"

"About a week, I should think."

The old man tugged on the huge door of the barn and shooed Jesse in. Venturing into the barn, before his eyes became adjusted to the dim interior, always required a little courage. Jesse was never sure what he might bump into.

Though the barn's structure was simple, it was the size that overwhelmed. Inside, a massive interior revealed itself, divided into thirds, like an early church. The middle section was large enough to accommodate two harvesting combines, front to back. Chickens roosted in the nooks and crannies of the machinery during the off season. In the east section of the barn, bales of sweet alfalfa were stacked ten high. On the other side, tucked under an eave, was Sam's workshop.

As Jesse moved through, he watched above, leery of the bats awakened by their entry and zipping around near the roof's steep peak. An owl stared from the highest rafter, on the watch for rodents.

Towards the back, by chance, he discovered another area that he had not remembered seeing before, revealed now by an open door. Cobwebs and thick dust blanketed the work benches—the place must have sat empty for years.

As he was turning to leave, an object caught his eye, covered in dust. It was a model of a steamboat about a foot and a half long, fashioned from redwood. A tiny railing ran the perimeter of the deck made from finishing nails and bailing wire. And set in the middle of the deck was a box to represent the staterooms and engine house. Two large wooden dowels on the top were the smokestacks. Painted in red letters on the side, though somewhat faded, Jesse could still make out "The Oakton."

Too soon, the call came, "Jesse. Where are you? We've chores to get done."

Jesse grabbed the model and ran to the front, where his grandfather waited.

"What's that work area in the back?" Jesse asked.

"The one covered in dust? That was your dad's."

It was funny, Jesse hadn't thought of his dad spending any time in one spot for any length of time.

"What is that you have there?" His grandfather asked as he slipped through the door. And then turned back. "I remember this."

"Who made it? What kind of a boat is it?"

"It's a model of the steamboat that would come up the river many years ago. Your father made this when he was a boy after I told him about the steamboat."

To imagine his dad working on a project in this workshop brought the elusive image of him a little closer. Jesse was happy to picture his face lighting up with a smile of satisfaction. Like an artist who can portray someone's likeness with a few roughly sketched lines, Jesse was forced to make do with the little he knew of his dad. But any additional strokes provided him a little more knowledge of the stranger he so wanted to know as a father. Here was another one of those bolder lines adding to his dad's portrait.

Checking his pocket watch, the old man left and walked to the stables to saddle his horse. He nodded towards the canal. "Why don't you go launch the boat into the canal, and we'll follow it on its way?"

The path bordered the main canal, which made a gentle curve through the orchard following the contour of the land. Walking his horse, Sam took note of the trees and the too dry ground beneath.

He loved order and economy. Many years back, he had converted the front pasture to neat rows of walnut trees. When Moses, his old foreman, and his crew had begun, he insisted the saplings be planted exactly twenty-four feet apart and in a perfectly straight line. Often, after dinner, he took a walk to check on the new orchard. Kneeling at the first tree in the row, he would get it in his sight, pleased when the row neatly lined up behind the first tree.

And his sense of order guided him when he had initially laid out the ranch. He was even a little envious of the blackbirds sailing overhead, imagining how orderly it might look from above. His property consisted of a five-hundred-acre rectangle that stretched from the road back towards the Buttes at the east. The rectangular farmyard on the river's side consisted of five acres. The perfect square of a farmhouse and its various yards and smaller buildings of rectangles and squares, overlapping and adjoining, filled in the south corner, while in the opposite stood the barns, stables, and equipment sheds. Though he felt, for the most part, that the Lord's creation was complete, he felt portions remained to be fine-tuned. Therefore, he believed any small adjustments he could make connected him to the grander scheme, making the Creator smile.

It pleased the old man to see Jesse enjoy himself following the model steamboat's progress on the first surge of the water. Every year, to mark Jesse's transition from the reluctant lad who had just arrived on the train to the one, a few days later, who smiled and asked lots of questions, was like watching a newborn foal. A little wobbly on its feet for the first time and uncertain of its surroundings, after a few days, the wholesome country air and good nourishment strengthened it. And growing more confident in its surroundings, its footing naturally grew more stable.

Soon, they came to an old brick bridge that connected one area of the orchard to the north end and stood to watch the boat pass under.

"When I was a young buck and first began farming, supplies were brought to the Eastside by the steamboat."

"Where did it come from?"

"From San Francisco up through the Delta, past Sacramento, and up the river where it would dock." Gramps reined his horse back and gestured past the farmyard. "Back over there, by the pump house."

"How often did it come?"

"Oh. About once a week." Staring off towards the river, he pictured the scene. "Didn't matter where we were, out in the fields or in the house, when its steam-whistle announced its approach, we'd come a-running to the Bluff to see if it'd brought us our latest supplies. I recall a few times in the summer," his shoulders began to shake in amusement, "when the rain was too little and the river was too low, the riverboat, like a fat sow, would get stuck."

"Stuck? Stuck on what?"

"Run aground on the sandbar at the Three Sisters' Place. A greenhorn pilot wouldn't realize the river had dropped so much. The sandbar was too close to the surface on the last turn before the Bluff."

"How would they get it unstuck?"

"Everyone would have to get off and they'd unload everything down there." Chuckling, he shook his head.

"What was it like to ride on the boat back then?"

The smile faded from his face. "I never rode it."

They arrived at the last field, where the thirsty corn shoots had poked through the dry soil. Sam slid from his horse and wasn't happy with what greeted him. He was sure they'd have gotten everything ready by now for the water's arrival. Scanning the horizon, he found the workers near the fence, busy hoeing. He kicked the crust with the toe of his boot. The land needed to be irrigated and soon, he thought. The spring rains had not been generous. The corn couldn't wait much longer for water.

Coming down the road, a beat-up old pickup trailing a dust cloud behind headed towards them. The old man led his horse to the side to avoid the pickup making a U-turn. The Ford had a cracked windshield, like an intricate spider web. And on the tailgate, someone had painted an L over the F. Out popped Sam's foreman, Guillermo, who was soon joined by a boy about Jesse's age.

"Why aren't the pipes in?" The old man furrowed his brow. "It's bone dry here. And I've brought the water. *Comprende*?"

"*Si*, Señor Hunter. But we need all the help we get. Still hoeing the back over there." He gestured to a line of workers near the eastern fence. "But we be ready this afternoon." Pointing to a trailer a few yards away, loaded with a stack of irrigation pipes, he added, "I put these here. This we do after siesta. Felipe will start that."

"And I see the orchard's bone dry, as well. We've got to get that under water, too. And we can't do that till we've completed this field. We've got a lot of work to do. *Vamos*, let's go see how far along you are," Sam said.

"Wait for me there, Jesse." The old man pointed to the grove of cottonwood trees nearby. "I won't be long."

Jesse plucked the boat from the canal.

Tracing the shape of the model with his fingers, he couldn't help thinking of his dad as a kid like himself—someone carefree enough to build models and float them on the canals. Boy, he wished he could have known his dad as a boy. Where was he really? He had been told that Dan was "up north, working." When his dad always forgot to send a birthday card or to remember Christmas, his mother would say he was probably up north, working. Once his mom had slipped and he had learned it was code for his dad drinking.

Jesse wondered how his grandfather got along during the year living by himself. But then he realized that, though his sons were gone, Tex and Brownie would never let him be alone.

This reminded him of the dog he had once brought home that he had picked from a friend's litter. He named the dog Tappan, or Tap for short, thinking that Jack might be coaxed to accept it. When he brought Tap home, all hell broke loose. A few weeks later, coming home after school, he discovered Tap had escaped through an open gate. For several days before and after school, he rode his bike around the neighborhood looking for Tap, but to no success.

A few months went by, and one night, after a particularly violent fight, Jesse was awakened by his mother's cries for help. Running to their room, he found Jack slumped over his desk with Lynn trying to shake him awake. After the ambulance had left for the hospital, with his mother following, Jesse was curious to go back to their room. On the desk where Jack had slumped, he discovered some scribbling on his stationery. In the note, Jack wrote that because no one trusted him at work or loved him at home, he had swallowed a bottle of sleeping pills.

Opening the top drawer to slide the note in, Jesse discovered a waiver from Animal Control authorizing them to put his dog down. It had Jack's signature and was dated the day of Tap's disappearance.

But there was one scene in the night's drama that stayed with him. On his mother's way out, she tearfully pleaded with Jesse to pray for Jack. And he felt guilty because he couldn't bring himself to do it.

Now out here far away on his grandfather's ranch, a pit began to form in his stomach. His eyes welled up with tears of anger and sadness. Anger because he once again had broken his promise not to think of Jack, and sadness because he wished, like the starlings overhead carving figure eights, he could just fly to his mother. When he was little, she would touch his cheek and tell him that he wasn't alone or worthless. But he wasn't a child anymore; that didn't work.

Then, coming from nowhere, he remembered a time his mother sang a hymn to him to make him feel better. He loved hearing her soothing voice while picturing the last stanza:

> *How lovely are Thy dwellings, Lord.*
> *Far from fear and worry free.*
> *Celestial castles from thee, afford.*
> *Peace to those who dwell in Thee.*

One of Jesse's favorite memories of his grandfather was when he was about six or seven. Gramps had insisted he get up early; he had something special to show him. Like a sleepwalker, Jesse followed him to his horse, which the old man had already prepared for the ride. In the dark, he managed to climb up and settle behind Gramps.

If he hadn't been with his grandfather, he would have been afraid to be in the orchard at that hour. The milky shadows from the setting moon reminded him of a scary movie, and he was sure he could see figures hiding behind some trees. He was just about ready to ask Gramps if he could see them, when at the orchard's edge, at the foot of the next field awash in sweet alfalfa, they stopped.

And then Gramps pointed to the Buttes and told Jesse he must wait very quietly for the sun to appear, explaining that this first light was the most important of the day. He told him that when the first rays touched the Eastside it was like the announcement that began a sequence of actions, and that Jesse was a part of it. The world was waking, and this was very significant.

And while Jesse waited, squeezing into the old man's back to keep warm, he concentrated very hard to keep his eyes on the Buttes waiting for the first light. Then, gradually, he saw the morning sky grow lighter and lighter, while above, at the same time, like someone blowing out candles, one by one the stars slowly began to fade.

His grandfather nudged him, making sure Jesse had not fallen asleep. Because it was at the instant before the sun appeared, the profile of the Buttes became illuminated, shimmering in an amber glow. And in the middle, between the two peaks, was a shape that reminded him of something. Was it something he had heard or was it something he had seen?

And then it dawned on him—here was the castle from his mother's song. When he asked Gramps about it, the old man replied he couldn't see it. Perhaps the sun was too bright, he said. But that didn't matter to Jesse. He knew it was there, and he knew why his grandfather had brought him here to see it.

Here was the castle his mother had sung about, up in the Buttes, where he could be safe and hide, far above slamming doors, screaming, and threats. A place where those dressed in pure white spoke to him kindly. And when he'd blurt out how afraid he was, they would smile, speaking softly that nothing could harm him there. And he liked the idea that if he lived in the castle nearby, he would always be able to see his grandfather waiting on his horse at the orchard's edge. A few summers later, he tried to share this with his cousins, but they laughed and told him it was nothing more than a rock formation.

When he was four or five, a Sunday school teacher had tried to teach Jesse to memorize the Lord's Prayer. Sometimes, words were just sounds and he couldn't remember them. But when he tried to put a picture to it, this would help. In repeating the line "… deliver us from evil," he pictured a postman safely delivering him to another family's mailbox.

Now, waiting for Gramps by the cottonwood trees, Jesse suddenly yelled as loud as he could, "Deliver me from evil!" He surprised himself with the force with which it escaped.

Checking in the direction of the workers and his grandfather, he realized they were too far away to hear. He shouted again, "Deliver me from evil!" He couldn't believe how good it felt to yell at the top of his lungs. It made him feel free to shout out how he felt.

And he wanted God to know how he felt. Maybe out here where buildings, cars, and crowds didn't clog the clear air, obscure the openness, or interrupt the quiet, God might hear him and do something about it. Remembering the Sunday school teacher telling him there was some significance about the number three in the Bible, he tried one more time, "Deliver me ..." but choked up before finishing.

About half an hour later, his grandfather returned to discover Jesse asleep, scrunched down in a ball against the tree trunk. He tied Nair's reins to a tree before finding a place to sit on a fallen branch. He took off his hat and fanned his face, then filled his cup of iced tea from his thermos and took a sip.

"Hey, Rip. Rip Van Winkle," he laughed out.

Jesse stretched.

"Fell asleep, did you? Not used to getting up so early, no doubt." The old man glanced at the boy, who stared at the workers.

"Are you all right, my lad? Anything wrong?"

"I'm fine." He brushed the dried tears from his cheeks. "Too hot, I guess."

The old man offered the cup of tea.

Jesse shook his head. "Gramps, how do they know what to do?"

"Who?"

"Over there." Jesse pointed to where Guillermo and about thirty other men, women, and children stood side by side hoeing the rows. The bright reds, oranges, blues, yellows of their clothing made them look like a giant colorful comb. Dragging themselves through the corn rows, they methodically hoed the weeds, clearing the shoots, and breaking the surface to prepare for the river's life gift.

"Them? They've been doing it for years. Fathers teach their sons. Mothers teach their daughters." He stopped to gather his thoughts and eyed a flock of squawking blackbirds landing on the freshly turned earth, anticipating what might be revealed.

"You know, out here nothing really changes. We follow the same cycles as others have done for generations. Of course, little things change. All things do to a degree, don't they? Like some new machinery to help with the chores, turning the work of many people into one."

Countless times, his sons had tried to persuade him to get some tractors in the fields. But there was something about the idea of people working the land without the cacophony of machinery. Their movements with the simple tools they used were beautifully choreographed, and their singing, keeping time with the rhythm of their movements, was sublime.

"The original things don't change, can't change. Seeds are planted and watered, and nature does the rest. We can't force anything to happen. We expect to harvest what we've planted. That's the basic difference between city and country living."

"The difference?" Jesse hadn't thought much about a difference. At home, the houses were closer together and with more people. Instead of growing things for their living, most people at home worked in buildings and dressed differently, but he hadn't given much thought as to how that might make them feel.

"Well, here it's just us and the land. It's what we put into the land that we count on getting back. We can't fool ourselves. We spend too many hours alone not to ponder what's in our mind. We're on our own; we have only our own resources to work with the elements.

"I'm not saying city living is wrong, really, it's just different.

Things change faster where people live close together. Too much friction when you get too many people in one place. But out here, where things are far apart, time slows down. Here, you see, we've got a bigger sky. Places where the buildings are closer together, the sky is small. Here, no one can force the clouds to burst forth, no one can make the seeds sprout and no one has yet to coax the plants and the trees to bear their fruit. But in the cities, there are those who try to harvest what they've not planted."

"What do you mean?'"

Sam set the tin cup on the dust. "Oh, I suppose, people trying to convince people to buy things that clutter their houses and lives, lawyers trying cases not for any convictions but mainly for the money or for the sport of winning. Folks spending money on wants rather on things they need. And I suppose when this doesn't bring them happiness, they get confused, wondering what life is all about. And yet, sometimes I feel it's not really their fault, either."

"Why not?"

"They just don't have the opportunity to witness the lessons of nature. That's all. If they did, they'd see there's no lack out here. Only plenty. The animals, insects, and birds are here to perform their tasks. The water's here to bestow its life on all. Then when the time's right, the trees and fields yield up their fruit to us. Only asking one thing in return before we've eaten and enjoyed the fruits ..."

"What's that?"

"To hold back a tithe to return to the earth a gift in gratitude to replant for the next season."

It was order and harmony and beauty to the old man, to watch his workers work side by side in a straight line. When he was young, not burdened with stiff joints, aching muscles, and shortness of breath, he would work alongside his hired hands, sharing in their banter.

Jesse let his grandfather's words sink in. Out here in the simple air with the sky above where clouds like puffs of cotton rode the thermals, it was easy to believe that fear didn't exist. If his mother and Jack could only see what he saw this very minute, they might feel differently. But this was hallowed ground. A world Jesse would not allow Jack to have.

Maybe Gramps was right about forcing things to happen. At home, Jack was always forcing them to think as he did and do things his way. It was always his way or the "hell's going to pay" way.

"Why are people so hateful?" he asked.

"I can't say for sure. But I can tell you that when I sow corn seeds, I'll get corn. When I plant walnut trees, I'm assured of walnuts. When we prime the pump, we get the river water." He glanced at Jesse. "The point is, my lad, we harvest what we plant. Some unhappy people still need to learn that. If they did, they'd stop being so unkind and selfish. They'd realize they get back in exact portions what they put in, and ..."

"And what, Gramps?"

"The cycle would stop." He swatted at gnats circling his tea. "You know, Jesse, an otherwise gentle dog will bite fierce when it's in pain. It's easy to see when a dog is in pain, you know. Not people. No. That's the rub. Most people will hide theirs. But they'll bite you just the same. And then you know."

"Know what, Gramps?"

"That they hurt, boy. Deep, deep down."

Jesse wondered. Did Jack hurt? Was this why he treated his mom so horribly?

All at once, the starlings took off from the field and flew over the fence. Gramps checked his pocket watch. Stretching a little, he waited for his joints to loosen before pulling himself up. "We'd do well to head back to the house. It's getting close to lunch."

That evening after supper, his grandfather retired to his office to go over some ledgers. Jesse sat alone on the porch for a while and then decided he had to do something; his legs ached with restlessness.

He poked his head in the office. "Gramps, I'm going to take a walk. I won't be long."

He retraced the path they had taken in the morning but took a detour over the brick bridge. In this part of the orchard, near the old granary barn, he counted five roosters and several hens roosting in the old English walnut tree. This struck him as odd; the other chickens and roosters never left the area around the farmhouse.

He decided he would call these roosters the "Five Brothers." Wanting to get a better look, he slowly crept around the tree, and surprised himself when he bumped into a marble cross, leaning on the other side. In the dim twilight, he could just barely make out the carving.

Daniel Jaeger
Born in Bavaria
Died here 1861
Aged 36 years, two months, 3 days

He ran his hand along the carving. How rough it had become over the years, he thought. Was there really someone buried below? The man's age was the same as his own father's now. More questions raced through his head: Had he a wife and children? How did he die? Was he killed?

The orchard, which before had been a familiar haven, now suddenly became a stranger to him—it held a mystery.

. . .

Later, in the kitchen, before going up to bed, he asked, "Gramps, when I was on my walk tonight, I saw five roosters and some hens, near the old granary barn. I thought all the chickens stayed close to the yard."

"Strange, isn't it?" The old man smiled. "What else did you discover? You must have seen something nearby. Eh, my lad?"

"You mean the cross?"

"Yes. I knew it wouldn't take you long to find it."

"Why is it out there?"

"There now. You've turned to the first page of the ranch's story. Let's go out on the porch, and I'll tell you more."

Jesse settled into a chair on the porch to wait.

The deep-pitched bellow of the bullfrogs near the river's edge drifted over. As the sky grew darker, he imagined the frogs, spreading out their sheet music and beginning their nightly recital. The crickets, too, joined in the song, their vibrations floating over the cooling air.

Above the oak tree, light years distant, multitudes of stars sparkled in the clear sky. Studying the constellations, he remembered that others had named and plotted them years before. Here, under this royal blue dome with the pinpricks of light set in their eternal paths, an awesome feeling began to overtake him. He had never had such a feeling before. It was almost tangible. It was like a presence.

Then as clear as the sky above, it came to him. He was a part of something spectacular! He was not alone! He mattered! That was it—he was a piece of some wondrous design. He had never felt this before. And he guessed it had something to do with being here with his grandfather and the ranch.

He tried to hold on to the feeling. He wanted to tell his grandfather about it, but it seemed to disappear with a speeding car up on the road, disappearing into the night. Watching the red taillights fade, he willed the car to return, but it didn't. Sinking back into the chair, he wondered how he could recapture the feeling.

The old man did not appear immediately, and Jesse knew he must have made a stop in the library, something he did most every night.

Finally, emerging from the house, his footsteps in sync with the old clock in the hallway ticking away the minutes and hours of the old man's life—as it had done for over fifty years—Gramps settled into his chair. Looking up at the fan, he sighed. His dogs lay down at his feet.

As though he had read his grandson's mind, he began, "The first owner of the ranch was a young fellow—Daniel Jaeger. He and his wife came from Bavaria, in Germany, about 1849, about the time of the Gold Rush. Like others, when gold proved elusive to most prospectors, they turned to something far more lasting and valuable—the land.

"They say he died of typhoid fever, drinking from the river. His family buried him near their farmhouse. I can't say for sure where the original grave is now because I had to move the cross when I planted the orchard. But I returned it to where I thought it was. I believe it's very close anyway."

"What happened to their house?"

Gramps gestured to the little building across the yard, now used for storage. "The only thing left of the original area is the stone cross and the old granary barn."

"Didn't he have a family?"

"Daniel's wife, their baby boy, and his brother, who had joined them, farmed until Daniel's son was old enough to take over. Years later, his son sold the land to me."

The old man pointed to the oak. "To mark the entrance to his property, Daniel planted that tree at the turn-off from the main road. After I bought the property, I moved their original house here. And there I lived until I finished this one for Grace." He fell silent, as though caught up in memories.

"Gramps? Where did your family come from?"

"Scotland in the early 1700s. They farmed in the upcountry of South Carolina. Not long after the War Between the States, the family moved to the Red River valley of Texas, where my dad died. Not long after that, my mother decided to move to California."

He chuckled, shaking his head in remembrance. "My brother Joe was a wild one. He had come here several years before. He convinced Mother this was the land of opportunity. Here they would recover all they had lost in the war."

He turned to Jesse, who couldn't stop yawning. "Well, my lad, you need your rest. It'll be another day tomorrow. Sleep out on the upstairs porch. It'll be cooler up there. It's always easier to wake up when it's cooler."

"Thanks for telling me about our family. Seems like everyone knows where they belong."

"What do you mean?"

"Just that everyone knows where their home is."

"Well, my boy. You know where your home is, don't you?"

"Sometimes."

"Sometimes?"

"Most of the time I wonder."

"Well, no matter what, your home is always here. You know that, right?"

"I guess. Sometimes … sometimes I feel like no one tells me anything."

"We're going to fix that this summer."

Jesse checked the constellations above. He wanted to take the picture of the stars with him to bed. It was a connection to that feeling of belonging he felt before. He wanted to tell Gramps about it, but it would wait until another time.

He shuffled over to the door, but then hesitated. "I was just thinking, Gramps."

"About what?"

"Well … I wish …"

"Wish what, my boy?"

"Just that … couldn't I stay here, with you? You said this would always be my home."

Sam wasn't sure how to answer in a way that the boy would understand. Not at this moment anyway.

Disappointed with his grandfather's silence, Jesse made sure the screen door slammed with a bang.

Sam considered calling him back, then thought better of it.

Resting his chin on his well-thumbed copy of Plato's *Republic*, a precious early gift from Grace, he studied the night sky. The doubt he had initially felt the other night, wondering whether he would be able to help Jesse was swallowed up by his growing conviction that this would be his last gift to his family.

He hoped a summer would be enough time to undo what three people had achieved. What was the Biblical saying, "There is no greater love than to lay down one's life for another"? Closing his eyes, he sent out a prayer to the stars for the courage and time to do just that.

6

_____

Seven days had come and gone since Jesse had stepped off the train, and still Dan had not shown up. And though Jesse looked forward to seeing his dad, there wasn't much time in the day for him to mope around, because his grandfather kept him very busy.

Beginning with chores, followed by trips to town for supplies, then a ride to the fields to check on the workers, before breaking for lunch (or dinner as the old man called it)—it all kept the morning moving. Then, with stomachs full, a little reading on the porch for Jesse while he waited for his grandfather to finish a catnap.

Next came afternoon chores, usually interrupted by leisurely visits from neighbors, before supper. After supper, more reading, or taking walks with the dogs in the orchard before the fading light surrendered to the shadows. And only when the mosquitos ate them up and the sky had turned a midnight blue did, they finally succumb, climbing upstairs to their beds, bone tired.

But for some reason this morning, Jesse found that all his busyness couldn't keep him from growing more impatient to see his dad. Whenever a pickup passed by on the road, he almost willed his dad to drive in. Several times during breakfast, he tried to find ways to ask Gramps if he had any news of his dad. But Jesse knew that if he attempted, his grandfather would bristle. The last time he had asked, Gramps muttered something under his breath and then quickly changed the subject.

Then several days later, Gramps surprised him with an update on his dad. Colton had told the old man that Dan had taken a temporary job up in the mountains with a heavy equipment crew. They were busy widening some roads, he explained. Colton also said that Dan hoped to make it down to the Eastside in the next few weeks after his work was finished.

It was when Jesse heard "hoped to make it down" that he decided, then and there, if he didn't see his dad all summer he wouldn't care less.

. . .

After breakfast, before joining his grandfather for the morning chores, Jesse aimlessly searched around his room. For what, he wasn't sure. Perhaps it was the room's stifling temperature, but he felt listless and drowsy. Shuffling through a drawer, he spotted the most recent of his mother's letters.

Clearly, she detected his reluctance in answering her letters; in her third unanswered one, she pleaded that he write her a "newsy" reply quickly. When he had retrieved this one from the mailbox yesterday, he had scanned it for anything new, anything unlike the other two. He was tired of the same two themes, how Jack was improving, and that Jesse should not forget to keep what happened at home to himself. So, he had tossed it aside with no intention of replying.

Flopping down on his bed, and against his better judgment, he opened her letter again. And because it reeked of her perfume and cigarettes, instantly he felt her presence in the room. He even glanced over his shoulder, expecting to find her at the door.

Jesse, Honey,

I'm sure by now you've written to me, and our letters are just crossing in the mail. I'm just desperate to hear from you and all that you must be doing on the ranch. Please tell your father hello for me. I'm sure you're having a wonderful time with him. Have you and he been horseback riding? Please be careful. I know your father can be so reckless. Please don't gallop in the orchard. Those horses can be very dangerous running under the trees.

Jack says hello. (Sweetie, you'd be so proud of him. He hasn't lost his temper once since you've been gone.) He asks about you every night. The other day at lunch he said he walked by a store and saw a baseball glove in the window. He thought of you and said that when you get home, he'll take you out to play catch. See? Isn't that nice of him? He really is trying. I think he's getting better this summer. And of course, I shouldn't really tell you this. He wanted to surprise you—he's thinking of bringing home a dog. Wouldn't that be wonderful? I know how sad you were when your dog ran away. He so wants us all to be so happy, together.

Oh yes. I ran into Mr. Tennen at the grocery store the other night. He says that he's putting together a Boy Scout troop and would like you to join. So, when you get home, we should sign you up. And I was going to keep this as a surprise, but you know how I can't keep a secret. Mr. Sester, down the street, is teaching guitar lessons. I would like to sign you up. See, honey, I think everything will be so good when you come home.

Remember our promise not to tell your grandfather or dad about our home life, here. It's really no one's business and would just cause more problems, anyway.

Well, Jesse honey, my boss keeps looking over my shoulder, so I better get back to work. But I'm just so looking forward to getting a letter from you. I miss you so much.

Love, your mother.
XOXO

Every letter was the same—lies, lies, and more lies pretending that everything would be normal. And the idea that Jack would think about getting him a dog was a laugh. Did his mother believe he'd fall for this? He crumpled the letter into a ball and tossed it towards his duffle bag. Why couldn't his life at home be disposed of as easily, he wondered.

It wasn't that he didn't want to let her know how he was doing; he just didn't want another one of her letters to remind him how awful home was. But he also knew if he didn't answer her, she would write to his grandfather, and he didn't want his grandfather to be bothered. Notepaper in one hand and pencil in the other, Jesse forced himself to go to the porch and, throwing himself into the chair, he began to craft a response.

> *Dear Mom,*
>
> *I'm sorry I haven't written yet. I've been very busy on the ranch. Gramps has been very good to me. I found a model steamboat that he said Dad had made when he was a boy. Can you imagine Dad as a boy?*

He erased that last sentence.

> *Dad is great. There is a new horse here. His name is Max. I've been riding him a lot.*

It felt good to tell the lie. She was free with her lies; he would be too. He didn't want to answer any questions about why his dad was not there. And he liked the vision of riding a horse that was supposed to be dangerous; especially the one that would slam-kick Jack against the stable wall.

> *I take lots of walks. I go to bed early and I'm getting up early. Gramps gets up so early. Gramps is still a good cook. He's letting me cook too! But don't get used to that because all I can cook is fried eggs and ham.*

*Mom, I don't want to be a boy scout. And I'm not sure
guitar lessons are for me. And I especially don't want to play
catch with that asshole you call your husband.*

He just wrote the last sentence in for fun. It looked good to see
it on paper. But he promptly erased it.

*I've got to go now. Gramps says hello. I really love it here
a lot. I wish you could be here. I haven't felt afraid all week.*

He knew the last sentence would upset her, but he left it in as
his way to get even for the lies in her letter.

Will write more later.
Love, Jesse

With the letter done and the obligation finished, he pictured
her reading it at the kitchen table surrounded by the broken
dishes on the floor. But he didn't want to think about that now.
There would be plenty of time after the summer for that. Here was
that feeling again, exactly what he did not want to feel. He was
sorry that he had re-read her letter. He quickly shoved his reply
in an envelope and ran it over to the mailbox. Back on the porch,
he waited, picturing the mail truck with his letter inside disappearing down the road, knowing that by tomorrow it would
reach his mother's anxious hands.

To wait for his grandfather and to get a little relief from the
mounting heat, he decided to go sit on the swing under the giant
oak. His mother had told him the swing was a gift Colton made
to provide Aunt Lil and her a little relief during their summer
pregnancies. It had been her favorite place to be while she thought
about the life that was growing inside of her.

What was his parents' marriage like before he was born? What
was it that drew them to one another? Did his dad act differently
with his mother? What made them decide they couldn't live

together anymore? Whenever he asked these questions, his mother found ways to dodge the topic.

He needed to put these thoughts behind him. He took huge gulps of air trying to get the smell of his mother and the letters to disappear.

"My lad." Lost in his reverie, he hadn't noticed his grandfather nearby. "Time to make our rounds."

Jumping from the swing, he followed Gramps. Jesse marveled at how each movement of his grandfather's seemed to be full of purpose and precise, no motion wasted. Slowly, deliberately, the old man ambled through the farmyard, savoring each moment's sound and sight, taking nothing for granted.

Halfway through their chores, they stopped to rest. Sitting on the horse trough, the old man searched the sky for any evidence of clouds. Seeing none, he absentmindedly doffed his hat and fanned his face. Then he noticed how low the water was and turned the spigot to replenish what the sun had stolen. Dipping his bandana in the water, he blotted his forehead and neck. Though it seemed one day blended into the next with the same routine, Jesse could spot the minute variations his grandfather added to keep it fresh.

At last, Jesse had put his mother and her letters out of his mind; he began to relax, glad to be here with just Gramps.

After he'd learned Grace's name, Jesse had searched every corner of the house for more clues about her. It was strange, but he could find nothing obvious. If Gramps had built the house for her, wouldn't there still be something of her to see?

Every afternoon, he waited for his grandfather to share his stories, but each day ended with no mention of Grace. Maybe it was too hard for him to talk about her, he thought. Maybe Gramps had second thoughts about wishing to share his story. Then Jesse began to wonder what it would be like if his grandmother were still alive. Would his grandfather still have as much time for him? But more importantly, would his dad have been any different?

"Gramps, where was Grace born?" he blurted out. "Did she live around here?"

Gramps knocked some dried mud from his boots, and reaching down, he scratched Tex between the ears.

"Funny ... I don't know if she ever told me. But she grew up in the hill country. Later, she and her sisters badgered their mother until they were finally allowed to come down here to live on a place their family owned, up the road a few miles." His eyes drifted over towards the farmhouse as he gave himself time to think about such a treasure.

Hoping he wouldn't stop, Jesse prodded. "Did she have lots of brothers and sisters?"

"Back then, every family was large. Let's see," his lips moved silently counting, "she had four brothers and five sisters. Her mother ran a hot springs resort called The Mountain House ..."

Suddenly, as though introducing his farmyard to a stranger, his hand swept across the yard, gesturing to the river and beyond, west to the foothills.

Oddly, Jesse became aware of an unusual sensation. He felt very strange, but he knew that whatever was happening was okay. The sensation wasn't uncomfortable, but different from anything he had felt before. He wasn't afraid or surprised.

Gradually, with each word of his grandfather's flowing to the next, he felt himself move slowly ahead with Gramps' nod of approval.

He was no longer listening to just words, the sounds the gentle voice made. The words seemed no longer sounds. Jesse could not explain it to himself, but it was as though each word or its sound was a bud of an idea, and from the idea it blossomed into a tangible place. Even the air, the temperature grew immediately lighter.

It never occurred to him to ask why—it didn't matter, because with each gentle word from his grandfather's lips, he was becoming aware of another time, another place. As though everyone had been waiting for him, once he was there, the entire scene unfolded before him.

7

March 1910

Mollie Pearson had just finished cleaning up the breakfast dishes and laying the dining room table for the noon setting. Dashing upstairs to her room, she longed for a few minutes of peace before the next coach arrived. Reading a few pages of poetry gave her a brief escape.

Later, she found time to slip away. Following the path up behind the pasture, she came to her favorite place at the precipice's edge, commanding a broad view of the little valley below. Tossing a scrap of cloth on the ground, she plopped down and plucked an apple from one pocket and a book of poetry from another.

In a few minutes, her attention was torn from her book to the valley below, where her brother and sister had emerged from the grove of oaks and raced their horses into the clearing, heading towards the stream. They always managed to escape when the stage brought its load of passengers, Mollie thought.

Grace tossed the reins of her horse over a tree branch, threw a blanket over some thick clumps of grass, and stretched out. Will tied his horse's reins to a tree and plopped down beside her.

"You know, Gracie ..." He plucked a handful of grass. "Mother's going to be mighty angry. The coach's due and we're not there."

Surveying the sky and the hills toward the west, Grace sighed. "I'm tired of this. I'm tired of being up here."

Chewing on a blade of grass, Will grinned as he always did when she landed on this subject.

"I want to go down and be with people in town," she said. "Why can't we go down to our place on the Eastside to live? It would be closer to town. Besides, Daddy says that with the new road being built south, the mail coaches will stop coming through here. Then where will Mother be? She'll be up here with no one to come. We'd all be better off down on the ranch. We can't live up here forever." Then a gleam came into her eye. "We all need to find husbands and ... and don't smile at me like that. Wives, too!"

He studied her for a moment, then sprung the news. "I understand there is to be a dance—"

"A dance." She sat up.

"Yes." The lines around his eyes burst into amusement. "A big dance down on the Eastside, next week."

"Why didn't you tell me this before?" Grace jumped up. "Here, Will, get up now." He moved aside to let her gather up her blanket. "What's the dance for?"

"One of Father's friends has gotten himself married, and he's throwing a dance to celebrate. I hear most of the people on the Eastside will ... Hey, hold up. I thought you weren't in a hurry to get back?"

She brushed her hands after putting everything in her side pack. "If I'm going to be allowed to go to that dance, I've got to get back and into Mother's good graces." She threw herself onto her horse and waited for Will.

"Oh now, Gracie. That's a hard one, you know."

"Come on. I need your help."

"My help?"

"Every woman knows you can talk the moon out of the sky, and they'll swoon, watching you do it!"

• • •

At the same time on the Eastside, Sam Hunter worked alongside his hired help—enjoying every minute of the labor. Under the relentless sun, with his face and arms dirt-encrusted and his muscles stretching to their limits, he found a satisfying fatigue at the end of each day. Paying with sweat and near exhaustion for what he claimed made him feel he earned this place, fair and square.

As the migrant crews worked their way up the state, they brought with them valued news and a little gossip. Sam counted on this to determine how the winter rains had affected the crops and what prices he could expect to earn for his harvest each year.

Moses was Sam's favorite. An interesting character, he had a story for every occasion. Though he couldn't exactly part the seas like his Biblical namesake, he could direct his chosen people to quickly follow him wherever he went. Sam could always depend on Moses' information as reliable and trustworthy because he had worked the valley's fields for most of his seven decades.

"Moses," Sam asked, "what prices are the walnuts fetching this year? Have you heard?"

Moses stared at him quizzically. "Señor." Pointing to the surrounding fields as though Sam might have forgotten, he proclaimed, "There no trees here."

"Been thinkin'. Doesn't matter if it's a dry or wet year, they always grow. I've decided to plant the riverfront area with trees."

The old patriarch nodded his head. "In that case, Señor, we help." He surveyed his people with pride.

Then a horse and rider stirred up a cloud of dust on the road. When he realized it was his brother Joe, he groaned in disappointment.

Within a minute, Joe brought his horse to a stop at Sam's feet. Jumping from his beast, he commanded one of the boys nearby to tie him to a tree.

"Good day, Brother."

"Good day, Joe."

"You shouldn't be working side by side with these people." Characteristically, Joe began, and taking stock of his brother's dirt and dark skin, he continued, "You're even starting to look like these damn gypsies. Don't forget you're the one paying them." Joe pushed him to a nearby tree, ignoring the look on his face.

While his brother continued to offer his unwanted advice, Sam's mind drifted. It was easy to recall why Joe was not his favorite. Joe enjoyed astounding the neighbors by continually boasting how prosperous his ranch was. He dressed in mail-order catalog clothes and insisted on eating supper in town. Then, late into the night, he gambled at the card tables, losing more than he could afford, piling up mortgages on his land to pay the debts of a lifestyle that his crops would never sustain.

"Where are you, Samuel? You're not listening to me. You always were such a dreamer. Well, no matter. I came to tell you there's a dance next Saturday."

"Oh?" Sam was relieved the subject had changed.

"You remember Martin, the fellow that was just married?"

"No. Not sure who he is."

Joe lit a store-bought cigarette. "Ah, he keeps pretty much to himself. At least he did until he got married." Joe winked. "Well, anyway he's holding the dance to introduce his bride to the neighbors. I've been sent to persuade you to come." He eyed his brother, who had begun to shake his head vigorously. "Now, before you say—"

"I don't think so." Sam waved his hands. "You know I don't go in for gatherings like that. Besides, I've plenty of work."

"A lot of people will be there. You know, Momma thinks it's time for both of us to get married." He blew a cloud of smoke towards Sam. "Where else are we to find a wife?"

"No. Joe, I can't go." Sam dodged the smoke, ready to get back to work. "And besides, you're older. You can get married first."

"You can't just work this place on your own. You'll spend all your money on the workers here. You've got to have a troop of sons to help you."

So now Joe was going to give him financial advice? Sam knew he would not be free of his brother until he agreed to go to the dance. Joe would bully him until he got what he wanted. "Alright, I'll go. I'll go."

Except for the wagons on the road heading to Sunday church, Sam seldom was bothered with what day of the week it was. But he was quite aware this was Saturday and was different from others. A neighborhood get-together never failed to generate excitement. It was like the north wind that kept everyone on edge.

He had been up at his usual time and had tried to squeeze in all his chores and work before the dance. During the morning, he made a pact with himself, if he finished his work in time, he'd go; if not, he'd stay home. Still, he knew that if he didn't show up, he'd never hear the end of it from Joe.

Finishing earlier than usual, he was a little disappointed he would have to keep his word and follow through. He dressed in his social best, although he would have preferred to relax, soaking in a cool bath on the back porch with a good book.

As he buttoned his high-collar shirt in front of the mirror, he spied the bookcase behind him, and with some difficulty, he resisted the temptation. He saddled up Rigel, his Rocky Mountain gelding, and started down the river road.

Allowing the gelding a slow walk on the road, he drank in the clear air and the view of the splendid Eastside with its blossoming orchards.

Where the road drew close to the river's edge, he noticed how the breeze shook the fluff from the tall cottonwood trees nearby. He was enjoying the summer sounds, the crunch of the gravel under the horse's hooves, and the squeaking of the polished leather saddle under him. The natural rhythm to all of it gave him a sense of security. *I am the luckiest fellow alive,* he thought. *I can't think of anything I'd change.* While still reveling in the stillness of the countryside, he heard a rumble, though faintly at first.

Suddenly, from around the bend behind him, a horse and buckboard raced down the road shattering the silence. Quickly he reined his horse over to the side of the road. Much to his surprise, he saw the rig was driven by a young man with four young women in the back, holding onto their hats.

As they passed, the women turned to wave and then broke out in laughter. Tipping his hat, he wondered if they were the family that lived up at the Mountain House.

Just as he thought the tranquility had returned, a young woman in control of a sleek chestnut came from behind and burst past him. With her hair loosed by the ride, the ribbon remained entangled, fluttering like a flag. She reminded him of Guinevere from his favorite boyhood story of King Arthur. So perfect was the picture that he was tempted for a moment to think she might be a figment of his imagination. But the instant she smiled, he knew she was no illusion.

Sam watched the rider continue down the road, disappearing around a bend. It took a few moments for him to regain his calm, and the Eastside was once again silent and remarkable. But he found his thoughts now rested not entirely with the fields and orchards.

Further down, joining a line of rigs and horses, he turned into the gravel road and then into the yard, touching the brim of his hat in hello to a few familiar faces.

He spotted the buckboard that had nearly run him over. Searching for the lone rider, he found her with the four other women. Once again, she smiled at him before joining what he guessed must be her sisters in amusement, as each gave him a glance. He was about to look for an attendant when his brother broke away from a group of men and strutted over.

"Well, little brother. You didn't disappoint me after all!" Seizing the reins from Sam, he threw them at a passing attendant and pushed Sam towards the barn.

Pointing to Sam's "Guinevere," Joe said, "Now there's a sassy little gal over there with her sisters. Their mother runs a hotel or something. Anyway, the sassy one is mine, but she came with a wagonload of sisters. So, I think you'll have your choice."

As Joe continued with his nonsense dialogue, Sam wondered why he had never called on Max Martin. He was surprised to discover this was, hands down, one of the most elegant properties in the county. A small hedge bounding a symmetrical garden surrounded the house. Benches rested under the shade of the trees, and pots of all colors and variety of flowers were scattered around the yard. Though his place would never be this elegant, he did make a mental note of what was here, if he ever had a chance to lay out a garden of his own.

Across the yard stood the barn where the dance would be. Red and yellow Japanese lanterns strung between the house and barn lent a festive air. Inside, everything had been cleared, and the dirt floor, swept clean and hard-packed, was ready for dancing.

Tables and benches were arranged outside the barn's doors. Around the corner drifted the enticing aromas of roasting meat. A crew of hired hands were grilling sides of beef, whole chickens, and venison for supper. Nearby, cakes and pies elicited the oohs and aahs from the women inspecting the Martins' hospitality.

As Joe continued his banter, Sam checked the yard for the few neighbors he knew. Groups of men stood nearby exchanging information on their crops and gossip about their neighbors. How strange, he thought, he almost couldn't recognize them not wearing their blue jeans, stained shirts, and old boots. But he had to admit it felt good to exchange the day's work for an evening of something clean and different.

The fiddlers, banjo players, and horn players had gathered in the yard, where the air was soon filled with the racket of their tuning. But before too long, the familiar starter piece, "Dixie," emerged from the din. Sam's mother would be proud to hear this tune, which would have instantly made her homesick. He was amazed that the South still lingered on all points of the compass. Then, like the pied piper, the musicians led a parade of women around the yard. Wandering around the trees and in between couples, the musicians captured more participants on their path to the dance. When they felt they had marshaled most of the women, the line disappeared into the barn.

It was the custom of the men not to appear too anxious, but to remain outside, chewing, smoking, and talking for a little while longer before casually drifting in to join the women. Joe did not make any move to join them but continued in his ceaseless chatter. Sam did a good job ignoring it, until he heard a mention of the girl who had smiled at him.

"… now I've just got to find her name … Are you listening to me, Sam?"

"Not really. I'm looking around for Max."

"Mind you stay away from the sassy one. She's mine. Hear?" He squinted at Sam. "Besides, I saw how she smiled at you."

"What are you talking about?"

"Oh, come on, little brother, don't think I didn't notice the way you looked at each other."

Taking a deep breath, Sam looked for a way to escape.

"But she doesn't look the dreamer type."

"Come on, Joe—"

"There." Joe pointed to one of the girls who had not followed the line into the barn but hovered around the tables slyly sampling a few of the dishes. "There's another one, a sister. She has the dreamier eyes. Granted, she's not bad looking, but not enough to entice me. I'll get her name for you." He poked Sam in the side.

Just as Sam had decided he would bolt, a friend who lived just up the road headed their way. "Joe Hunter! You vile devil! Where the hell you been keeping yourself? We're trying to get a poker game up in the back. And by all accounts you owe me some money."

Wishing now he hadn't come, Sam was almost tempted to retrieve his horse, but realizing his brother would soon be deep into poker, and deeper into debt, he knew he had nothing more to fear. Not interested in joining those in the dance, he decided to see what the house was like. Taking the front stairs two at a time, he crossed the porch and slipped through the front door.

In the front hall, he felt a tap on his shoulder. Thinking his brother had followed him to ask for poker money, he spun around and spat out, "God-damn it—" He found himself face to face with a dark-haired man his own age. "I beg your pardon. I thought you were somebody else."

The man broke out in a smile. "Quite all right. Just remind me never to get on your bad side." He offered his hand.

Sam shook it. "Look, I'm sorry. I'm not usually so impolite. Anyway, my name's Samuel Hunter. Sam for short. I live up the road a way."

"I'm Will Pearson." Inspecting the huge hall, he said, "Quite a spread, don't you think?"

"I should say. How can anyone take care of something so big?"

"Beats me. They say there's quite a collection of books in the library."

"Do you like books?" asked Sam. It was so unusual to find a fellow like himself on the Eastside who read. Most were consumed with the work and were suspicious of those that had time to read just for pleasure.

"You bet!" Will gestured. "I've a passion for it. I find reading sort of allows me to discuss great ideas with the authors."

"My brother Joe says I'm too much of a dreamer. He says I spend too much time in my books." Examining his palms, he continued, "But I have the hands to prove that's not true."

"Strange. My family says the same thing about me."

"Actually," Sam looked around a little and admitted, "I'm beginning to start a book collection of my own."

"Really? Well, then. Let's go see if this collection will inspire you."

Though it was little more than a decade since the turn of the century, the house retained the same splendor as when built in the high Victorian era, forty years before. Making their way to the other side of the front hall past a wide staircase, they found themselves in the main hall. Sam trailed Will through an arched doorway further down a passage where it became dimmer.

At the end of the hall, they decided the library must be behind the double doors. And opening one, they slipped through, to find themselves in an elegant room, unlike anything they had imagined. Most of the bookcases had glass doors that protected the leather-bound volumes from the country dust. Persian carpets with intricate patterns in faded colors were spread about. Comfortable chairs surrounded a table in the middle. And dozens of candles in sconces on the walls cast a soft glow, completing the enchantment.

Sam slowly made his way around the room, inspecting the contents of each case and, finding a book of interest, carefully pulled it free.

Will came over. "What do you have there?"

"It's Plato's *Republic*." He flipped through the pages, searching for a passage.

"Isn't that where he writes about the men who sit in a cave and watch the shadows made by those outside? And because they've lived in the cave their whole lives, they think the shadows are real," Will said. "Think there's something to that?"

"I'd have to say it's an interesting idea that what matters might be beyond what we can see." Sam put the book back into the case and closed the door. "But I'm fascinated with what you can do with that idea."

"How so?"

"Don't try to change the shadows themselves but do something about what's causing the shadows, and then they'll change necessarily."

"Interesting. But how do you change shadows? I'm not sure I understand," Will said.

"Well, if there's a shadow in your yard preventing the sun from shining your way, you can't grab the shadow and move it. You must move the tree. Likewise, if you have a problem, you don't remedy the problem directly, but discover the cause and remedy that instead." He thought for a moment. "You know, the Bible says, 'As a man thinketh in his heart, so is he—'"

From the open door came a pleasant voice. "Was I interrupting a philosophical discussion?" Startled, Sam saw it was the girl he thought of as Guinevere. "One always chances that, speaking to Will," she said.

"Oh, there you are, Gracie." Will gestured to Sam. "I'd like you to meet a new friend of mine—Samuel Hunter. Samuel … I mean Sam, this is my sister, Grace."

"Are you a preacher, Mr. Hunter?"

"No. no. I was just talking to your brother here about an idea."

She had tucked her hair back up to the nape of her neck, which disappointed Sam. He had preferred the look of it flowing in the wind. Though she wore a simple white blouse, tucked into a long black skirt, appropriate for an evening dance on the Eastside, it was how she carried herself that impressed Sam most. The women he knew were mostly shy, but Grace kept her shoulders back and looked him in the eye.

"My friends call me Sam."

Grace returned his look and smiled. "Actually, I think we owe you an apology.

"An apology?"

"Yes." She turned to her brother in amusement. "Will, we nearly ran Mr. Hunter off the road on our way here."

"Oh, now I do remember. We do owe you an apology, Sam."

"No apology necessary," Sam replied. Recalling the feeling it gave him as she rode her horse by, he felt as though he should be the one to express his appreciation. Her daring riding was part of what captured his attention.

Turning to Grace, he said, "And please call me Sam."

"We must be friends, now," Will interjected. "He likes books as much as we do."

Grace strolled a few feet to the middle of the room. She traced a pattern in the fine dust that had settled on the table and turned to Sam. "I never feel at home unless there are books around. What makes you feel at home?"

"There is only one thing that surpasses that. To be on my ranch, outside on the porch, reading my books." He felt proud to mention that he had a ranch.

"Oh. So, you're a farmer, too."

Sam wasn't sure, but he believed he detected disappointment in her voice. Ready to explain a little further, he was horrified to see his angry brother at the open door. But before he could say anything, Joe abruptly turned, and stormed down the hall, and, like a dog scattering a flock of clucking hens, plowed through several women on their way to the library.

"Good Lord! What was that was all about?" Will shook his head.

Sam once again wanted to fall through a hole. "That was my brother, Joe."

Moving to the door to see what the commotion was about, Will was surprised when he discovered the "who" of the source. He scoured the room for another exit. "Gracie. It's the three sisters, and there's no way out."

"Oh well." She smiled at Sam, which increased his curiosity. "We'll have to face them now."

"Cousin Amanda, Hattie. Hello, Polly." Will bowed, as they pushed their way into the room.

Amanda, clearly in the lead, took a quick look around the room. "Does anyone know who that uncouth field hand was who just plowed through us, without so much as a word of apology?" She studied the silent group. "How on earth did such a brute even get in here?"

Sam cleared his throat. "That was Joe Hunter."

"And who is Joe Hunter?" Amanda sniffed.

"My brother," Sam admitted.

"Oh. How unfortunate. I'm very sorry." Amanda left it at that. But not quite satisfied, she examined Sam from head to toe, verifying his resemblance to his brother. "And what is your name?"

"Cousin Amanda, let me introduce my new friend, Samuel Hunter." Will beckoned to Sam.

"Pleased to meet you. Miss …" He glanced at Will for help.

"Lungreen. Miss Amanda Lungreen," Amanda interjected instead. But she felt no obligation to return the introduction and looked at everyone who remained silent.

Spotting Grace, she examined her dress. "Oh. Hello, dear. We haven't seen you in some time. I didn't think your mother allowed you to leave the hills. How is she, still waiting on people at the boardinghouse?"

"Very well. Thank you. Cousin Amanda. But as you know, it's a resort, not a boardinghouse which she runs. And I manage to escape when I can." Grace rolled her eyes at her brother, who didn't catch it, although Sam did. She went on, "Cousin Hattie, Polly. I didn't know you bothered yourself with these get-togethers."

"We usually don't," Polly said nervously, "but we wanted to—"

"To meet Max's wife and catch up with the news," Amanda interrupted.

"Sam," Will broke in. "Amanda, Hattie, and Polly just moved onto their father's place here on the Eastside just across from town. You know which one?"

"Ah. You have a nice piece of earth. I've admired it since our arrival from Texas," Sam offered as a gesture, knowing that he wouldn't have given them the satisfaction if they hadn't been cousins of Grace and Will.

"Well, our daddy loved that ranch. Though we were perfectly content where we were, we are trying to carry it on since his death. You're from Texas?" Amanda proclaimed apologetically. "Well, at least it's considered the South. But it doesn't matter anymore. Does it?"

Sam bit his lower lip. Now he understood Grace's and Will's desire to escape. An awkward silence filled the room, while Amanda scanned the contents, mostly with a scowl.

"How are you all related?" Sam tried to think of anything to say, though he would like them to vanish so that he could spend time getting to know Grace and Will better. Amanda was extremely bossy. And there was no point in trying to engage Hattie in a conversation; her only role was to be Amanda's shadow. But Polly was worse. She looked so nervous that she'd fall to pieces if someone slammed a door.

"I believe our grandfathers were brothers." Grace turned to Will. "Do I have that right? Back in Kentucky, they had—"

"Our family had extensive land holdings and a sizeable fortune before the Unfortunate Incident," Amanda declared sadly.

"Amanda, here in the West they call it the Civil War." Grace interjected.

"And how is Cousin Griffen, Amanda? We haven't seen much of him." Will tried to steer the conversation away from the traditional disagreements.

"Yes, dear Griffen." She glanced around as though he was purposely hiding from her. "He's here somewhere. Probably dancing already. He is to leave for San Francisco in a few weeks. Refuses to be rooted in the Eastside. He's determined to live in a city. Before Father died, he tried to get Griffen to promise not to go. But stubbornness is so foreign to our family ..."

Will diverted his laugh into a cough, trying to dodge the gleam in Grace's eyes.

"But Griffen won't stay."

"I would like to go with him," Polly announced, surprising Sam that she had a voice.

"Polly Lungreen!" Amanda's face turned dark. "What on earth has gotten into you? The city is no place for a young lady."

"Cousin Polly." Grace jumped to find an entrance into that subject. "I would love to come visit you if you do. I'd give anything to get away. I'm sure Mother—"

"Don't waste your breath, Grace. Polly's not going anywhere.

Father would turn in his grave if he knew one of his daughters was in San Francisco."

"Amanda," Polly said, moving towards the door, "we really should go. I'd like to see the rest of the house."

Amanda seemed to think this made for an acceptable exit. "You're right."

Now that the room had once again become theirs, Will caught Grace's eye. "Well. That wasn't so bad. Was it, Gracie?"

"Are they really your cousins?" Sam had heard they were a difficult bunch.

"Yes." Grace nodded. "They aren't so bad, really. If you steer clear of them." She laughed.

Having stayed too long indoors and missing the dance, she grabbed her brother's arm. "We'd better let Sam get to the barn to get a dance or two in."

Sam spent the remainder of the evening on the sidelines in the barn, watching the dancing couples. When he was a boy, his mother had insisted that he and his siblings take some dancing lessons, saying it would impress the girls. But he almost laughed out loud while watching these couples. No one here seemed to have taken any lessons. They danced as though they were making up their own steps as they went along. He was glad he wasn't out there making a fool of himself.

But still they all seemed to be having a good time, laughing, and calling out to each other. What did it matter about dance steps if they were having fun, anyway?

"There you are," Will startled him. "How come you're not out there dancing?"

"Guess I'm not much of a dancer."

"Say, isn't that your brother dancing with our sister Mollie?"

Mollie worked hard to keep up with Joe. Her face was beet red, and she was breathing heavily—but from the look of it, was very pleased to be dancing with such a handsome partner.

"Yes, that's Joe." What the devil was his brother up to, he wondered. Why would Joe have any interest in Mollie? Sam hoped he wasn't playing one of his cruel jokes on the poor girl. He didn't want his brother to jeopardize his new acquaintance with Will and Grace.

The musicians played a lively arrangement of "The Yellow Rose of Texas," and the caller yelled out the steps in his singsong voice, though few followed the directions. Suddenly, Grace appeared dancing past them, her face flushed, clearly amused at something her partner was saying.

"She certainly loves a dance," Will said.

Sam detected disappointment in Will's voice.

"Why don't you ask her?"

Sam stopped tapping his foot.

"You could get the next one with a little effort."

"Who's she dancing with?" Sam thought the fellow held her a little too close. "She seems pretty interested, as far as I can tell."

"Oh. That's our cousin Griffen. The one Amanda was bragging about. I don't much care for him."

"Why not?" After listening to the conversation in the library, he could begin to understand that the cousins weren't the sincerest people, and, judging from the way this man held Grace and looked at her, Sam didn't particularly like him either.

"Don't trust him, that's all." Will poked him in the ribs. "Come on. Go out and take her away."

What was this feeling that was making him so shy?

He had to admit, that though most days were full and satisfying, there were others when he was beginning to feel a little emptiness, because he didn't share his life with someone. That was the spark of whatever he was sensing tonight, and he began to wonder if Grace wasn't the flint. She seemed to awaken a need he didn't know he had until now. She was beautiful and full of life with joy and confidence. He had never met anyone like her. Was this what he was missing?

But in the library, his heart had skipped a beat when he

detected the disappointment in her voice, discovering he was a farmer. Some girls on the Eastside knew all too well how hard it was to be a farmer's wife. They were anxious to escape and see other places and what life could offer them. And as difficult as it was, watching her eyes light up at her cousin Polly's mention of moving to San Francisco, he knew she had the same aspirations. Damn! She was like the north wind that snuck up and blew fierce, cutting right through a man, stirring everything up in circles.

At midnight, the musicians played the last dance, "Good Night, Ladies," while the attendants began retrieving the horses and rigs.

Outside the barn, Griffen was escorting Grace to her horse, when Will deftly scooted in between them and led her towards Sam, who was about to climb onto his horse.

"Sam, it's been a pleasure to make your acquaintance." Will said. "Now that we're friends, let's not be strangers."

"Please come and visit anytime," Sam said, tipping his hat. Rather self-consciously, he added, "Grace, it was a special pleasure meeting you this evening."

"I'm sure you and my brother will be great friends," she said, then quickly freed herself to get to Griffen before he reached a group of girls.

Riding out into the darkness, with the moonlight reflecting brightly on the river's glassy surface, Sam thought it strange how the familiar countryside had changed a little. Somehow it seemed different; something he hadn't felt before.

8

Summer 1960

T he sun had scarcely risen above the Buttes when Sam had eaten breakfast and ridden to the back field to check on the irrigation. Measuring the progress, the old man was encouraged that the crew was making up time and would be on schedule with the east field flooded. On the road, he had run into Guillermo, who assured him that the walnut orchard would be under water as well. On his way back to the house, the old man was pleased that, as it always had, everything happens at the right time.

Because Jesse still struggled with getting up early, Sam had let the boy sleep in a little. At the table, Sam drummed his fingers to a jingle in a radio commercial while his grandson poked at his half-eaten hotcakes and moved his cold eggs from one side of his plate to the other.

"Okay. That's it." Sam stood up. "If they're not going to give me the weather, then the devil with them," he muttered under his breath. Stretching the stiffness out of his joints, he said. "I'll be in my office. I've got to finish up some paperwork. When you're done pushing your eggs back and forth," he winked at Jesse, "I thought you'd look for the gray cat."

"Why, Gramps?"

"Haven't seen her in a while. She may be having her litter."

"Where d'ya think she is?"

"Seems like the stables are a good place to start looking."

After breakfast, Jesse made his way out to the yard, led by Tex and Brownie. It didn't make sense that a cat would choose to have her litter in the stables, he reasoned, where there was so much activity. Seemed a quieter place like the barn with a hundred good nooks and crannies would be a better place to hide kittens.

Lifting the rusted latch, Jesse tugged on the barn door and was nudged in by the dogs. Half searching for the cat and half just exploring, he found himself standing in his father's workshop. Instantly, he envisioned a young boy, leaning over the workbench, busy measuring and cutting the pieces that he'd assembled to make up the model steamboat.

The familiar question came again: What was his dad like when he was a kid? It must have been different living here with his grandfather and Colton. Nothing like Jesse's life at home. If only he could be here on the ranch, that would be heaven. But then, the other night, his grandfather had answered that with silence.

Wait a minute ... he stumbled over it: His dad had grown up here, so why wasn't he happy now? If he could answer that, he thought, many mysteries would be solved. After a few moments, he retraced his steps to the foot of the stairs leading to the hay loft.

"Wait here," he told the whining dogs. "You might scare the cat if she's up there." Tex and Brownie barked their disapproval before deserting him.

Nearly halfway up the stairs, he stopped when he detected a rustling sound somewhere above. It sounded like something was struggling to break loose. Maybe it was the cat in her search for a place to have her litter, he thought, and now trapped in something, needing help. At the top of the stairs, he hesitated to see if he could tell where it was coming from, when a small dark object flew straight toward him. He quickly ducked, so it missed his face but somehow got entangled in his hair.

His hands flew up to grab it, but try as he could, the creature became more ensnared. Jesse was sure it was a hurt bird because of the squeaking sound it made. Finally, he got a grip and pulled it loose. When he saw it was a bat, he yelled out in shock and let it go, where it escaped out the window.

Disgusted by the experience, he didn't care where the cat was—he was getting out of there. And turning to leave, he froze, when he heard more rustling. It didn't sound like one bat this time; it sounded like a cloud of bats heading his way. Instinctively, he fell flat with his hands covering his head. When they didn't pass by but seemed to be hovering above, he was puzzled and scared.

Peeking through his fingers, he saw they were a cote of mourning doves. If he hadn't seen this with his own eyes, he wouldn't have believed it—the doves formed into a circle and flew around him. There was nothing he could do but watch. Sunlight, through the window, illuminated their wings and made him feel he was enclosed in a cloud of light.

But before he could begin to reason what it all meant, one dove broke free and flew out the window, drawing the others with it. Once again, the barn grew eerily silent, with tiny feathers raining down on Jesse, the only signs of what had just happened.

The marvel of this magical encounter was not to last. Outside, the dogs were barking wildly at something near the river. But before he could leave, a strange feeling convinced him he was not alone. He rushed down the stairs, and at the door, he paused to make sure no one was following him, but silence prevailed. Only when he was out in the yard did he stop to get his breath, but even then, he couldn't shake the feeling someone had been there.

Intent on discovering why the dogs were so wild, he ran through the yard and barely stopped to look for cars before leaping across the road. By the time he reached the shoulder of the road, the dogs had disappeared over the embankment.

Just as a warning light went off in his head about being so close to the edge, the gravel under his feet gave way. Landing on his tailbone, he yelled out in pain, then caught his breath, shocked to realize he was rolling down the embankment. He threw out his hands to grab at anything to stop his slide, but the loose gravel tore at his palms. A few yards from the river's edge, he closed his eyes and held his breath, waiting for the plunge. But, balancing at the edge, he came to an abrupt stop. Despite the pain of his stinging tailbone, raw palms, and a sore rib, he felt relieved.

Without warning, the edge of the bank under his arm collapsed into the water. Quickly, he shifted his weight to his other arm. Though he knew how to swim, the current here was too strong. And even if he could fight it, he could become entangled in the tree roots and debris hidden below the surface, or worse be sucked into the intake pipe from the pump. Besides, his fall down the embankment had worn him out and banged him up; he was in no condition to swim.

And then it came to him; if he were swept into the river, it could be days before anyone would discover his body.

"Yoah! Boy! Move away from there!"

At the sound of their master's powerful voice, Tex and Brownie scrambled up to the road above.

Again, the command came, "Come away from there. Now!"

Not sure what to do, Jesse willed himself to stop his shaking. On the embankment behind him, he grabbed an exposed root that lay just a few feet above. Getting a toehold in a squirrel's hole, he began his crawl up the embankment. Minutes later, though seeming to slip back once for every two steps forward, he finally made it to his grandfather.

Motionless and pale as one of the marble statues on the courthouse steps, the old man stared through Jesse. He seemed to be searching for the depths of his being.

"Gramps?" Jesse whispered when he could bear it no longer. He noticed his grandfather shaking slightly and taking shallow half-breaths. "Gramps. Are you okay? I'm so sorry. I didn't—"

"How many times ... have I told you ... to stay away ... from here?" His hand trembled as he pointed to the river. "Do you realize ..." He tried to control his breathing. "... how treacherous this river is? How could I ... have possibly saved you? My lad, you ... you have no idea what our family has suffered ... because of this river!"

"But, Gramps—"

"Don't ever come near here again!" His grandfather's words whipped through him.

He would have given anything to be one of the dogs, who sat obedient and unrattled near his grandfather. To see the distress in those eyes, which gave him such comfort when he needed it, was breaking Jesse's heart. At once, he was grateful for the stinging tears that began to blur his vision.

Sam's chest began to heave in and out, and his breathing grew more distressed. Searching his pockets, he grabbed a small pill and shoved it under his tongue. Glancing from the house and back to the river, he seemed to weigh a decision. He pointed to a stump a few yards away. "I must sit down."

The silence was soon broken when the dogs ran barking in pursuit of a squirrel. But Gramps remained still and stiff, taking shallow breaths. He seemed to concentrate on an unknown point across the river. If Jesse didn't know better, he'd say his grandfather was waging some sort of battle.

Mercifully, a light breeze began to stir, carrying a little coolness with it to fan their faces. A hawk soaring effortlessly on the thermals above captured the old man's attention. He blinked a few times, and the corners of his mouth turned up slightly. Finally, his shoulders relaxed, and to Jesse's relief, his grandfather's breathing gradually returned to normal.

"Here, let me see your hands." Jesse stretched them out.

"Foolishness!" The old man fished his handkerchief from his pocket and blotted Jesse's palms, shaking his head. "Anything broken?"

"I don't think so. Just kind of hurt all over."

"Suppose so. You must've taken quite a spill." The old man tousled Jesse's hair and smoothed it down again.

And with that touch, a sense of peace washed over him.

"Gramps?"

"Yes." Though he answered Jesse, he could have been responding to something that he was allowing to gradually appear in his thoughts.

"When I was in the barn, a bunch of doves flew circles around me. It was weird."

"I expected this." It was as though he were commenting on a familiar scene only he could see.

"Why do you say that?"

"They sometimes intuit what we are thinking and provide signs to help."

"Strange."

"Not so strange when you've seen what I have, over the years."

Jesse would have to ponder what this might mean, later. "Gramps, I didn't find the cat."

"She'll seek us out soon."

Jesse wondered what Gramps was thinking. He got the impression his grandfather, in answering, was really addressing other questions well out of view.

"When did you see Grace again?" Jesse asked.

His grandfather, seemingly so far away from him, was very close to the place he had asked about.

"Several months after the dance."

"Why so long?"

"She left soon after the dance to visit with her cousin Polly in San Francisco."

"But you said Polly wasn't allowed to leave the Eastside."

"No. I said Amanda didn't want her to go. Evidently, Polly and Griffen persuaded Amanda to allow her. And not long after, Grace followed her there. Will and I became good friends. I would ask after Grace. You see, I began to worry she might not return. Then, one day in town I saw her with her mother. But it was difficult then to talk to her."

"Why?"

"Many reasons, but one in particular. Her mother was very angry with my family."

"Why?"

"Hold on. A book must be read front to back." After taking a few moments to collect his thoughts, he continued. "I well remember the day when I saw her again. I was out at the foot of the Buttes, mending fences, alone with just my two setters, Mars and Jupiter, when two horses raced down the road near the pond. When I saw who they were, it was almost as though she was so close in my thought, that she jumped from my heart out to the road."

9

June 1910

"Y ou're not going to win this time, Will Pearson!" Grace shouted over her shoulder. She leaned forward and dug her heels into the horse's flanks. The wind grabbed her hat and tore her hair loose, but she paid no attention. She squinted, keeping her focus on the figure at the fence as the goal.

"We shall see, Gracie," Will yelled over, half laughing, half serious. He shouted into his horse's ear. "Let's show her, my friend."

He jerked right on the reins, attempting to get around her. "I'm gaining, Gracie. She's too tired. You've ridden her too hard today," he warned.

Grace threw her weight to the right and slapped her horse with her crop, pushing to cut her brother off. He quickly pulled back to avoid colliding. Galloping ahead, she left Will in the dust.

"No fair," he yelled.

Sam climbed on the fence to get a better look. He was amazed at how well Grace rode. For years, his family had bred and trained

85

horses in Texas and even raced a selected few, but he never believed anyone could handle a horse better than a man. But here was Grace, proving his theory false.

A few more paces and the horse and its rider landed directly in front of him. Will burst through the dust cloud.

"I told you I'd win." Grace loosened her grip on the reins. "You mustn't taunt me. You know I'll win every time."

She gave her horse a pat on the neck, allowing a walk to cool down. "You're a good old girl."

"Hello there, you two." Sam hopped from his perch and grabbed the reins as Grace jumped down.

"Thank you, Mr. Hunter." She smiled, trying to regain her breath.

"What a great surprise. What are you two doing?" Sam asked.

"We were just out riding … on the Pond Road and decided … to stop by, once we knew … we were near your place," Will said between gulps of breath. "But we don't want to take you away from your work."

"Nonsense! In fact," Sam made up quickly, "I was planning to head in myself."

Grace's thick, golden hair was long and loose. And Sam imagined that Guinevere's hair couldn't have been more beautiful. Strands stuck to her face, moist with perspiration. Shoving her hair back, she blotted her forehead with her handkerchief. Her cheeks glowed deep pink, and her chest heaved as she tried to catch her breath. The night of the Martins' dance all came back to him. Afraid she would catch him staring, he suggested, "Let's go to the house for something cool to drink."

"Will. We really shouldn't keep Mr. Hunter." Grace said. "I promised Mother—"

"Oh, come now and stay," Sam pleaded. "I haven't seen Will in a few days. I'm looking forward to catching up. And I understand you've been traveling. I'd like to hear about your adventures." He searched his brain for anything to say that would persuade her to stay.

But it was Will's pleading look that did the trick. They allowed their horses a slow walk to the yard to cool down.

"Isn't Sam's ranch large?" Will asked his sister, hoping to start a conversation between them.

"Oh. Yes." She glanced around quickly but seemed more involved with her hair. "Damn. I've lost my comb!" She did the best she could to untangle the strands, before rolling them up and securing them at the nape of her neck with a ribbon she found in her pocket.

"I suppose it's bigger than it looks from the road," she commented. "Do you have much help?"

"Well, we didn't when we first started out." Sam was perplexed by her tone. "But since I bought my brother out, I keep a crew busy during planting season."

Will winked at Grace.

"You owned the ranch with Joe?" Grace asked.

"Yep!" Sam interjected. "When my family moved here from Texas, Joe and I became partners. But after a while I found it best to be on my own. More freedom, you know? Although I often wonder if the youngest in a family of eight brothers can ever attain—"

Will watched Grace as her face showed she was reasoning something out and he grew more uncomfortable realizing she was making a decision contrary to what they had decided before embarking on their ride.

Sam studied the lines of her neck and the highlights of her hair, which the sun reported in colors he could not name. Her face changed expression a dozen times while she spoke. During these few months, too many times to count, he'd tried to picture her and wondered if the image he conjured was accurate. No, he decided. The image he had tried to hug close was flat and colorless. When he had tried to summon up her likeness, it wouldn't come at one time. It was as though he could remember the style of her hair, but he had the shape of her face wrong. Or if her smile materialized, then he couldn't picture the sparkle in her eyes.

She was good-looking, no doubt. But that was wide of the mark, as there was an animated quality that infused life into her face. Somehow, Sam had forgotten this. Though her features were almost too chiseled to be considered feminine, she was a beautiful woman, but her true charm was evidenced by how her face was modeled with each thought she contemplated. He guessed that she could never completely hide what she was thinking. She would never have maintained a poker face at any of Joe's card games.

"Does your place extend past the pond near the road, too?" Grace interrupted his reverie.

"No. Back where I was working is the property line." When their eyes met, it was like a spark that etched her likeness on a photographic plate. And that image was now fixed in his mind.

"Who owns the pond?"

"Belongs to old man Simmons. In fact, I often go there on Sundays."

"What? No church on Sundays, for a Bible quoter? Sacrilegious!" Her eyes twinkled in amusement.

"No." Gesturing above, he explained, "My contemplation is out here. I find a man brings too much of himself into church to do anyone any good. Besides, what domed church could compare with this vaulted sky?"

"You were a book lover, as I recall. Do you 'read' your sermons out there?"

"No, the pond is for fishing and thinking only." Though Sam enjoyed the questions, he was beginning to think she was mocking him. And he knew it wasn't his imagination—Will's shoulders tightened with each of Grace's questions.

"No, my place for reading is in the shade of the oak over in the yard. In good weather, I'm rarely indoors. If the mosquitos don't eat me up, I usually take my meals out there as well."

The eastern paddock near them was fully planted in barley. Thirsty green shoots soaked up the water flowing down the parallel rows. At the edge of this field was the next one, planted in alfalfa. Swarms of bees hovered around the miniature yellow flowers. The deep blue sky above and the Buttes behind had inspired many a local artist to attempt to capture the vision.

"I can't think of any place I would rather be but here."

"So, you've traveled?" Grace sounded a little incredulous.

"No, not really."

Determined to find a subject they might have in common, Will interjected, "Sam, you traveled from Texas."

"You can't call my trip from Texas to California traveling, really."

"Come now, Mr. Hunter, don't you ever desire to see other places and people?" Grace persisted. "Doesn't getting up with the same chickens every day get old?"

Sam picked a sprig of alfalfa blossom and offered it to Grace. "Call me Sam, please. Working a ranch takes all I've got. To be honest, I've not given it much thought." He gestured. "What could anyone want besides this?"

Grace sniffed the alfalfa sprig and cast a mischievous smile to her brother.

After tying their horses at the stables, Grace and Will made their way towards the yard, while Sam pumped water into the trough.

"Make yourselves comfortable," Sam said, catching up. Pointing to a makeshift table surrounded by four chairs, he said, "I'll bring some drinks out." He disappeared into his little house.

"Gracie, see," Will said. "Contrary to your prejudices, not all farmers are illiterate and dull. He reads and is a great thinker. And I know you protest that you've no interest in a farming life, but Sam is a good man. I've gotten to know him well these past few months. He's ... he's different than most. And he's very different from his brother, Joe. I know if you gave him a chance, you'd find him this way too."

"Will, nothing will come of it. I mean to leave for San Francisco. I don't care what you all think." Will poked out his bottom lip and made a funny face. "Oh, Will. I mean I care what you think, but no others. This is no place for me. You know me well enough."

"You mean I know your stubborn streak. It's like Mother's, through and through."

"What do you mean?"

"Gracie. There's a willfulness deep inside—"

"Oh, let's not start that—"

"Hear me out. You know how protective of you I've always been. I'm concerned over these plans of yours to live in San Francisco. You're naïve. To one who's been raised in the simplicity of the hill country, the city has too many temptations. Finding your happiness here would save you from many dangers in the city."

"We've been through this before. As you say, I'm stubborn, and my stubborn mind is made up. I've no interest in this place or in Sam for that matter. I'm here as a neighbor making a call. At your insistence, I might add. My aspirations lie elsewhere and not around this country."

"Gracie. You know the old saying, 'The higher the horse, the greater the fall!'"

"Really!" She pushed the sprig of alfalfa into her hair. "Besides, I've changed my mind—I should do something for Mother here. I know I agreed not to get involved, but this is an opportunity I can't pass up. Perhaps she'd let me go back to San Francisco, with her blessings, if I could help."

"What on earth ...?" Will whispered, eyes getting bigger as he realized she would do it. "Gracie, I was worried you were working that out in your mind. You promised me you wouldn't touch that subject. Besides, nothing is to come of it. It's a waste of time. You leave that alone. Don't you dare get involved."

She stuck her tongue out at him and giggled wickedly.

"Gracie, so help me God. I'm warning you—"

Sam returned with three mason jars of tea and set them on the table in front of Grace. "I'm glad you feel so comfortable here that it makes you laugh," he said.

Making sure she had her brother's full attention, she coyly smiled at Sam as she guided a strand of hair back behind her ear.

Sam fell into a chair between the two and fanned his face with his hat.

Handing a jar of tea to her brother, she commented, "How relaxing it is here under this tree."

But Will looked anything but relaxed.

"What an unusual little house you have." She dodged her brother's pleading glances.

Glancing over his shoulder, Sam nodded. "'Tis, isn't it? I guess I've become accustomed to it."

"You didn't build it?"

"Nope. You see it was built by the original owner of the ranch. I'm told he brought the design with him from Bavaria. His wife was homesick, so he built it to remind her of their home there."

Sam waited for Grace to hand him a glass and decided that she had forgotten. Noticing her lapse in manners, she went for the glass at the same time. When their hands collided, his heart jumped, and she seemed startled as well.

"On your last visit, you said something about your family leaving their hotel up in the hills. Have they decided to live on their place down here?"

"Daddy prefers the ranch," Will explained, "but Mother refuses to leave the Mountain House. And the girls are determined to spend more time on the Eastside. I guess they need more refinement. Daddy sides with the girls. He only tolerates the Mountain House because Mother is so attached to it."

"But we've convinced Mother," Grace spoke up, "that we should spend more time down here."

"I hear a new road is going in up there?" Sam asked.

"Just south of the place. I'm afraid the Mountain House will be a thing of the past." Will shook his head.

"Then you'll have to work your ranch?" Sam asked him. "Or are you still planning on going to college?"

"Not sure. Right now, I'm obligated to finish out my lease on the three sisters' ranch."

"Their brother never came back, eh? Sworn off the Eastside?" Sam asked.

"He was the smart one," Grace said.

"Smart one?"

"To get out of this country and experience what a city offers."

"Too bad. It's a good piece of property. Especially on that stretch of the river," Sam remarked, disappointed with her obvious ill comments of farming life.

"What's so special about one plot of dirt from another?" Grace asked, gesturing around her.

"Just like a woman, eh, Will? That's why a man needs to work it."

"And the sisters have it!" Will said, shaking his head.

"Shame. A man would know what to do with it." Sam thought for a moment. "And they won't marry?"

"They're a loyal group and—"

"You see," Grace, growing impatient for this subject to end, butted in, "the youngest, Polly— you met her at the dance— anyway, while she lived with her brother in San Francisco, she met a man ..."

Sam could see Will was amazed that Grace would divulge this. Obviously, there was more to this story than she might say.

"But he called it off after I—" She caught a glimpse of her brother, who seemed to sink down in his chair each time she said the word *I*. "Well, shortly after I arrived. And you know how loyal those sisters are? Amanda made Polly and Hattie promise they'd never marry."

The expression on Will's face confirmed for Sam that this might be the abridged version.

"Very strange." Sam was confused.

Grace seemed as relieved to abruptly end the explanation as she had seemed in such a hurry to start it.

When a man riding up on the road called out asking for directions to a neighbor, Will leaned over to Grace. "Why would you even bring that up? Your carelessness will be your downfall."

"I'm sorry." Sam rejoined the conversation. "Did I miss something?"

"No, nothing. I just said, not too popular with the townspeople right now either," Will filled in quickly.

"Who?" Sam asked.

"The cousins."

"Oh?" asked a puzzled Sam, feeling like he was back in the schoolyard, playing monkey in the middle.

"You haven't heard? They want the town to pass a bond to finance a bridge where the ferry is."

"Why?"

"They claim it's unsafe. But I think it's because they don't like the horses and wagons lingering on their land waiting for the ferry."

Then, for a moment, silence fell on the three. A mockingbird in the oak tree chattered frantically, filling the awkward silence.

"So, it seems," Sam announced, breaking the lull, "Joe has been seeing quite a lot of Mollie, I hear."

Grace did a poor job hiding her look of surprise behind her jar of iced tea.

"Yes, I suppose it's true." Will held his hand out toward Grace. "And there, Grace, you've won your second contest today." Then to Sam, he said in resignation, "A large family in a small town. Difficult combination to keep anything secret."

"I'm sorry. I've missed something. What's the second contest?" Sam asked Will.

"Nothing, Sam. Just a family joke." Grace smiled. "Once I start something, I always finish it." She made sure she had Will's attention and that he saw her expression of victory. "It's the stubborn streak in me."

Sam returned her smile, growing more bewildered. "I'm glad, though. What we have begun as a friendship, because of Mollie and Joe could end up joining us together as a family!"

Grace's eyebrows shot up. "Well, Sam, now that you've brought the subject up—"

"Oh Lord." Bolting to his feet, Will motioned to Grace. "I think we've detained Sam long enough—"

"William! Where are your manners? We may have been raised in the hills. But we're not hillbillies."

"Hold on. What's going on?" Sam's puzzled glance was met with Will's of resignation. Will fell back in his chair, powerless to stop what would follow.

"Sam." Grace turned serious. "I wasn't going to broach the subject, but now that you've brought it up ..."

"Brought up what?"

"It's regarding your brother and our sister."

"What about them?"

"Let's be honest here. We all know it would be a mistake—"

"A mistake?" At least this part of the conversation he was beginning to understand.

"Mother would never allow Mollie to marry someone like your brother. We can't let this thing go further. It falls to us—"

"Why? What's so awful about it?" Sam felt his blood begin to boil, understanding that she didn't think his family was good enough for her sister. It was one thing to think that Joe might not be suitable for Mollie, but to have an outsider make judgments regarding his family was intolerable.

"Awful? Come now. You mean to tell me that you don't know that your brother owes everyone in—"

"Grace!" Will barked. "I won't have this interfere with my friendship with Sam. You can't insult a family and hope to remain friends."

"It's all right, Will," Sam said, surprised by his own self-containment. Turning to Grace, he asked, "And how do you know my brother owes everyone in town?"

"In a small town like this? Everyone knows everything about everybody."

"Well, now that's not really our business," Sam explained. "Besides, he's a good farmer, he'll turn it—"

"And the fact that every girl in town and most in the neighboring counties won't marry him?"

"What's that got to do with Mollie?"

"I'll tell you what it has to do more really with your brother than with Mollie."

"How so?"

"It means that every girl has wisely refused Joe. Mollie is simply his last choice."

"Gracie! Really." Will hissed.

"He doesn't love her." Grace ignored him. "He's desperate. That's no reason to marry."

"Surely you don't mean that he's marrying because no one else will—"

"What I'm saying is that Mollie is a dreamer. She can't see reality. She doesn't know what it feels like or tastes like. She spends her days immersed in her poetry. Father has filled her head full of fairytale stories of what life was like in the South. He's as much a romantic as she is. And this has prevented her from seeing what's real."

"And what's real, Grace?"

Will fidgeted with his hat.

"I'll tell you." She looked from one to the other. "It's not living your life on a dirt farm on the river. Stuck at home nursing baby after baby. And watching your husband squander all your money on gambling and other diversions. It's not spending day after day on your hands and knees in the dirt scraping for a living. And waking each day with nothing but the same awaiting you. Watching your youth and beauty dry up in the hot Eastside sun. That's what's not real! Besides, the Bible may say that we're made of dust, but that's no reason to crawl in it."

By God! Sam thought. Here was a woman unlike the giggling girls his mother tried to introduce him to. Though he had to admit he admired her for her strong opinions and her ease in sharing them, she was mistaken—a farming life was not all bad. And though Joe was ... well ... was Joe. There wasn't much a man or woman for that matter could do about that. Although a thoughtful woman might set Joe straight. Might make him settle down a little. At least Sam found himself thinking in this direction, now confronted by Grace.

"What do you think I can do about it, Grace?" he asked.

Though he was angry that she was so adamant about Joe and Mollie, in different circumstances he probably would have taken Grace's side. Instinctively, he knew a marriage between Joe and Mollie wouldn't be successful. He knew it! But damn! He would have agreed with Grace if she wasn't so irritatingly, condescendingly right. How could she equate his sacred ranch as no different from one plot of dirt from another?

"Sam. Look." She leaned towards him, her stretched-out hands pleading. "Will speaks to your praises. I'm asking you to use your influence to persuade your brother to stop pursuing Mollie. Marriage would be a mistake. Your brother isn't the kind of husband Mollie thinks she's getting. I want you—"

"To interfere with my brother's life?"

"To prevent a mistake from occurring. A mistake even you must admit—"

"Grace. It's clear you don't know me. Someday, I hope to persuade you to know me. But if you knew me now, you'd know that what you're asking is not for me to do."

"Do you mean you could sit by and let a mistake happen and do nothing about it?"

"Dreamer or not, your sister is an adult, and so is my brother. It's up to them to make their own decisions. Surely, you know that's true."

"You're right, Will." She began tapping the side of her leg with her riding crop. "We must be going. We've kept Sam from his work long enough."

"Stay," Sam pleaded. "Let's change the subject to something else."

"Will. We must go. Clearly, we are just wasting Sam's time." She turned to Sam. "Thank you for your kind hospitality."

"No, wait. I was polite enough to hear you out. You can do the same." Sam's look made her sit still and listen.

"Mollie's head isn't the only one being led astray by dreamy nonsense. The city isn't going to bring you any satisfaction," he said. "I know what brings satisfaction and contentment. Spending hours in a field with the deep blue canopy overhead, the birds in the trees, singing their song, the smell of freshly turned earth, a full day's work that ends in sweet exhaustion, the full autumn's harvest of the spring's promise, and the powerful river nearby— this is genuine happiness. You just haven't allowed yourself to be open to this. This is your problem, and this is your solution."

Grace glared at him and sprang to her feet. "How dare you presume I have a problem and you have the solution!"

"I guess we should leave." Will dragged himself from his chair to follow his sister, who had quickly mounted her horse. Turning to Sam, he offered, "I'm sorry, Sam."

Later that night, before retiring, Sam walked to the yard to stretch his legs. Lighting a cigarette, he blew smoke rings on the evening air and watched them float towards the oak. After a moment, he came to where Grace had pleaded her case earlier that afternoon. Sitting where she sat, he surveyed the farmyard, the river, and the house, wishing to see how it must have looked to her. From their conversation, there was no doubt what she was thinking, but he wondered what she saw, sitting under the oak?

Could she see that he was consumed with her beauty? Could she know his head was drowning with thoughts of her? He had to admit that Mollie wasn't the only dreamer, of sorts. During his daily chores or during his days in the fields, he would find himself daydreaming what life would be with Grace. Ever since the dance, he had felt differently about being alone.

Admitting to himself, lately, that he wished to share this with Grace, he began to picture her in the house, eating their meals together, and later in the evening sitting under the oak reading to each other. She was clever and strong, and that appealed to him. It was strange how he determinedly told his mother whenever she insisted on meeting the girls from her church, that he'd stay single and bury himself in his work before he'd marry one of those silly girls. But Grace was no silly girl; she was a woman who knew her mind and had strong opinions to prove it.

Ah, yes. Her obstinacy. That was another side. She was intent on going to the city to live while claiming to feel so little for the country. And that mystified him to a degree. There was something woven throughout this afternoon's conversation. Something about her decision about going to the city. Somehow it involved Polly and herself.

He couldn't put his finger on it, but it seemed they were not sharing the entire story. He had overheard Will tell Grace something about her carelessness. And yet, it was almost as if Grace wanted this carelessness to be used as an excuse, wanted it known—whatever it was, to be discovered.

He located a bright star in the constellation of Orion, the hunter, and sent up a prayer asking that the afternoon's disagreement wouldn't prevent him from the opportunity to prove to her what she really needed was to be here, with him.

10

A few miles north of Hunter's Bluff, at the old Giffen place, Grace and Will had cornered Mollie. Since the day she had announced her engagement, Mollie had taken to staying with her friend Daisette Giffen. Their mother, Eliza Pearson, had declared that if Mollie was determined to make the mistake of a lifetime, she could make it away from her. The family became divided over their mother's position. At least once a week, Mollie received visits from her brothers and sisters, who tried to convince her to break it off with Joe.

"And what good is money really, Grace?" Mollie said, smoothing the wrinkles from her dress.

"Money is important, dear, and has a great deal to do with happiness. Convince her, Will."

"Joe's ranch is highly mortgaged, and he can barely obtain credit in town for necessities." Will's voice was firm.

"Doesn't matter. You two are just envious."

"Envious?" They looked at each other.

"Yes. Especially you, Grace. I've watched you ride around the county, dodging Mother's pleas for help. I've stood by as you've convinced her to allow you to visit the cousins in San Francisco, the cousins you don't even like, just so you can selfishly enjoy yourself while I stay behind, following Mother around like a shadow. I've watched you come home with beautiful clothes while I wore rags—"

"Mollie Pearson. That's not true. At least not accurate. You're listening to Papa too much. He's filling your head with those silly stories."

"They are not silly stories—"

"And burying your head in your poetry books."

"My poetry books. I'll have you know they've kept me sane these years. They're my friends while you two are riding around the countryside. They're always there for me." Her hands flew to her face to cover her tears.

"Now, honey." Will got up and wrapped his arm around her. "That's not true. We've always been here for you. We love you. You know that."

"No." She choked back her sobs and pointed accusingly at Grace. "You don't love me. You're just jealous. You've taken Will from me, and now you want to take Joe away."

"What?" Grace couldn't believe what she was hearing.

Motioning to Grace, Will put his finger to his lips.

"But I have a secret that you don't know." Mollie lifted her face, which had brightened a little through her tears.

"What kind of secret, dearest?" Will enfolded Mollie's hands in his.

Pulling her hands back, she used her handkerchief to wipe her eyes. "Well, now. A secret's not a secret if it's told."

. . .

Her secret wasn't kept for too long as she and Joe eloped the following week. But the other, more important secret was that at Mollie's bidding, her father had secreted some money away and from this used it to settle a portion upon her as her dowry. It was just enough to entice Joe to realize he had no choice but to marry with the prospects that he could pay off some of his debts and keep the shopkeepers at bay for another year or two.

The couple set up house at Joe's ranch, preparing for their family's congratulatory calls, but none came. Growing impatient with Mollie's moods, which ranged from hysterics to silent depression, although it was uncharacteristic of Joe to exert effort on anyone's behalf, he rallied to her defense and successfully convinced both families to call.

During their first year of marriage, it appeared that he had turned over a new leaf to become the attentive husband everyone had doubted he could be. He worked his fields and spent less time in town except for the occasional Saturday night drinking bouts and gambling with his friends. He even boasted to his drinking companions that he was pleased to find Mollie was becoming more beautiful as one month turned into the next.

. . .

And with Mollie and Joe's marriage behind everyone, the bright star of Orion partially granted Sam's prayer. At first, it was awkward when Grace accompanied Will on his frequent visits. She did not give up her insistence that happiness could only be found away from the Eastside. At times, though, her longing for the city subsided while in the company of her brother and Sam.

Over the ensuing months, she had to admit to herself she was coming to admire Sam. Encouraged by subtle clues that he detected in the ways she looked at him or the excuses she made to ride by his place, his hope increased. Sam's joy lay in that day he prayed would come, when Grace would admit how wrong she had been about his ranch and the Eastside.

On days when the harvest could wait, they made excuses to race their horses on the path through the marshlands in the back. In the wet, foggy days of fall, they hunted ducks in the marsh; in the lengthening, warmer days of spring, they hunted jackrabbits in the fields. And on mild evenings, rarely an hour passed under the oak tree without a lively discussion of some sort.

And as the fall of 1910 gave way to the spring of 1911, Grace seemed content riding and spending evenings with Will and Sam. But some days—it seemed to come from nowhere—she paced around like a caged animal. Picking up on old subjects where they had dropped them, she shared with Sam her desire to travel and see what the world had to offer. Farming was all he had ever known, all he ever wanted. He couldn't understand why she couldn't feel the same.

Finally, weary of hovering between two worlds, she chose the one that didn't include Sam. Convincing her mother to let her accept a teaching position in San Francisco, she kept her plans from Sam and made Will promise to do the same.

The night before she was to leave, she and Sam rode home from town. She was unusually silent and pensive. Just at his place, they could see the moon's illumination of the river, turning the surface a soft silver.

"Isn't the river beautiful tonight?" she declared to the silence. "Don't you find it curious that the river we both see here will eventually flow to its end, where we are unable to see?"

"Yes. But isn't that a reflection of life in general?"

"I suppose. But it could also be relevant now."

"What are you trying to tell me?" Sam held his reins tighter. He knew her well enough to see this was leading somewhere.

Reining her horse abruptly, she turned to him, "Sam, surely ..."

"What, Grace?" He sensed her struggle.

"I wanted to tell you sooner. I don't know how to tell ..."

"Tell me what?" His stomach churned.

"I leave tomorrow on the riverboat. I've taken a teaching position in San Francisco."

"I don't understand."

"Cousin Polly is there keeping house for her brother. Mother wouldn't consider me going to the city unless it was with family."

Sam's face grew tense; his animated, friendly features had turned to stone.

"Sam, please say something."

They resumed their ride, but now in strange muteness, the crunch of gravel beneath the horses' hooves the only sound between them. It was all he could do to keep from yelling out. In his daydreams, over and over, he had rehearsed the moment when he was sure she would come to him and declare her love and her wish to be a part of his life. Daily, he grew confident they were drawing closer and that she realized she would never be happy without him.

During the last several months, she had dropped many clues that she was feeling the same. She had suggested several ideas for improving the ranch, things he was surprised he had not thought of. One day, she even remarked that his little house was too small for him to live in for much longer. Content with his simple needs, he was sure she had suggested this based on their eventual marriage. His sense of security grew as last year's harvest prices were higher than he had expected, and banking the profits gave him great comfort, knowing it was for their life together. But to hear that she had made plans to leave. How could he not have seen this coming?

Although he had told himself he would not ask Grace to marry him until she changed her feelings about the Eastside, he couldn't let her leave without telling her one more time how he felt. If he didn't, the regret would be intolerable.

"Grace, I wasn't prepared to ask this, tonight. I didn't think—"

"Sam! Please. This is difficult enough. Let's not make it more ..."

"How could we make it more so?"

"It's just ... I'm certain what you're going to—"

"What, Grace?" Sam tugged on the reins to stop his horse. "What do you think I'm going to say?"

"I know—"

"What do you know of my feelings?" His blood began to boil. It was rare that he allowed anything to get under his skin. Maybe anger would be easier to endure than the sorrow it would hide.

"Yes. Of course, I do." She hesitated, searching for the right words. "I never expected to feel this way either, but—"

"Then let me say what I have to say. Though I can offer you nothing but a simple life, it would be with someone who loves you deeply."

The full moon had traveled to the peak of its course. Illuminating the neighboring fields, it cast a soft silver glow that made the alfalfa look like a lush carpet. So deep and thick did it look that she could almost lie down and fall asleep, so exhausted was she of battling with this decision. How could she make Sam see? She studied the moon, as though the answer lay on its surface, but in hieroglyphics she couldn't possibly begin to understand.

During their times together, she had nearly completed her profile of Sam. He had led her to believe he was very happy on his land and needed only his books for companions. How could she live here, awaking every morning, knowing the city lay at the end of the river? Every morning when she rose, glancing at the powerful flow, she would have to face this reminder, and couldn't bear it.

And yet, the idea Sam might marry another, and their friendship no longer be the same would be unthinkable. It was awful to discover she had found and grown to love the right man, but that his life was in the wrong place.

"Oh, Sam. I'm sorry this isn't the right time. I must leave. Mother just wouldn't approve. I can't bear to feel Mother's disapproval, like Mollie has endured."

Life was meant to be simple. Why couldn't this be simple? He loved her, and he was certain she returned his love. He had land, some money in the bank, and was respected in town. As far as he could tell, what more could a woman need? But then it struck him! That was it—needs versus wants. Maybe that's where life became complicated. She spoke of wants, while he spoke of needs. She spoke to him of what she wanted from life, what she wanted to find in the city, and what she wanted to discover about herself.

And yet when he thought about it, he always spoke in terms of his needs—what crop was needed to make a profit, what weather was needed to make it grow, what food was needed for his health, and his need of his ranch for his happiness. How could they be reconciled? How could he convince her that what she wanted was what she needed—to be here with him?

Approaching the gate, he jumped from his horse and held the reins of hers while she climbed down. They led their horses to the trough.

"I'm sure it's no secret that I've grown to care for you, too," she said, "and I am honored that you want me to be a part of your life. I will come back—"

"You'll come back?" He was incredulous.

"After I've fulfilled my plans and, if you feel the same about me then, I'll come back to you."

Battling to end the uneasy atmosphere, an idea popped into her head. "So many times, I think of the many days we've spent under the oak. It also has become my favorite spot. You must promise to build your own house near the oak."

"Why? Why must I build a house when I already have one?" He was indignant that she would suggest this when she had made it clear this was not where she wanted to be. He was tired of trying to make her understand what he believed was clear as the sky above. But he consoled himself that at least, his competition wasn't another man, just a city.

. . .

In bed that night, he tossed and turned, mulling over the night's conversation. Racking his brain, he tried to come up with something he could give to convince her, that her place was here with him. Suddenly it came to him. Jumping out of bed, he walked out to the giant oak. Here, in the moonlight, he paced out the foundation of a house he had pictured while lying in bed. Then he surveyed the space and, assured the house would fit close by the oak, only then did he crawl back into bed.

In the early dawn, perched on the horse trough across from the oak tree, he sketched out the house he had imagined a few hours before. Satisfied that it was close to the image in his mind, he rolled the paper up and tied it with a knotted bow.

Half an hour before the departure, he waited near the wharf. Leaning up against a tree, he watched the river's eddies swirl within the swift current. He grimaced as it occurred to him that the same vessel that brought the needed supplies was the same one that was now to take someone away; someone he very much needed to remain.

He asked himself if he could watch the riverboat drift down the river with her on it. He took a step back towards his place, thinking it would be better to begin his day's work than to wait here for his heart to break. But what if she thought he didn't come because he didn't care? His dilemma was solved when Will drove up with Grace.

Sam was surprised no other family members came to see her off. Maybe she had come to cancel her plans. But when he saw her luggage, he knew otherwise.

"I am pleased you came." Grace smiled a little distantly. "I thought you'd be too busy."

"You know I couldn't let you go without seeing you off." He would try to be light. This wasn't the time to restart old arguments about her leaving. "Here. Take with you the vision of a sad man." He took off his hat and looked down at his feet.

"Oh, Sam. How could you say that to me now?" Grabbing his hat, she stuck it back on his head.

He studied her face looking for any doubts, but she returned his gaze, revealing none. "Well, it looks like it's a fine day for travel," he said, sighing as he checked the sky. "I guess your trip won't be too long."

"No. I must be fully rested. I begin teaching day after tomorrow."

Noticing the roll of paper with the tied twine in his hands, Grace asked, "Is that for me?"

He pushed it into her hands. "A going-away present."

"I have nothing to give you."

"But you have." He pointed to his heart. "It's right here."

When the whistle signaled the time for the *Oakton's* departure, she tearfully kissed her brother. Turning to Sam, she grabbed his hands and squeezed hard and surprised him with a kiss. She would not look him in the eye but backed away before taking her bag from her brother's hands. Then, she walked resolutely aboard the vessel. Finding a place at the deck's railing, she waved a final goodbye to Sam. Waving back, he was certain he noticed her glance over in the direction of the oak.

Even his dogs barking and dashing back and forth above the landing area couldn't stir him from the trance of watching Grace standing on the deck, holding his gift. Only was the mesmerism shattered when he caught her brushing tears from her cheeks. He almost shouted at the top of his lungs to stop the riverboat. He wanted to dive into the river and swim to catch up. He needed to save her from her mistake.

But firmly rooted where he stood, he didn't leave until the boat churned around the bend, out of his sight. And even then, he would have stood there longer willing her to return, but that Mars and Jupiter growling reminded him where he needed to be.

Summer 1960

Gaining nothing from their hunting, Tex and Brownie howled their impatience to leave the roadside, just as the old man finished the story.

Glancing at the river to catch the riverboat drifting down, Jesse was surprised it wasn't there. And what had become of the wharf, he asked himself? Only one or two of the old pilings remained stuck where the wharf had once been.

Little else had altered in the ensuing years. The unchanged sounds and landscape made it easy to persuade Jesse he was there, witnessing the boat's departure. But he needed no convincing, he knew somehow, he had been there.

Induced by the dogs to return to the house, the old man slowly got to his feet. "That's enough for today. I'm too tired to go on, my lad."

For a few more moments, Jesse stood baffled, before running to catch up with his grandfather.

11

Summer 1960

For the most part, Sam could tell that Jesse was adjusting to the rhythm of the summer days. When he wasn't busy with chores or out riding horses, the boy spent most of his time exploring every corner of the place. As Sam had discovered years before, the ranch transformed those who breathed its fresh air, ate its wholesome food, and trusted in its stability. Of course, he knew this was only true for those who were open to it.

And this timeless effect was confirmed by Jesse's appearance. His hair was now bleached white by the sun, his skin transformed to a deep brown, and his hands sported many cuts and calluses. As his pudginess faded to leanness, he stood up straighter, which cast him more in Dan's likeness. But unlike his dad, a smile came easily to his face most days.

Sam also knew Jesse's days here were temporary, and he grew more irritated each time his grandson received another letter from Lynn, which only reminded the lad of what loomed at summer's end. He wished she would back off and let the lad enjoy the little time he had. When Jesse saw the typed envelopes, the spark in his eyes would flicker, and his smile would fade. Later that night, Sam would hear Jesse cry out from one of his frequent nightmares, which the boy would not recall—or at least never mentioned—the next morning.

The early mail brought another perfumed envelope, which Sam slid across the table to Jesse, which he quickly jammed in his book. Sam noticed Jesse was still restless afterwards, so he suggested that he pick some oranges.

.   .   .

On the way to the fruit orchard to check on the boy, he was forced to stop several times to catch his breath. After a few more steps, at the foot of the tree where Jesse labored, he reached a packing crate to rest. Counting the jigsaw shapes on the ground's dry surface allowed him to get his mind from his ever-increasing companion—the pain in his chest. The unrelenting mosquitos didn't make for the best place to rest, but he had no choice but to wait there until what felt like a bird in a cage, fighting to escape its confines, would give up and settle down for a bit.

Gradually, after a few minutes, as the pain receded, his strength returned.

Fanning himself with his hat, he warned, "Don't let the mosquitos get the best of you."

Somewhere hidden in the tree's foliage, he heard an orange drop in the bucket. "Gawd, Gramps. These bugs are awful. How d'ya stand it?" It was all Jesse could do to pull the oranges with one hand and swat at the haze of mosquitos with the other.

"You get used to it. Comes with the territory. If it's too much, you can quit."

"You said you'd bake us an orange spice cake. I'm not giving up."

"And it's not just any cake," Sam reminded him, "but Grace's recipe."

Swatting at a mosquito, Jesse fumbled two oranges. Bouncing on the ground, they rolled to the old man's boots.

"Westy says a fellow's to demo a new piece of equipment to-day. He'd like me to come over. Want to go?" He pocketed the two oranges. Standing up, he stretched and felt strong enough to continue—the caged bird would stay calm, for the time being.

"Sure," Jesse said, before picking his last.

Getting out of the muggy orchard and away from the mos-quitos was reason enough, but to exchange it for a ride up the road was better.

Wedging the last orange into his bucket, Jesse followed his grandfather to the yard. At the arbor pump, he threw handfuls of cold water on his face.

"Let the water run over your wrists," Gramps suggested.

"Over my wrists?"

"It'll cool you down."

Instantly, he felt the effect of the cold water, as though the tem-perature dropped ten degrees.

"Saddle up the horses. And be sure to grab a couple jars of preserves from the pantry. We'll take them to Mrs. Westland. And you might want to bring a book along if it goes on too long."

Jesse dashed down the back stairs after collecting his things and grabbed the preserves on his way out.

In the stable, the dogs sniffed around while Jesse brushed the horses. He led Nair, his grandfather's mare, out to the yard and fastened the lead rope to the post.

Nair was a Quarter horse. She had been named after the star Nair al Saif, which means "bright one of the sword." She was good mannered and had a comfortable gait, making her an ideal mount for Gramps. Aside from fast and steady, she was also affectionate, gentle, and intelligent.

Next came Nilam, his dad's Rocky Mountain gelding, a little smaller than average and a solid light brown. Though he was gentle, he would test the limits with each rider. Dan rarely rode him, and with his absence, Nilam became Jesse's horse during the summer. The gelding trusted the boy and could almost sense his uncertainties, which, unlike another horse, Nilam would not take

advantage of. The old man had named him after the star—
Alnilam, after the pearls in the middle of Orion's belt.

Jesse carefully carried out his grandfather's beloved saddle. He
had learned years ago that Moses had brought it from Mexico as
a present, one the old man had always cherished. The finely
tooled black leather and polished silver edging contrasted with
the shiny, well-used seat and stirrups. Years ago, Sam had rarely
used a saddle, preferring to ride bareback; the way his brothers
taught him. But as he grew old and stiffer, he preferred the stability of a saddle.

After preparing the horses, Jesse led them out, one by one, to
the water trough to wait for Gramps. Running back to the arbor
(suddenly remembering he'd left the preserves and canteens
there), he stuffed the jars into his backpack. As he filled the canteens, a ruby-throated hummingbird danced around the trumpet
vine.

When his grandfather appeared at the kitchen door, Jesse had
to ask, "Gramps? Did Grace plant this vine?" Since his grandfather had begun his story, Jesse saw that most everything related
to something else, and a story tied them all together, the story he
was anxious to hear.

"My mother gave it to Mollie, after little Letty's death." Picking
one of the blossoms, Gramps rolled it between his fingers before
sniffing it. "I brought a slip back here to plant and built the arbor
to support its growth."

"Who was Letty?"

"Let's get going." He tossed the blossom away. "We don't
want to keep Westy waiting."

Mounting their horses, Sam and Jesse turned north onto the
road. Jogging down the bridle path adjacent to the road, Jesse
knew from prior rides that his grandfather would soon become
immersed in taking inventory of the neighboring ranches and
comparing the crops. But Jesse could also see that his grandfather
seemed curiously preoccupied with casting glances at the river.

Before long, they came to a place where the path split into two, running side by side. Jesse pulled forward so that he could ride by the old man's side the remainder of the way.

In a few moments, Gramps sighed, then spoke. His voice seemed to match the cadence of the horse's hoofs. "Such ... a ... sad ... affair. Such ... a ... tragedy. Tck ... tck ... tck!" Clucking his tongue like the ticking of an old clock. "Such ... stupidity!" he said.

"Joe was the most selfish man I knew." The old man spoke out as though he saw Joe in front. "To him the only person that mattered was Joseph Hunter. I don't know why he just couldn't get it through his thick skull that others had hearts that beat, too." He fell silent, letting the horse's cadence fill the void, like the clock's measures tying each moment to the next, from the past to the present.

Jesse grew impatient waiting for more. "Was Letty their daughter?"

"You remember I told you the other day, the misery the river caused our family?" His grandfather took a deep breath and knew he had to tell it.

"Joe and Mollie seemed to get along well for the first year of their marriage. And everyone thought he must have changed. But you wouldn't think that if you knew him like I did. There were little things that showed. In town, shop owners would pull me aside and tell me Joe had begun to charge up his accounts again, missing his payments. They wanted me to talk to him. And his place started to show some sloppiness. The trees weren't pruned or dusted, and the machinery wasn't maintained. Or the workers were sloppy with no one to tell them what to do.

"But then, just as it seemed everything was at a low point, Mollie was to have a baby. Joe came to my place as soon as he found out. He was finally going to have his sons. And he wasn't to have just one—no, sir; this was to be the first of an entire crew. They were all going to look up to him—their papa. He'd have to buy more land on the Eastside because his place wouldn't be big enough to raise all these boys. We let him have his say, because we were happy for Mollie. We thought everything would be all right for her. But then, like so many of his poker games, he cursed his luck when his little king turned out to be a princess—a precious little girl."

"How could he not be excited for a little girl?" Jesse said. "They would have more children, right?"

But Gramps didn't seem to hear the questions.

"By the way he carried on, you'd have thought he'd been cheated in cards by his own flesh and blood. He wouldn't keep his mouth shut about how awful it was and how he shouldn't have married a hillbilly like Mollie—someone that could only give him a girl. Then he went on a drinking binge that lasted weeks. We, that is, the family, tried to lift her spirits and convince her he would return. He was just disappointed, we told her, that's all. And if she was patient, she'd see that he'd come to accept Letty. But it never got any better. Lord. That man was the most selfish man I ever knew ..."

July 1914

Sam had a difficult time digging in the hard ground near the oak roots for the basement, but with stubborn determination and many months, he got that part of the construction behind him. The year after Grace left, he felt it was really happening, when he finished laying the brick foundation. On days when he wasn't working his land, he was near the oak tree, laboring on his house.

Today was no different from any other. He had been up well before sunrise to add a few hours to his day. Each minute was valuable, as the time was approaching when he would be completely consumed with the harvest and would have to leave off from building until after.

Will was always busy by his side. Together they had covered the foundation with the sub-floor, and the framing had been raised and enclosed. Will had plenty of his own work to do, but he enjoyed helping Sam. And it worked to his advantage, as Sam, who had a knack for anything mechanical, often fixed the worn-out machinery on the three sisters' ranch that Will had continued to lease.

"Will, bring me a handful of ten-penny nails, won't you?"

"Sure. Sure. Hold your horses." Will dropped a handful at Sam's feet. Surveying their progress, he admitted, "You said you'd have a beautiful house someday. And truth be told, it's going to happen.

"It is, isn't it." He stopped to think about it. "Hey. What do you hear from Grace?"

"She writes occasionally. Tells us how well teaching suits her. Right now, I believe she and her students are on a train coming back from St. Louis."

"Imagine that! What do they want to see back there?"

"Museums, I'm told. Gracie certainly has gotten her wish to see the sights."

"Seems to me there are enough museums and such in San Francisco. Shouldn't have to go all the way to St. Louis." Sam missed driving the nail straight in. He gave it one swift hit and buried the crooked nail in the wood. Picking up another, he sank this straight in with one blow.

Will smiled, and inspecting his pocket watch, he saw the time had gotten away from him. "Well, I must go. Cousin Amanda and time, in that order, mind you, wait for no one." Picking up his jacket, he made his way to his horse. "I'll be seeing you later."

Sam had to admit it was a good idea to build a new house; he found that he needed a larger dwelling. As the seasons brought an increase in the harvest, it made sense to convert the former Jaeger house as a place to feed and bunk the laborers traveling up the valley looking for work. So, though he began building the house because Grace had suggested it, he felt comfortable justifying the time, expense, and effort with practical reasons as well.

Though the demands of the ranch allowed Sam to borrow only a few hours a day for construction, which was not progressing as quickly as he would like, still he discovered that building in this measured means was useful in two ways. It provided him with plenty of time to plan his library—the house was designed to embrace this most cherished room. Each step they took on the house's construction, though small, brought some tangible evidence that time was passing, and that Grace would soon come back.

As the seasons progressed from planting to cultivating to harvesting, he assumed Grace was following some similar cycle of her own. He grew more convinced that she would be ready to return to the Eastside before too long. And he wanted to have the library ready, as it was in this room he planned to ask her to be his wife.

A few weeks later, Sam and a field hand had spent the day far out in the eastern paddock digging post holes for a new fence. Intent on finishing, he didn't return to the house until late. After dinner, he cleaned up and was looking forward to a quiet evening of cards with Will. As the hour grew late, he paced the porch and finally went out to the road to peer into the growing darkness. This was so unlike Will. If he said he'd be somewhere, then he always showed up when expected.

Concerned, Sam strode to the stable, threw a bridle on his mare, and rode up the road in the direction of the Pearson ranch. Just around the bend, he saw Will walking beside his horse, staring vacantly out at the river.

"Well, hey there," Sam shouted over, instantly relieved to see Will. "I was beginning to worry about ..."

But Will acted as though Sam wasn't there.

"Everything all right?" Sam slid from his horse. "What's going on?"

He was now close enough to see Will's face wet with tears. "What's happened?" His heart seemed to stop. "Is it Grace?"

"No, Sam. It's not Grace. I guess you haven't seen anyone to-day?" Will said.

Sam felt a wash of relief. "I've been out on the east boundary working all day. I haven't seen anyone. But what is it?"

"It's Letty. She's drowned!"

Sam was sure he had not heard right. "How can this be?" As difficult as it was to wait for an answer, he realized Will was fighting something inside.

"This morning," Will cleared his throat, "Mollie was going to town with Sister Kate." Then giving Sam a look, he hesitated.

"What is it?" Sam demanded.

"Well, you know how Joe is with …"

"Letty. That sweet little girl … yes, I know." Sam exploded. "What did he do?"

"The little one insisted on staying behind with her daddy, but he wouldn't have anything to do with her. Kate worked hard to convince Mollie it would be all right to leave Letty with Joe. They left Letty playing outside with Joe on the porch.

"After they'd gone, the banker rode in from town to talk to Joe about settling some debts, I guess. Apparently, he and this fellow went inside for a few minutes ... maybe he got distracted, I don't know. Mollie's always been fearful of the river." Will swallowed hard. "She always made sure Letty was never near it."

"Poor Mollie," Sam whispered to himself. "Poor Mollie."

"The fellow from the bank told us that suddenly Joe thought of Letty and ran from the house towards the river calling for her." Will tried hard not to let his voice break.

Sam moved over to squeeze his arm.

"The river. He said, 'Oh God, no. Not the river, not the river.'"

"Sweet Lord, how awful." Sam let go of Will's arm.

"That's not the rest of it."

"What do you mean? The rest of …?"

"When Mollie and Kate were getting ready to leave town, they noticed a crowd gathering by the river. A man yelled out that something was floating on the surface, and they hurried over to catch a glimpse.

"By the time they got there, a boy had grabbed it and laid the body right at Mollie's feet. Kate said Mollie's screaming curdled everyone's blood, and she wouldn't stop until she mercifully passed out."

"Oh, dear God!" Sam moaned.

By the time the two reached Sam's place, the darkness had swallowed up what remained of the sunset. After securing their horses, they walked in a somberness that was so foreign to them. He guided Will into a chair under the oak before throwing himself into another. Grace's chair separated them. He wished more than anything that she would somehow materialize.

Sam wanted to offer some words of comfort. He would like to snatch anything and give it to Will, anything that would ease the obvious pain his friend was feeling. But he felt powerless under the grief and darkness beginning to overtake him, knowing nothing he could say would prevent the darkness enveloping them both. Jumping up, he disappeared into his little cabin to get a lantern.

Returning, he discovered Will was no longer under the tree.

"I can't stay here." Will was already on his horse. "I must go home to see if I can offer any help. We're waiting for Gracie. We wired her as soon as we found out. She'll be on the morning train."

"Let me pick her up in town for you."

In the dim light of the lantern's glow, Will studied his friend's face for a moment and shook his head. "No, Sam. It's not a good idea, right now. The family's beside themselves. They blame your family for this."

Sam felt his chest tighten.

"I'm sorry, Sam." Will turned his horse toward the road. Sam hated the feeling of powerlessness in watching the darkness swallow them up.

12

—————

Summer 1960

As they turned into the Westlands' yard, Mrs. Westland, anticipating the morning visitors, stood on her porch, waving feverishly while Westy, her husband, stood nearby.

Jesse was noticeably shaken at hearing of Letty's drowning. Though Gramps had told him earlier the river had affected their family, he wouldn't have imagined it was like that. In a way, he was glad that he would have to wait a bit for his grandfather to resume until their way home.

"I see you've brought some help with you. Tie your horses up over there and come on up where it's cool." Westy beckoned to them.

After tying the horses in the shade and loosening their girths, Jesse returned to the porch and rummaged through his backpack for the gift.

"We brought you something." He pushed the jars toward Mrs. Westland.

"Oh, how nice. How thoughtful. We'll have them tomorrow at breakfast," she assured him.

119

"How're your orchards doing this year?" Westy asked Sam. "Are the dust spiders bothering you like everyone else?"

"No. Not much this year. Thank goodness."

From the road, a succession of backfires announced the arrival of a faded blue Chevy pickup. Out poured PJ Heeg and two other neighbors who had ridden up the road, packed tight like sardines, in the front seat.

"Glad you could make it," Westy yelled from the porch.

"Hell, I'm always interested in new equipment, progress," PJ replied, making his way towards the porch, skirting around a bewildered Shep.

Taking a pipe from his pocket, PJ packed it with some tobacco, scraped together from a Prince Albert pocket tin. Sucking on the pipe, he lit it before taking notice of Mrs. Westland. "Hey, honey. The mister treatin' you all right?"

"Good as can be expected, PJ." Mrs. Westland smiled at the age-old greeting.

Sam scoured the yard. "Where's that salesman, Westy? He didn't cancel, did he?"

"Oh, no. He's out behind the barn getting his contraption ready."

In a few minutes, a skinny, balding man appeared from around the barn. "I think we're ready. The name's Mr. Edward Snowley. But just call me Ed." His entire body seemed to tremble; he was so nervous. "Now, if you'll kindly follow me, I'll show you what you'll wonder how you've done without all these years."

"Well, my Lord," PJ snorted, pointing to the barn. "The man's got a pot o' cash over there."

When the group burst out laughing, Mr. Snowley's face dropped, wondering if he'd have a tough time keeping their attention.

"Come on, gentlemen," Westy said, slapping his hat on and waving them forward. "Let's allow Mr. Ed to show us his prize."

Deciding to stay behind, Jesse rummaged through his backpack, where he had stuffed a book. Scrunching into a chair, he settled in for some quiet reading. When the book fell open, his mother's latest unopened letter slipped out.

He was tired of reading the same old stuff, but he guessed this would be as good a time as any to see what was new. And he hadn't gotten to the second line before he read that because he had only written once this summer, Jack had offered to drive his mother up to the ranch to make sure Jesse was all right. She assured him they would plan to come up next week if she didn't receive a reply before then. His stomach churned, picturing Jack and his mother pulling into the ranch in their convertible. He could not let that happen.

He promised himself the minute he got back to the ranch, he would send her a long letter. He thought of things he'd write so he could quickly get it down on paper and into the afternoon mail.

Suddenly, he was startled by an empty Prince Albert can sent flying across the porch. Mrs. Westland had inadvertently kicked it when she came out to clean up the porch. She paid no attention to the flying Prince but was intent on grabbing the glasses when she noticed Jesse's startled face.

"You look downright parched. You need something more to drink?"

He slammed his book shut, with his mother's letter in it.

"You just sit there. No trouble a-tall. Take me but a second."

Moments later, she returned with two large glasses of iced tea and a plate of homemade cookies. She dropped into a chair next to him, where she began to examine her rough hands.

"You know, it's such a shame we never had any children," she said wistfully.

Jesse listened politely, but wished she'd leave. He needed to come up with something to write to his mother.

"Sometimes it gets so lonely out here without any young people." She sighed, looking up from her hands to the Buttes. "How're you enjoying your summer vacation so far? Do you know how lucky you are to have such a good man as your granddaddy?"

"Actually, I like—"

"Yes, son. You're very lucky!" She craned her neck to look over in the direction where the men had gone. "Not a finer man. Not a finer man," she repeated mostly to herself. And then as though it had just occurred to her, she asked, "Did you know we've lived here for many years?" She fell silent as though she would begin reviewing each of the years.

"In fact," her eyes lit up, "guess you already know this place used to belong to the Hunters."

"To my family?" Jesse sat up a bit. "Gramps didn't say anything about that."

"Oh, then he didn't tell you this was his brother Joe's place. He must've told you they lost a child here?"

Jesse nodded.

"We bought the land from the bank not long after," she said. Seeming to weigh something in her mind, she scooted her chair closer.

"After the little girl's death, Joe drank beyond reason and allowed this ranch to stand idle. And any squirrel knows that if you're not going to farm the land, you've got to lease it out. He couldn't even do that. Then, mind you, your grandfather, in Christian goodwill, took pity on his poor sister-in-law and farmed it himself, even though he had plenty of work to do on his own place.

"And do you know what Sam Hunter did with the money? Why, he took nothing for himself, only just enough ..." she took a sip from her glass, apparently waiting for what his grandfather did to sink in, "to cover the expenses. He gave the rest to Mollie so she could survive."

Mrs. Westland shook her head. "Joe was never the same. Never. His guilt became too much, even for him. Oh, and mercy, Mollie! The poor dear. She was beside herself living out her life in such sadness. My, that woman was devoted to Letty. You know, after Letty was born, there were some sort of problems. Female problems, I mean. And the doctor told her she couldn't have any more children. Joe never forgave her because he wanted a bunch of boys to help him farm."

She stood up abruptly. "Then, she lost Letty. Too much for any woman to bear. Especially Mollie. Well, I had better get back to my work," she said as she picked up the plates and glasses. "It was nice to talk to you. You're a good conversationalist."

She gave her flowerbed a glance. "I probably said more than I should've. But, oh, child, 'twas a sad affair." Shaking her head about the tragedy as though it had occurred only just yesterday, she disappeared into the house.

Jesse tried to find his place in his book, but he could think of nothing but what he'd just heard. What happened to Mollie and Joe after their child drowned? Remembering that Mrs. Westland said she and her husband acquired the ranch shortly after, he wondered what had become of them. He could barely wait for his grandfather to return.

About half an hour later, all the men reappeared from behind the barn except for Ed Snowley.

"Well, imagine that," PJ declared. "If I've said it once, I've said it a thousand times—they ought to send out someone that knows what he's doing and not one of those factory salesmen. Hell, what do they know about anything? The minute I saw it, I could've told that bird that it wouldn't work!"

They all nodded and grunted in agreement.

"Nothing substitutes for common sense and hard work," Sam said.

Setting his glass down, he turned to Jesse. "Well, my boy, why don't you go bring the horses around."

In a few moments Jesse returned, riding his horse and leading his grandfather's up to the porch steps to make it easier for mounting. The old man grunted as he threw himself over Nair.

"See you all later." Sam turned to Mrs. Westland. "You've been very kind to entertain my grandson here."

"My pleasure." She looked up at him, shielding her eyes from the sun. "I can see that he takes after his grandfather."

Tipping his hat to her, the old man turned his horse out of the yard and onto the road with Jesse following.

On their way home, Jesse's curiosity got the best of him "Gramps. I hope you don't mind, but Mrs. Westland told me how badly Joe treated Mollie, and how she couldn't have any more kids."

"What?" His grandfather turned instantly. "She told you about that? She had no business telling you family things."

The old man adjusted his straw hat and waved a fly from his face. He repeated, "No business at all!"

They rode silently for a few minutes before Gramps turned to Jesse and sighed. It was time to share more of the Hunter story.

July 1914

"I'll not hear of it!" Eliza stamped her foot. "We will not push it off until after church on Sunday. That little girl deserves services during the week."

"But, Mother," Will stumbled, "the weekdays are as valuable as the harvest. You can't ask these people to give up one of their precious days for a funeral."

"These people can't sacrifice an afternoon? Look at us. Look at what we've sacrificed. That angel deserves services during the week. Now if it was some old person ... like me ..." Eliza stared at her hands. "You can roll me in a ball and toss me in the ground at midnight—"

"Mother! How can you speak of such a thing?" Grace couldn't believe her mother's methods.

"That little dear is going to have services on Friday. It shows more respect. Besides, if we can't count on people doing this for our family, then friends we have not."

After the burial, the family decided that Will would take Mollie back up to the Mountain House where she could rest quietly away from the gathering.

Family and friends met at the Pearsons' Eastside ranch for refreshments. The storeroom had been raided for empty mason jars to hold dozens of flowers the neighbors had brought from their gardens for an offering. Planks had been thrown across sawhorses, set under the shade trees, and yards of light muslin protected the array of food.

Sam found Grace sitting in the yard apart from the others. "May I?" He pointed to the space next to her.

Moving her dress to make room, she instantly began to feel the calm that she had been longing for since she had spotted him in the back row in the church. But her throat felt constricted, and she could not form any words.

"Grace, I'm so sorry." He had rehearsed what he planned to say, but now forgot the words. The tears made her eyes sparkle; that and her sadness bestowed such beauty on her that it took his breath away. "We … I just want you to know that I am here. If there is anything I can do …"

"I'm trying so hard to make sense out of this," she said. "During the sermon, the parson read, 'Behold, what manner of love the Father hath bestowed upon us…' What kind of love does God offer when He can let a child like that die? What kind of God causes suffering to His children? What did she ever do? What did Mollie ever do to deserve this suffering?"

His heart wanted to break for the grief that prompted these questions. Yet he was moved that she was searching for the strength outside herself to weather this. He was encouraged that she didn't fling it off as one of life's unexplainable mysteries but struggled for some degree of understanding.

"Grace, if it were in my power, I would sweep away all the pain that you and your family have endured. I believe there's an explanation for everything and when this is found, peace will be yours. I believe there are no unsolvable mysteries in life."

"You seem so convinced," she whispered, shaking her head.

"I think times like this force the gold in our characters to come to the surface. It tempers us, makes us stronger. Perhaps," he struggled, wondering if he was saying too much, "we need to look at it from a different point of view."

She looked shocked. "So, you believe this tragedy is divinely driven?"

"Nothing of the sort. I'm just suggesting that most of our heartaches come when we stubbornly refuse to look for the solution that has been there the entire time. I don't claim to understand, but ..."

"Thank you for being here. Besides my brother, you're one of the deepest thinkers I've ever known."

He smiled at the treasured compliment.

She wiped her tears and took a deep breath, seemingly determined to escape from this unsolvable mystery.

"On my way here, I caught a glimpse of this new house of yours," she said. "You've been busy, haven't you?"

A little surprised at her abrupt change, still he was relieved to be able to turn from this as well and tell her what he was doing for her. "All my time is spent in building the house and working the ranch. I have done little else since I saw you last. A few more months and the house will be finished."

He took a deep breath, nodding to a friend passing by. "I will finally have my library. And when I'm done, it's going to be almost as nice as the room we saw at the dance that night."

She glanced across the lawn to where her mother stared at them.

"How could I forget?" she whispered under her breath. "I think of it often. If I can get away, I'd like to come and see what you've done."

"Then come and see the house before you return to the city." He had to ask. "You do have to return to the city?"

"Sam, it'd be wonderful to escape from all this and visit with you, like old times."

The next day, Sam was measuring a space for a planting near the pump when his barking dogs announced Grace.

"I'm so glad you came!" Sam glanced behind her. "Did Will come with you?"

"No. There's too much going on at home. Mother's still in an uproar. I was barely able to sneak away. I can't stay long."

She slid off her horse, tossing the lead around the fence. "Look at your house. It's really taking shape."

"It's slow coming," he said, brushing dirt from his hands. "But it's steady."

"Show me around. Won't you?" She walked ahead of him and up the kitchen porch stairs.

"No. You can't approach it from there for the first time."

"What do you mean?"

Taking her hand, he led her around the house to the front door. "I want you to see it from here. The front porch is here, straight back from the oak tree. Like I drew it in the picture for you," he explained, as he led her through what would be the front door.

Standing in the middle of the house, he pointed out the various spaces that would serve as the kitchen, dining room, and living room.

"Where's the room?" she asked, peering through the framing.

"Room? They're all rooms. Pretty soon—"

"No. I mean, where's the library?"

"Over here to the left just off the hall there."

"Show me what it will look like."

"It'll have bookcases here, and the windows will be there on the east wall. And the fireplace will be right there with bookcases on either side." As he walked out the dimensions, indicating where everything would be because he had pictured it over and over in his head, he almost felt the finished result couldn't be more real.

"It'll be beautiful." She strolled around.

Weaving in and out, she drifted through the framing trying to imagine how it would all look when finished. Satisfied that she had a good grasp, she went down the porch stairs and waited for Sam, who quickly followed.

"It's very nice, Sam." She glanced toward where the library would be. "You've done a fine job."

"Come over here. I need to finish something." He pointed toward the pump.

Grace rested next to the well, watching as he finished planting a small cutting. "What is it? Seems so tiny," she said.

"It's a slip of a trumpet vine that my mother gave Mollie."

"Why not a rose or pretty flower?" She gave him a puzzled look.

"In Mother's time, some plants were given to convey particular messages."

"Does this one have a meaning?"

"I looked it up last night in an old book," he said. "This vine symbolizes, 'One must look to hope and faith for comfort.'"

Tapping the last of the dirt around the green shoot, he drew water from the well, giving its first drink from the life source. Grace meandered over to the circle of chairs and found hers.

Finished with his planting, he was glad to take a seat next to Grace; he longed for her closeness and to take in the scent of her perfume. Suddenly he turned to her. "So. How's life away from the Eastside? Do you still enjoy teaching?"

"The city is fine. Certainly nothing like it is here, though." She looked wistfully around. "You know what I miss the most?"

Sam shook his head.

"I miss the river."

"Living in the city, you're surrounded by water. And you miss this old river? Why's that?"

"I suppose because it means I'm close to home. But there's so much more. It's deep and dark and mysterious, and yet its surface reflects all that's light and beautiful above it. Strong enough to support a riverboat, but soft enough to yield to a finger's touch. Its power cuts a channel through the earth, and yet it's so pliable that it will follow your lead to irrigate your fields. Without it, nothing would be here. Even that little vine you've planted needs the river."

"Yes, but don't forget, the river is extremely dangerous. As you say, it gives life, but it snatches it away. Often too soon."

"Sam. When will your house be completed?"

He sensed that she wanted to get her mind away from this newfound guilt. Ignoring her question, he leaned in and took her hand. "It's been long enough. Isn't it time to come back to family and friends? What could possibly be in the city that you can't have here?" He took a deep breath.

"Oh, Sam—"

"Stay and be my wife."

She pulled her hand away. "Because this is not the right time."

He stared at her, bewildered. "What do you mean? Seems to me there couldn't be a better time."

"So much has happened recently. There are things in the city… Life here is simple. Life there is complicated. Or I guess we make it complicated. Sometimes I think I know my mind, and then at other times, I feel so confused. I ... I must return. I'm sorry."

Jumping to his feet, he tried to keep the rising anger down. "Grace. For God's sake. Don't you realize everything I do here is for you? Can't you see that the house is for you? The ranch is for you. How can I make you understand that?"

"Do you think it's easy for me?" she pleaded. "Easy coming here? Seeing you? Sitting here? Loving it here? But I can't remain here. You don't understand. Perhaps someday you will."

"Grace. At least, let—"

"Sam. If you say anything more, I'll leave. Please, no more. Can't we just sit here in peace?"

Later, as she climbed on her horse to leave, and far from the moments when the conversation had been so solemn, she turned to him. "I don't know when I will be able to return, but when I do, I look forward to seeing your finished house."

Shielding his eyes from the sun, he strained to read her face. "Will you promise to come back when it's finished?"

Gazing past him towards the Bluff, where she had climbed aboard the riverboat that had promised such adventures, she searched for an answer.

"I promise." She smiled before turning her horse toward the road.

Sam knew her well enough to realize there was nothing he could say to change her mind. Maybe Will had let it slip to his mother that he had planned to propose to her in the library. He knew Eliza would never consent to another marriage between a Pearson and a Hunter and reasoned this was why Grace said the time wasn't right. But he couldn't help feeling that she was keeping something more from him.

Later that afternoon, an idea popped into his head. He went to the barn where the firewood was stored. Searching through the stack, he found the right size piece that he had trimmed from the oak tree the previous winter. He took it to his workshop and sliced it into three sections. Discarding the outer sections, he worked the middle piece into a small tablet shape.

After dinner, sitting under the oak tree, with his pen knife he carved in the letters:

Built for Grace,
with much love,
in the year of our Lord, 1914

When he was done, he climbed down the cellar steps and attached it to the foundation of the house.

With his dedication complete, he took a walk out to the recently planted orchard. Checking the new growth, he discovered the jackrabbits had gnawed on a few of the new trees. Tomorrow, he would wrap those in protective cloth. But now, he would clear his mind of this day and try not to think of Grace.

13

Summer 1960

By Sam's calculations, Bella should have foaled before now. During the day, for no apparent reason, he sensed something was not right, though Bella hadn't shown anything out of the ordinary. Before retiring for the night, he had checked on the mare. He scattered some fresh hay in the stall and wrapped her tail in case her water broke before morning. Realizing there wasn't much more he could do now but wait, he returned to the house.

A few hours after midnight, the dogs' whining woke him out of a deep sleep. A few minutes later, the old man stood at the mare's side checking the foal's position. Though Bella didn't seem uncomfortable, she poked her head out in the direction of the yard and snorted the night air as though she'd jump over the gate if her belly wasn't so heavy. But he could tell she still wasn't ready to deliver. Too awake to go back to bed, he returned to the house to wait.

He tossed a few spoonfuls of coffee grounds into the pot and thrust it on the stove. And by habit, he pulled a side of bacon from the icebox, carved off a few slices, and threw them into the pan.

A pickup backfiring on the road drew his attention. Glancing out the window, he could see a pair of headlights eerily illuminating the fruit tree orchard. *Who the devil would be out on the road this early?* he thought. Dan was working on the road up north, so he couldn't imagine it would have been him, although Dan was known to come and go at any hour of the day.

"Sam! Whoa, Sam. Old man?" The voice came from the yard.

He pushed the frying pan off the stove. "Well. What do you say, Jerry? What're you doing up the road so early?"

"I was up at Westy's place. Their old sow started to deliver last night but had some problems." Removing his glasses, he rubbed his dry eyes. "Lasted quite a while. I was headin' home when I saw your lights on and remembered your mare was just about due."

"Your timing is good. I think she's getting ready."

Jerry tossed his hat onto the table and fell into the chair. "I just knew the minute I'd get to town, you'd probably send for me."

"Have you eaten?"

"Nah. Not hungry." He sniffed the air. "But that coffee smells good."

Sam slid a steaming cup to him, then cocked his head, straining to hear something.

"What? What is it?" Jerry cupped his hand behind his good ear.

The vet followed Sam into the stable where they heard low grunting. Though the mare persisted in moving back and forth, it was the alarmed look in her eyes that got their attention.

"Her water broke." Sam shook his head.

Jerry passed his hand along her underside and then checked under her tail. He shook his head and pursed his lips.

"What's wrong? Something not right?"

"I might be wrong." Jerry bit his lip. "Seems far along, though. It may turn yet. But the foal's still transverse. Not turning fast enough."

Sam stroked the mare's forelock. "It's okay, Bella. Come on now. You cooperate."

"Well, something's happening here," Jerry said after a few moments. "One foot just popped through." Sam came around to look.

Suddenly the mare flopped down on her side.

"Look here, there's the other foot popping through." Jerry gestured. "Okay, that's a good sign. But she needs to get up." He stooped down and began rolling his sleeve up to check her.

Suddenly the mare bolted up on all fours.

"Her contractions just aren't right, Sam." The vet performed some mental calculations, shaking his head. "Don't know what's going on."

Finally, the foal's nose popped out a bit, becoming visible behind the membranous sack.

"It's not trying to breathe," Sam said.

"Nah. Just looks that way. It'll be fine now. Just got to get the shoulders out. Help me pull."

Sam grabbed one foot while Jerry grabbed the other one. Gently they tugged, but it wouldn't move.

"Looks like the foal's trying to breathe a little now," Jerry commented. "But there's some obstruction."

Without warning, the mare fell, bellowing and grunting. "What the hell!" Jerry yelled. "Get her up. She's got to stay up!"

Rushing to her front, Sam yanked on her bridle. "Come on, girl." But she just snorted, her eyes wild, stretching to look behind her.

Sam tried every which way to get her to her feet, but to no avail. At the other end, Jerry tried his best to move the foal out. But all he could do was shake his head.

"It's crushed!" Jerry's words hit Sam square in the face. "She God-damned crushed it."

＊

Jesse had been captive in one of his frequent nightmares. He was back at home and had noticed his dog, Tap, was missing. Drifting through the house to investigate, he bumped into Jack, who smiled, but in an evil way, giving Jesse the impression that he was hiding something. Then instantly, behind Jack, the dog began barking. And now Jesse could see that he had interrupted Jack trying to smother Tap. Somehow, the barking woke him up, and he realized it was his grandfather's dogs that were making such a racket. At the window, he saw the vet's truck, and he knew that Bella must be delivering. Slipping into jeans and throwing on a T-shirt, he ran to the stable, where he found his grandfather and the veterinarian leaning over the mare.

They were trying to extract the crushed foal from its bloody confines. Since his uncle Colton had spilled the beans, Jesse had anticipated this day. He looked forward to watching the foal develop over the summer, knowing it would be his. But instead, he confronted two blood-spattered men, grunting in their attempt to clear out Bella's dead foal.

Aware of his grandson's presence, Sam directed, "Jesse, go fetch an old blanket from the tack room." As a second thought, he added, "And let the horses out to give them some room." Bella's distress lingered in the stable air like the smoke from the fall's torched fields.

In a few moments, Jesse had all the doors unlocked and the horses quickly moved out to the paddock. Then he returned with the blanket. Leaning up against the stall, he waited while the vet cleaned up the mare.

"Here, Sam." The vet gently wrapped the foal in the blanket. "Let's put him in my pickup."

"No. He stays here. I'll bury him in the orchard. Jesse can help."

"Gramps." All color had faded from his face. "Do I have to? I mean—"

"No, lad. Jerry will help me. Go on back to the house then."

Back in the house, Jesse's stomach began to churn. He ran outside to get some fresh air. Wandering aimlessly, but keeping a safe distance from the stables, he found himself at the edge of the orchard. Waking up in the middle of the night was catching up.

The hollowness in his head moved into a dull headache and was worsened by scratchy, dry eyes. And his stomach wouldn't stop churning. He desperately wanted to be with his grandfather. Squatting down, between taking deep gulps of air, he tried to see if Gramps was on his way back. Why hadn't he gone, Jesse thought. He hated to disappoint his grandfather.

Suddenly, the picture of his dad came to him. He wished more than anything that his dad was there. He wanted to confess his sadness and watch the side of his dad's mouth crinkle with a rare smile as his dad explained there was nothing to be sad about. To wash away Jesse's concerns with the wave of his hand and a reassuring arm around his shoulders, to know that good feeling inside would never leave, because his dad would always be there.

The knot in his stomach grew hotter, and before he knew it, he was leaning over, retching nothing from his empty stomach. After a few minutes, the convulsions stopped, and his stomach stopped rumbling.

He stumbled back to the house. And, instead of going upstairs to bed, he ended up in the library. He loved how the many volumes had a way of absorbing all the jarring sounds of his thoughts and brought a calmness and peace to him. And the smell of the books—like an old librarian imbued with her perfume—convinced him that he would be watched over and nothing would be allowed to harm him.

Scanning the shelves, he came across a tall, thin book that had white binding embossed in gold letters: *A Child's Book of Victorian Verses*. Hugging the book to his chest, he sank down into the window seat's cushion. On the flyleaf, inscribed in flowing script, he read, "To Letty. All my love, Mama. 1914."

Turning page after page, he saw simple drawings in faded watercolors, illustrating the poetry and short stories. On a page where the verse was laid out symmetrically and the illustrations captured human-like animals, clothed in Victorian-style garments, he saw a red robin, an arrow piercing its breast, lying on the ground surrounded by other animals dressed in black.

He began to read.

The Death and Burial of Poor Cock Robin

Who killed Cock Robin?
"I," said the sparrow,
"With my little bow and arrow,
I killed Cock Robin."

Who saw him die?
"I," said the magpie,
"With my little eye,
I saw him die ...."

Who caught his blood?
"I," said the fish,
"With my little dish,
I caught his blood."

Who'll make his shroud?
"I," said the beetle,
"With my thread and needle.
I'll make his shroud."

A breeze caused the lace curtain to dance side to side, tickling his arm. Instantly, his muscles relaxed, the aching in his stomach stopped, and he no longer felt lonely or sad, just increasingly sleepy.

Who'll dig his grave?
"I," said the owl.
"With my spade and ..."

Overwhelming drowsiness drew him into a realm where words return to ideas. In this place, where objects no longer express ideas, thoughts are not always bounded by logic or reason; ideas do not need words for movement, but flow freely on their own. Here they dance, separating, joining, changing, separating again, and then rejoining, until they take on different forms and expressions.

. . .

Back from burying the foal, the old man looked around the house, concerned about Jesse. Finding him in the library asleep, he crept closer. Recognizing the book of verses, he shuffled to his chair with a sigh.

His weary eyes fell on the floor where the first rays of sunlight burst through the window above, marking the doorway to the library. And at once, he remembered a day many years ago when the light was the same.

14

Summer 1916

S am, sparing a few minutes from an already full day, realized he had neglected the kitchen garden in his busy days and decided to try to catch up a little.

When an automobile honked as it passed by on the road, he cursed. Lately, it seemed more Sunday drivers were finding great sport driving up and down clogging the roads. The farmers had pitched in to have the gravel macadamized to make it easier for themselves, but those pleasure drivers seemed to think it was for their convenience—while the additional wear and tear would cost the farmers.

Not only did the automobiles frighten the horses on the road, but when the drivers couldn't find their way on the maze of unchartered roads, they thought nothing of turning into the nearest property and honking until someone came out to give them directions. Convinced these drivers were a nuisance, farmers began closing the gates to their properties.

To his disappointment, this automobile roared into his yard, honking the entire time. He cursed himself for not closing his gate. His dogs deserted him, adding to the noise, howling to see who it was. Sam decided he'd not bother this time. The driver could find his own way out. Besides, he knew they wouldn't last long with the dogs nipping at the car's tires.

But the horn didn't cease. Throwing down his hoe, he took off towards the yard. He had patiently given directions to the last two touring automobiles, and enough was enough, he decided. They would get the directions to their destination all right, but it may not be the one they were expecting.

Rounding the corner of the house, he was faced with a man climbing out of a brand new 1916 Ford Model T to join a young woman standing nearby holding a basket. The audacity of this pair, he thought. Who did they think they were? He would take pleasure in setting them straight. But the way they stood gave him pause. These two seemed different somehow. These city people certainly were out of their element. They were as stylish as their new automobile. Judging by how they were dressed, they must have taken a wrong turn on their way to a wedding.

There wasn't a woman on the Eastside who wouldn't have envied this young woman's clothes, although there would have been no place to wear them. And the Eastside would never have turned out someone like her companion. He was too clean, too polished, and looked as though he could have walked out of an ad for Arrow shirts.

"Aren't you going to ask us to sit down?" The woman asked, gesturing to the table and chairs under the oak tree.

Only when he heard her voice did the scales, as they were, fall from his eyes. It seemed to take hours for him to pluck himself from his dreamlike trance. His heart leapt to think that Grace was in front of him.

"Wait a minute!" he whispered to himself. What the hell was going on? Every idea that popped into his head to make sense of this wouldn't work. He forced himself to say something, anything. "Is it really you?"

Grace took a few steps towards him, then decided to wait for her companion. Picking up the basket, she traded it from one hand to the other.

"It's been much too long. How are you, Sam?" She extended her hand. "I'm sorry we've come unannounced."

What the hell was going on? The refrain repeated in his head. Who was this man? Then his stomach churned with the fear of who this might be.

Taking her trembling hand, he squeezed it tightly. It was icy cold.

"Sam. This is Lou Landon." She glanced from Lou to Sam and then quickly down to the basket. "And this is Kate's child, Elizabeth. You remember my sister Kate? Anyway, I promised to watch after—"

"Grace, honey," Lou said, not taking his eyes from their clasped hands. "Your introduction might confuse Mr. Hunter."

"Sam ..." She took a deep breath, as though it was hard to say the next words. "Lou is my husband." She released Sam's hand and stared at the ground a few inches from his boots.

"Good afternoon." Lou's expressionless lips barely parted. "Mr. Hunter." Both hands remained buried deep in his pockets.

How could this slicker drive in here and introduce himself calmly—as Grace's husband? What the hell had happened? The thoughts reeled over and over in his head.

Sam glanced into the basket where the infant lay sleeping. "So, Kate had a baby? I hadn't heard. But then she has quite a brood. One could lose track." It was all he could come up with.

How innocent children were, so unaware of the deceit of those entrusted with their care. How backwards the world had gotten it. It is we that should be under their care. Perhaps then ... ah, ignorance being bliss ...

"Here. Come sit down under the tree." He struggled to cover his astonishment. Jupiter and Mars followed, sniffing around and generally making pests of themselves.

"Mars, Jupiter. Sit!" At the snap of his fingers, they quickly lay down behind him.

"So? What brings you all to these parts?" Sam said, amazing himself that of all the questions buzzing around in his head, this was the one that escaped his lips.

Grace couldn't take her eyes off the house. "Look at that," she said too nervously. "It's beautiful. My, you've been busy." She turned back to him. "Has Will had time to help you?"

How Sam wished that she could hear the thoughts and anxieties bouncing around in his mind. He didn't wish to share them with the city slicker next to her. But he could only stare straight into her eyes, willing her to read his thoughts.

"I haven't seen much of Will lately. He's planted quite a crop on the three sisters' place. And I hear he's making plans to enroll in college. Guess his hands are full. Obviously, we haven't talked enough."

Grace's husband coolly watched Sam, who could sense his scrutiny.

"Hell, where're my manners?" Shaking himself from the moment, he took the opportunity to escape into the house to get drinks.

Lou's eyes followed Sam. "My dear, I can't believe you grew up in this—"

"Back country?" she anticipated. How foolish she had been insisting on coming here. One mistake after another ...

"You were sure you wanted to stop in. He ... and you certainly seem very uncomfortable. Are you sure there are no ...?"

"No. That's long gone. It's fine!"

The dogs brushed past him. "Shoo. Get!" Lou spat out.

Grace felt sorry for her husband. When they had first met, she tried to explain how much the countryside meant to her, but he cut her off by pronouncing that the country was just the space one endured to get from one city to the next.

"You know, I'll confess the house is handsome and the yard

looks well kept," Lou pronounced. "Though how a rough cowboy like him would even know anything about style is beyond me."

Grace glanced back over at the house.

"But what I don't like is knowing that this farmer is still in love with you."

"Lou, keep your voice down," Grace pleaded. "He might hear you." She bent down and adjusted the mosquito netting on the baby's basket.

From the kitchen window, Sam had a clear view of Grace and her husband. He couldn't remember the last time he had seen a suit of clothes like Lou wore. His old blue jeans, oil-spotted and dirty; his work shirt, sweat-stained; his boots, dirt-encrusted, were no challenge to a tailored suit and shiny leather shoes. And recalling his mother's words of wisdom from long ago, "The value is in the package, not in the wrapping," gave him little comfort right now.

In a few moments, he returned with the drinks and placed them in front of Grace. She handed a jar of tea to Sam and offered the other to Lou, who refused it.

"So how long have you been here? On the Eastside, I mean," Sam probed, he would have a huge argument with Will and even Mollie realizing that they both had purposely withheld this. He was beginning to understand why Will had not been around lately. And lately Mollie's melancholia had rendered her difficult to engage in conversation other than what needed to be decided about farming her ranch.

"Well, hardly—" Grace began.

"Just a few days," Lou interrupted, "but even that is long enough." He gave the old Jaeger cabin, Sam's former house, a questioning look.

"I miss my work and my associates in the city," Lou added.

The dogs walked over again, sniffing his hand. He was quick to wipe his hand with his silk handkerchief.

"Do you like horses?" Sam crossed his legs and swatted a fly from his jeans. He sure would like to see those fancy brown shoes buried deep in a stall full of fresh horse shit. "A mare just had a foal." He turned to Grace. "You remember Cassie, your mare?"

"Yes. I gave her to Will when I left. I didn't realize she was here."

"Would you like to take a walk around to the stables?"

"No, I don't think so," Lou said, turning to Grace. "You said we would only drop in for a minute on our way into town. We must be going. We don't want to miss our appointment."

Grace looked around at the yard. As though taking some sort of stand, she told Lou, "You go ahead. I'll stay here and rest a bit. I don't want to wake Elizabeth."

He stared at her. "No. That's a mistake. We must go together."

"No. It won't make a difference." She shook her head. She looked comfortable with her decision even though she evidently had not planned to stay. "In fact, it's probably wiser if I'm not there. You can take care of it. I'll rest here and wait for you to return."

Lou glared at his pocket watch and then ground the cover shut. Glancing from Grace to Sam, then back to her, he said through lips that seemed not to move, "You don't think it's wiser to come?" She shook her head.

Sam grew perplexed, trying to figure out what the appointment could be for; then he decided it would interest him only if it was with a divorce lawyer. And from the looks of things, if she didn't get in the car, that could be likely. What made his blood begin to boil was that they had not planned to stop—this was just a quick diversion from their intended destination.

Lou gave her a quick kiss on her forehead, dodged Sam's outstretched hand, and raced to the car. Forcing the Model T into gear, he drove away towards town.

15

As the sound of the engine faded down the road, an uncertain silence enveloped Grace and Sam. Knowing he was staring at her, she met his gaze a few times but could think of nothing to break the stillness. She knew that the minute she opened her mouth, he would have many questions. Fidgeting, she knew she shouldn't have persuaded Lou to turn in. But the sight of the oak from the road and her curiosity had made her insist that they stop. She hadn't realized that conjecture is very different from reality; she hadn't counted on how it would feel with a real Sam there. This was a mistake.

Yet she also admitted to herself that she didn't want to go to the meeting, and perhaps, this was why she chose to put herself in this position—gaining an excuse not to go, but at what price—alone and vulnerable?

If only she could make Sam understand why she had married Lou, perhaps then he would not be so hurt. Of course, he was shocked to see them arrive unannounced. She knew how she would have felt had Sam arrived in San Francisco with a woman, at his side, announced or unannounced. Would she have remained as gracious as he? She didn't think so.

"So. Now I'm just a stop on the road?" Sam broke the silence.

"Sam. It's more involved than—"

A car stopped at the gate, and the driver popped his head out of the window. "Wonder if you might be able to direct me to the Giffen place?"

"What's the matter? Horn broke?" Sam yelled over.

"What?" The man yelled back.

"It's up a ways. Not more'n a mile." But he groaned at the driver's quizzical look. "I'll be right back," he told Grace.

She remembered how much she loved Sam's gait, confident and full of purpose. Her heart skipped a beat as she faced the gulf that existed between Lou and Sam. Lou would not waste any time with a stranger unless he could see some selfish benefit. Whereas here was a man who found no one and nothing too unimportant for his attention. He was a rock.

In the oak above, the squirrels danced across the branches, climbing higher to disappear in the upper ones. Mercifully, the birds' chatter and the other country sounds began to blanket her in the comfortable feeling she longed for.

With the traveler on his way up the road, Sam returned, shaking his head.

"Hell, Grace. I just can't believe you're married. I had no idea."

"I scarcely realize it at times myself." She stared over his shoulders into the orchard.

"Can't believe you fell for a city man. Where did you meet?"

She took another sip of iced tea. How complicated everything had become. To think there was a time when she was bored with the country simplicity, and now, she yearned for it. She must try to explain to him how her life had changed. This was the price she must pay to enter his place and enjoy a brief peace.

"When I was teaching ... uh ... living with Cousin Polly, we ... my students and I met Lou at an art exhibit. He was a friend of Polly's. We've many things in common. His family lives in St. Louis. Very charming." She smoothed an imaginary wrinkle from her dress. "Lou travels often between the city and St. Louis on business."

Restraining himself no longer, Sam said, "You can't be serious? Surely you don't believe what you're saying. Grace, what could you possibly have in common? You're from the country. You love to ride, hunt, and sit under a tree. From the looks of it, his skinny butt has only touched a horse's hide on a horsehair sofa."

The expression on her face laid her wide open. Sam could tell that she already knew this, and the effect of his words was to hurt her. What good was all this? He knew everything he said hit her hard, and he also knew there was nothing she could say that would change her situation now. And that bothered him the most—seeing her so defeated and sad. She was married now. The deed had been done. She had made the choice.

"You couldn't have told me?" he asked. "I had to meet him head on with not so much as a warning—"

"I'm sorry, Sam. There wasn't time."

"Don't I ... didn't our friendship mean anything to you?"

"Of course, it did ... does!"

"And what the hell? Why didn't Will tell me?"

"Until I could tell you myself, I made him promise not to."

From where he sat, Sam had the perfect vantage point to contemplate the fields where the barley he had sowed earlier that spring had begun to shoot up. Once the fields were cultivated and irrigated, the seedlings would grow. It happened as it was always supposed to happen, as it always did happen. And then when the time was right, all he had to do was harvest its yield. The reward was inevitable. How could this have turned out so differently?

Each time Grace had returned, he had convinced himself that he should patiently wait while she worked to get the city out of her blood. Each time she came, she'd spoken of the house and the land. He was convinced he was building it for her, for them. What had gone wrong?

The silence grew until she blurted out, "Mother writes that Mollie is not well most of the time and that Joe's never around."

Sam continued to study the field.

She searched for anything to say. "You've been very good to Mollie," she went on. "Will says you work the land and give her the money to live on."

He wondered what she was really trying to say.

"Do you take anything for yourself?" she asked. Taking out a handkerchief, she blotted her neck and face. He almost began to take pleasure now in how uncomfortable she was becoming.

"I mean, you must take something for your labor?"

He took a deep breath and bent forward. "My joy is in helping someone in such need."

He leaned back in his chair and leveled his gaze at her. She returned his look momentarily and then glanced away, stuffing the ball that she had made of her handkerchief into her pocket. Picking up the ribbons that decorated the side of her dress, she began to braid them.

"You mentioned Will has planted another large crop on the three sisters' place," she said. "Do you think he's in over his head?"

"Over his head? He's smart and knows what he's doing."

"Really? I don't trust Cousin Amanda. Will is much too kind."

"Yes, your brother is kind, but he won't let Amanda take advantage of him. He knows what's fair."

"Is it fair to work the land on a promise that they'll help send him to college?"

"A promise?" Sam jumped to his feet and began circling the chairs. "You mean there's nothing in writing?"

"Sam. It's all right. Daddy says he'll have some hard lessons to learn. He's always—"

"Goddamn it! It's not right! Will's too trusting. He just thinks that because he works hard and trusts those that shouldn't be trusted, everything will turn out all right. It's not fair. It doesn't work that way. I don't want to see him taken—"

"Sam. There's nothing you can do about it now." She sighed.

He stopped circling and flopped down in the chair, brooding.

Grace seemed to be looking for anything to say that would

calm him down. Settling on the house, she stated, "The house is just beautiful. How proud you must be."

He was amazed that she could voice such feelings, when only that last time she was here he had made his second offer to give it all to her in marriage. What about her promise to come back after her obligations? He searched her face but could detect nothing of this.

Fearing that he might say something he would later regret and wanting her to know what he had done for her, he stood up abruptly.

"Come on. I'll show you!" Noticing her look at the basket, he added, "The baby'll be all right for a few minutes."

At the front door, Sam paused, glancing over his shoulder at Grace before motioning her in. She hesitated, then entered the front hall ahead of him.

"It's so bright." She gazed around her. "And see how the window upstairs allows the sunlight to flow in."

"Over here on the right is the living room." He brushed past her on his way through the hall. "Do you recognize the stone on the fireplace?"

She went over and touched it. "Should I? Where did you get it?"

"Will and I brought the stones down from Cliff Rock Springs near your mother's place."

"Ah ... yes ... Mother's place."

They moved to the next room.

"Another living room? How extravagant!"

"Not really. I designed the house to be symmetrical. I needed another room here to balance it out, that's all." He smiled at the expense of having things balanced.

They drifted to the back hall.

"And there to the right is the dining room. Beyond that is the kitchen."

She went over to the table and poked her head up the back stairway. The breeze, sifting through the screen door, loosened her hair, making strands of it dance on the currents. The folds of her dress gently rippled, looking as though she floated lightly forward. The steady ticking of the clock in the front hall traveled down the corridor.

"Here, let me show you the most important room in the house."

As though it had been planned, the sun's light streamed through the upstairs hall window down through the hall, illuminating the entrance of his cherished library.

"Oh my!" Entranced, Grace moved through the doorway.

Following her in, he studied her carefully, noting her impressions. For this was the room he had done all to complete to ask her to marry him. And now all he could do was show it to her. He gave her time to examine it as she searched the shelves and noted the books. Moving over to the library table, she fingered the books lying there as well. Her hand drifted across the smooth wooden table as she looked past the open window into the sunlight outside.

"Oh, Sam, it's so beautiful. I never imagined ... It's very much like the one at the Martin house. So lovely! It seems so long ago."

She picked up a book from the table. She read the inscription on the flyleaf aloud and then looked up in surprise. "Who gave you this?"

"Mollie."

"Why?"

"She knows me and books. She gave it to me to remember Letty by. She said she was grateful to me for working her place. She said Letty loved to hear the poems and stories from that book."

Perhaps it was the mention of Letty, together with being here, knowing the house was for her but would not be hers, that it became too much. She turned away from Sam trying to hide her tears. She wiped them away and, fanning through the book, stopped at a page that had been earmarked. She read a few verses:

> Who'll dig his grave?
> "I," said the owl,

> *"With my spade and trowel*
> *I'll dig his grave."*

> *Who'll be the parson?*
> *"I," said the rook,*
> *"With my little book,*
> *I'll be the parson."*

From memory, Sam picked up the lines:

> *Who'll be chief mourner?*
> *"I," said the dove,*
> *"I mourn for my love,*
> *"I'll be chief mourner."*

Grace looked up and recited,

> *Who'll carry the coffin?*
> *"I," said the kite,*
> *"If it's not in the night,*
> *I'll carry the coffin."*

Sam carried it forward:

> *Who'll toll the bell?*
> *"I," said the bull,*
> *"Because I can pull,*
> *I'll toll the bell."*

Finally, Grace hesitated, then tried:

> *All the birds of the air*
> *Fell sighing and sobbing.*

But then stumbled and couldn't remember the rest.

Sam finished it:

> *When they heard the bell toll*
> *For poor Cock Robin.*

"How this poem reminds me ..."

He wished to hold her to comfort her, but in a way, he wanted her to suffer a little, at least feel a little of the pain that gnawed at his heart. He waited a few moments before asking, "Reminds you of what?"

"When we were children," she laughed between her tears, "and a little rambunctious, to get our attention and settle us down, Mother would recite the first stanza. Then each would recite a verse or make one up, adding to the poem." She looked at him. "The one who could think of nothing to add by reciting the last verse would be the loser."

Bringing the book with her to the front window, she sighed. Hugging it close to her, she sat down in the window seat and appeared to stare at the circle of chairs. But Sam sensed she was really searching for the many years before.

He studied her expression and would have given anything to know exactly what she was thinking. She must have shoved the memories of previous conversations to a distant alcove in her mind to make the decisions she'd made. Allowing her to sit for a time, he had no wish to hurry her. The room seemed to take on a new life with her in it. But that didn't surprise him.

After a few minutes, it seemed as though she had decided something. Taking a deep breath, she stood up and moved towards the doorway. There she caught a glimpse of herself in the mirror and straightened a wisp of hair.

As she brushed past him, he caught the scent of her hair. Impulsively, he touched her cheek. She did not step away, but hesitated and looked him in the eyes, and didn't move when his hand drifted down her cheek and around her head.

When he pulled her towards him and their lips met, it seemed nothing existed around them—no house, no time, no space, no sound. In a moment, he tasted the salt of her tears in his mouth. As the clock began its hourly chime, she backed away.

"Goddamn the clock! Goddamn the time!" he muttered under his breath.

And as though on cue, the baby began to fuss.

"I must get back." The expression on her face was mirrored in her sad voice.

Following her out, he was taken with how easy it seemed for her to move from what just happened to picking up the baby and rocking it. It came to him what a wonderful mother she would have made for their children. He could almost make himself believe that this was their baby and that their lives were here together, and all had turned out according to his plan. That Grace had come home to him and to their house, and all was well. And that everything before had been just an unfortunate dream. But he was not the sort that could make believe. He lived in reality and in truth. And though this was the reality, he was not fond of what was now true.

"Oh, Sam, will you ever have anyone?" When he did not answer at once, she asked again, "Is there anyone you can share this with?"

"No. Not now." What could he possibly say? Having her here was so bittersweet. "I thought as much at one time, but then she never came back."

She knew the moment in the house had to disappear. "Well, I'm sure there will be one, someday." She rocked the baby, trying to forget what his kiss tasted like.

"I don't think so. I guess I'm learning that I need no one! Besides my needs are simple, and the work here is hard."

And as though the last cue was perfectly timed, Jupiter and Mars announced the arrival of Lou with howling and barking.

Jumping from his automobile, Lou aptly sidestepped the dogs as he walked toward Grace and Sam. He took a deep breath and stared at Grace. "The business has gone well. The agreement just needs to be notarized. We need to get into town now before the banks close."

She nodded absently.

Lou glanced from Sam to Grace. "Everything all right?" He began to bristle.

"Yes," Grace answered. "Everything is—"

"Just fine, Lou," Sam interrupted. "It's as it should be. Grace was feeling faint from the heat, and I'll be damned if you didn't come back at exactly the right moment."

Surprised by the response, Lou stared at him. "Then we must get going."

While Lou dodged the dogs to stow the basket on the floorboard of the car, Grace whispered to Sam, "Thank you so much for the pleasure of the shade of the oak."

"Grace, honey. We've got to get going," Lou shouted from the driver's seat.

With the baby snuggled against her shoulder, Grace took advantage of the moment; leaning over, her lips brushed Sam's cheek.

His heart jumped. He pictured himself reaching out and grabbing her, after he had picked Lou up by the lapels of his brand-new suit and thrown him into the river. But, what could he do? She had made her choice. He slammed the car door shut after she had taken a seat next to her husband.

Sam stood as still as one of his new saplings and did not turn away until the Model T was back on the road and well out of his sight.

Drifting over to the grass, past the table, he noticed that Grace had left behind a folded scarf on the cushion of her chair. Unfolding it, he brought it to his face and breathed in. He willed her scent to be buried deep in his lungs forever. He lay down under the oak tree. The dogs came over and, lying down next to him, licked his face. Rubbing their heads, he looked up in the direction of the branches of the oak tree.

Tracing along one of the main branches, he followed the antics of two squirrels. He watched one as it made its way, far up to the top, eventually disappearing from his view, while the other went the opposite direction down the trunk to land on the ground and out of his sight. He knew that was exactly how it must be for Grace and him. He had worked hard to make her a part of the ranch. And now, he would work equally as hard to let her go.

16

Summer 1960

When alone, after the dinner dishes had been washed and put away, the old man liked to bring one of his well-worn books out to the front porch to help end the day.

Writings of the great thinkers, who recorded their contemplations of the universe and their place in it, comprised his most treasured. Plato taught him that for every visible object in the world, there was a perfect model in the invisible. Meditations by Aurelius taught him lessons on self-control and self-awareness, while St. Augustine addressed the enduring spiritual questions.

In his favorite chair, lost in silent dialogs with these familiar friends, occasionally he would glance up to catch the sun painting its strokes of twilight on the sky and feel the darkness descend around his home. Only when his eyes grew too heavy and it became too dark to see the words, would he retire to bed.

. . .

This midsummer evening, as Jesse was on his way out to the porch, he stopped in front of the gun case in the front hall. The old man, following, watched his grandson study the contents.

"Interested in rifles, eh?"

"They look pretty old. Are they antique?

"Well, they're not all quite that old." He chuckled. "A few belonged to my brothers, and that one," he tapped the glass, "is an 1852 Sharp's carbine, used in the Civil War. It belonged to my daddy."

"What about this one?"

"That's a 1917 Eddystone, 30-06 caliber rifle, U.S. Army issue with a sling. I brought it back from the Great War."

"You were in a war?"

"I fought under Pershing in France. Many years ago."

The mention of the war had unleashed a slew of memories that Sam had not revisited lately. In depots with flying flags overhead, young men crowded into trains. Mothers tearfully waved good-bye with their husbands standing stoically nearby. Youthful heads filled with duty, adventure, and a time to get away from the ranches and clerking jobs shouted back, cheering and waving.

Anxious to see countries they had only read about in school; their optimism was greeted by that which the old veterans in their families could never have prepared them for. Finally, after months of service, these ill and war-ravaged young men, stepping from trains to meet their families, cast guilty glances at the baggage cars where some friends came home in pine boxes. To those who returned in one piece, it would take many seasons of planting and harvesting to put behind the horrors of their great adventure.

He realized Jesse was far older than Colton and Dan had been when he showed them how to handle guns.

"I don't suppose your dad ever showed you how to shoot?"

"No."

"Hmm." Gramps stowed his book on the hall chair. "It's time you learned."

Fumbling to remove the small key from his pocket, he unlocked the cabinet. Taking out a rifle and a box of ammunition, he handed the rifle to Jesse. It was a Remington Model 700 BDL .308 WIN caliber—almost too heavy to hold but with a comfortable, solid feel. The woodwork on the handle was a heavily polished burl.

In the clearing on the other side of the barn, Gramps instructed him to set up a few cans on the fence.

Satisfied that he had had enough, wondering if he would be able to hit any, Jesse joined his grandfather sitting on the bale of hay.

"Do you know why it's called a rifle?"

Jesse shrugged his shoulders.

"That's because inside the barrel, called the bore, are many spiral grooves. The process of making these grooves is called rifling. When the bullet travels through the barrel, the grooves cause it to spin. And the spinning motion keeps the bullet steadier to the target."

With the rifle resting on his lap, his grandfather pointed to sections of it. "The end here is called the butt plate. It's attached to the heel. Resting it against your shoulder when you fire steadies the rifle. This rifle has a scope, but some don't. You line up the rear sight, here, with the front site on the barrel. Then get your target lined up, and you should be able to hit it. And of course, this is the trigger."

In one smooth movement, Gramps unlocked the bolt, shoved in a shell, pulled the rifle up to his shoulder, squinted through the scope, and pulled the trigger. *Pop!*

The dogs backed away startled and began whining. One look from the old man and they quieted down.

"Your turn." Gramps pushed the loaded rifle into his hands. "Sit here facing the target. Remember to do as I tell you. Okay?"

Jesse nodded. His mouth went dry.

The old man got up.

"Where're you going?"

Moving around to the other side of the bale, facing in the opposite direction, Gramps sat down. "Lean up against my back. I'll support you when the rifle kicks back," he instructed.

"Okay, aim the rifle. Now get the can in the crosshairs. If you have the target dead in the middle, put pressure on your trigger finger. But very gently. Keep your eye on the crosshairs. Don't hurry. Take your time. Keep squeezing."

Jesse fired quickly as his grandfather absorbed the shock of the kick-back.

"Gramps, I missed."

His grandfather moved around to reload the rifle before taking his place again. "Now, try it again. Relax. Just concentrate on getting the target in the crosshairs. When you get close, take a breath, hold it for a second, then slowly squeeze the trigger. No jerking. Just smooth as silk."

Jesse fired again. *Pop!* And missed. After a few more tries, Gramps took the rifle from him.

"What was it like?" Jesse asked.

Gramps gave him a puzzled look.

"I mean the war. Did you ever shoot anyone when you were a soldier?"

His grandfather ran his callused fingers along the rifle's smooth gray metal shaft. "I was there because of Will."

"You don't say much about him."

"Because, my lad, sometimes words are just plain inadequate. And no words could do Will justice. He wasn't like any of my own brothers. He was a deep thinker and saw things differently. He wasn't like most men on the Eastside."

"What made him so different?"

Gramps gazed into the distance, thinking. "Didn't matter if it was a book, an idea, or person, Will wanted to know why it was written, what it meant, or what made a person tick. And he had the rare capacity to appreciate the beauty around him. He saw the symmetry in a tree where others saw knurled branches ready for firewood. Or the brushstrokes in the sunrise, where others saw a hot day coming. And where others saw a nuisance in someone needy, he saw an opportunity to share."

He searched the horizon for the first stars.

"Though it's been many years," he sighed, "I think of him often ..."

April 1917

"Anyone home?" A voice came from the yard.

"That you, Will?" Sam peeked over the top of the book he read while cooling off in the old tub on the kitchen porch.

Will rounded the corner of the house. "None other than."

"Well, pardon me if I don't get up."

"On the contrary, looks like a great way to finish off a day." Will pulled up a chair and straddled it.

Sam gently closed his book and let it drop to the porch. Sinking back in the tub of cool, soapy water, he closed his eyes.

Will studied him for a few moments. "I've noticed lately you don't seem yourself. You seem just a little ... I don't know ... distant. Can't put my finger on it."

"I should be very happy. I've got the barley planted. The walnut trees are in. And the cattle are spoken for."

"Then what's bothering you?"

Sam sat up, glancing from the field to the recently planted orchard, and reluctantly admitted, "I'm sure you can imagine."

"Uh-oh. Still her, huh?"

"What do you hear from her?" He looked Will in the eye. "Is her husband treating her all right?"

"Well, she writes seldom. But when she does, she tells us about her city life and travels." Will stuck some chew inside his lip. "I thought you'd put that behind you."

Sam reached for his shaving mug and stirred up lather with a brush. Staring into a mirror fragment propped on a chair, he dabbed the suds to his face. "I don't know. Some days I work so hard, that I fall into bed asleep without thinking about her, but ..."

"Sam, what is it about her that you can't let go?"

It was difficult to put into words how he felt about Grace. He guessed it would have to start with the first day he'd seen her riding to the Martins' dance. It was the way she snuck up on him, breaking into his world. It was the way she handled her horse and how she smiled at him with her hair loosely flowing behind her.

But what made him sometimes stop in the middle of his day was picturing her eyes. Those hazel eyes that sparkled lightly, mischievously one moment, only to change darker when wrestling with something profound the next. It was also the willfulness she kept concealed, a kind of stubbornness that impelled her to venture beyond the boundaries set by her family. It was the restlessness that plagued her when she was trying to do the right thing. But what grabbed his insides was her vulnerability. This moved every fiber of his being in his desire to protect her.

"Sometimes when I can't sleep, I'll take a walk between the newly planted trees to search the sky. Studying the constellations reminds me there's something bigger to life than this piece of earth I've claimed."

Sam gave Will a glance. "You've heard all this before. Before I knew her, I was content to work the ranch, thinking I needed no one. But like a shooting star in the dark, she made me aware. The sky is different now."

He had tried very hard to let this all go. And because his friend said nothing now, he felt even more awkward. It was so unlike Will, who was always good for making one see the issue from another angle.

Gazing out to the fields, Will remarked, "Well, you haven't asked me about my crops."

Sam began shaving. Now that he had opened his heart to Will, he wished he hadn't. These things were best kept back and not discussed. He was glad Will had changed the subject.

"I suppose now that everything is in, you'll be leaving soon for school. Guess you'll be getting your money for tuition?"

"Well, you told me not to trust Amanda." Will spat to the side.

"What?"

"She told me that she can't afford what she'd promised. She said the taxes this year ate up most of the profit."

Sam hurled his razor into the tub and stood at attention. "The devil!" he shouted. "How can she do this to her own flesh and blood?"

Will smiled at Sam's reaction.

"Tell me you're not going to just sit there and take this? If you don't do something, I will!" Sam said, despite Will's giggling. "And what the hell is so funny?"

Will gestured to him to sit back down, making Sam aware he must look funny standing there displaying his pale, naked body. "It doesn't matter now. I've another plan," Will declared. "Is that all it took to rouse you from your melancholy? Good, now I'll tell you why I've come."

Sam sank back down into the soapy water and searched for his razor. "I don't know why I bother to be so stirred up if you can calmly sit there with a smirk on your face, saying nothing."

"You didn't hear me. I've got something that will cure your melancholy and make me forget about the cousins."

"And what's that?"

"The war in France."

"What about it? It's a long way away."

Will pulled out a rolled-up newspaper from his back pocket and thumped the front page. "Look here—Wilson's declared war on Germany." He shoved his hat back off his face. "Sam, Germany's announced unrestricted submarine warfare against England. And they say England won't last six months on her own."

"Here, let me see that." Sam grabbed the paper.

As he scanned the front page, Will continued. "Wilson says we're no longer neutral. He's assigned General Pershing to lead the first troops. They begin training in France."

He glanced at Sam sideways. "Some of our friends are signing up in town right now at the train station."

Tossing the paper back, Sam asked, "Who? No one said a—"

"Westy ... AJ ... Grover ..."

"Then they're fools! Who'll farm?"

"Are you ready for this?" Will asked.

"For what?" Sam knit his brows together.

"You and I are going to—"

"What!"

"We've got to, Sam. It's our duty."

Sam sighed. "Now I can see how Amanda could cheat you." He tapped his forehead with his middle finger. "She wasn't all that shrewd; she was just dealing with someone a little touched. And you want to be a lawyer?"

Shaking his head, he stared at Will. "I'm many things. I'll admit I may be a love-lost fool. But I'm not a stupid love-lost fool. I'm not going to fight in some war halfway across the world. My only duty is here. Besides what would I do with this place? I can't just walk away."

⁕

Five months later, Grace and her sister Kate, with Elizabeth, finished their shopping at Union Square and rode a cable car from the shops up to Grace and Lou's apartment on Mason Street in San Francisco.

Kate tossed her hat and heavy coat on the sofa—one never knew how to dress for the city weather. "Are you sure Lou won't mind my dropping in to stay for a few days?"

"Of course not."

They were startled when the key jiggled in the lock. Barging around the corner, Lou nearly bumped into Kate.

"Kate. I didn't know you'd be here." He was halfway out of his overcoat. "Grace didn't tell me we'd have visitors."

"I thought you said you had an appointment and wouldn't be able to make lunch," Grace said.

"My schedule changes without notice." He glared at her.

As they took their seats at the table, Grace noticed a stack of mail next to Lou's plate and cursed herself for not checking it.

He flipped through the stack. He held up one envelope and carefully examined the front and back, then whistled. Grace bit her lower lip.

"Well, well." Lou turned to Kate. "Some interesting mail here. Looks like our friend from the Eastside continues to write about his adventures in France. Why he thinks anyone at this address is interested is beyond me."

Grace glanced at Lou and then at the envelope. "Who is it addressed to?"

"Why to you, my dear." He tossed the letter to her. "You know, I almost forgot," he shoved his chair back abruptly, causing the dishes to jump, "I do have an appointment today over in Oakland. In fact, it'll last late, and I'm sure to miss the last ferry. I'll spend the night there ... with friends."

Kate stared out the window at two squawking seagulls.

Grabbing his jacket and briefcase, he left, slamming the door behind him.

"I'm sorry, Kate. It's difficult right now," Grace said.

"He still sends you letters?"

"It's what keeps me alive."

"But what about Lou?"

"It's all right." Grace said, staring at the envelope. "What can I do? I'm getting used to—"

"How long can you live like this?"

Grace jumped up as though the letter would disintegrate in a few moments. "I hate to leave you. I must know how he is," she said, running towards her room.

The second she opened her bedroom window, the wash of fresh air flooded the room, and she was grateful it would soon clear the room of Lou's lingering scent. She fell into the chaise next to the window, fanned her face with the envelope, and watched a fishing boat drift across the bay. The silence provided a golden calm. Unable to resist any longer, she opened the envelope carefully, unfolding the water-stained paper.

July 31, 1918.

Dearest Grace,

I'm sorry it's been so long since my last letter. After we completed our training, we had to move our quarters and do more work digging the trenches. It rains here constantly, and we are forever pumping the water out of the trenches.

I wish I could write everything we're doing but they tell us the censors will delete anything that might endanger our troops if it fell into enemy hands.

The conditions here are so much worse than anything I could have imagined. Sometimes, I wonder if I will ever make it home. But Will, as always, is nearby. His companionship has made it almost bearable. He won't stop trying to convince me that our great adventure is selfless and that we're here because we're needed.

Here, where I sit, man's hatred and distrust of one another has cut its path through the land. Here, only a trench divides men from each other and reeks of death.

It's not the dirt that bothers me; I'm used to having the soil a part of me. I thought all the soil of the earth was the same. But I'm wrong. The colors and textures vary.

I try to keep my thoughts dwelling on the peaceful Eastside where we spent many happy hours. I long to see the giant oak but instead I see a war-ravaged apple orchard. The land is littered with holes where bombs have hit and where they've stretched the barbed wire. The fruitless trees reach out for mercy but are shown none. I spend hours watching the gray sky crying tears of despair and remember the spring rains back home where orange blossoms gently sip it. The rain here washes away what once was fertile but now barren topsoil, leaving open wounds and deep scars.

In the distance is an abandoned stone farmhouse. Before this, I imagine a man much like me awakening every morning to the sounds of the farm as I did. I try to picture the land supplying everyone with its abundance before hatred poisoned the air and soil.

People think the conflict is here on the land but that is not the truth. The battle we really fight is the one in our mind. We fight every day for courage and survival in these wretched conditions. Strength comes from many sources. Some say they think of their families. Others say it's their determination that keeps them sane. And there are those who stay strong due to their love of the fight. We have little to say to those.

But I'll tell you what I see when I'm in the trenches smelling death and listening to the gunfire. I see my farmhouse and my land. This is what keeps me strong.

When I am overwhelmed with fear, I go home and sit in my favorite chair out on the porch, secure and content, enjoying a book or the view of the wide-open fields. I let the scent of the orange and lemon blossoms come to me on the cool breeze.

Even at this moment I can close my eyes and see it.

I see the huge oak tree. So strong and lasting. And the river. The cool emerald river.

I see you sitting under the oak now. I think about our kiss in the library the day you came to visit. I watch you as you listen to the chattering squirrels climbing higher and higher. Then you smile at me, and I hear your laughter. And yet to think of you in this way is just too difficult.

My watch has just ended, and they are asking for mail. Please keep us in your prayers.

Love, Sam.

With tears running down her cheeks, she released the sheaves of brittle paper to the breeze that made them dance before landing on the floor. The mild draft warmed by the sun caressed her, and she sobbed again, in the comfort that Sam was still safe and would always remain so, hidden deep in her heart.

17

Summer 1960

Jesse had followed closely as his grandfather repeated the lines he recalled from his letter to Grace. "Gramps, sometimes I get so into your stories it's like I'm there. Is that what you meant in your letter?"

"In one sense, yes, but in another, not really. It's one thing to engage in a story to understand it better. But it's another thing altogether to use it to escape a dangerous situation. You can't bury your head in the dirt; there's no running from anything; you must resolve it. You can't be passive, or you'll suffer."

"I don't understand."

"A story is a story. You can take part if you want, or not. But a dangerous situation—you must resolve that head-on. If you don't, eventually it will destroy you, in one way or another." The old man thought for a few minutes. "Here, I'll show you my way of meeting it head-on. You must really concentrate. You must put your entire being into it. Do you think you can try?"

Jesse nodded and began to feel goosebumps in anticipation.

"Okay, now close your eyes and try to quiet your thoughts, by thinking about the ranch. Feel it."

Closing his eyes, he could hear his grandfather's labored breathing. This was easy. He could think of no other place he would rather be than here, near his side. Before he knew it, though, he pictured himself with his mother. This was not where he wanted to be, he thought. But because she seemed happier than he had ever seen her, he allowed himself to remain there. Her smile was warm, and she beckoned to him. And as though he were a toddler taking his first steps, he moved in her direction. With this movement, a gentle, warm feeling began to grow inside him.

And just as he was about to fall into her arms, an explosion blew them apart. The rifle must have misfired. His stomach took a blow, and then his lungs hurt as though he had taken another. Suddenly Jack's red face jumped out from the grayness. Gasping like a fish for air, Jesse leaped up. His hands flew out in front.

"I know. I know. 'Tis no good running from it. You've got to face it down," his grandfather commanded. "You can do it."

"I can't! Gramps."

"Yes, you can face it down."

"Really, Gramps. I can't! I've tried before. You don't know how awful it is." He felt a tremor from his feet all the way up his spine.

"Show me you can, my lad!" Gramps squeezed his arm. "I know you can do it."

He shook his head in determination that he wouldn't be able to do it. And they sat there for several minutes until it dawned on Jesse, if he couldn't trust his grandfather, then who could he trust? However, to continue, the image of Jack must disappear. Somehow the picture had to be deleted from his mind.

When his breathing slowed down and with his grandfather's encouragement, he grew more confident and would try again. It seemed within a few minutes without effort, he saw a raven flying overhead towards the river, and with the bird's disappearance over the trees went Jack. Jesse's muscles relaxed, and with a sigh of relief, he felt safe again.

The breeze tousled his hair and tickled his ears and eyes,

coaxing him into a feeling of perfect calmness. The melodic cooing of the mourning dove as it guarded its nest called out only to him. And as if someone had turned up the volume, he heard sounds surrounding him that he had not been aware of. He had never felt this awareness before.

The evening music of the bullfrogs pierced him. It was as if he had ceased to be in this somewhere; instead, this somewhere was now in him. He could feel nothing of his body—it was as though his five senses had melted together, resulting in just being. Suddenly, he felt the effortless weightlessness of becoming the evening breeze that, moments before, had gently stroked his face.

Though he had been in danger once because of the river, now there was nothing to fear of the river that had carved its course before bringing its life to the fields. The rushing current making its way down the canal, but still part of the river, began to fill his veins with its vibrant being. And he felt his chest expand outside its boundaries to accommodate a force as powerful as the river.

His mind had no boundaries ... it was the open field, his thoughts, the many birds that flew circles, figure eights, descending and ascending. His body—his substance—was the rich dark soil. But even this was not solid; he knew it would move and shift with the rains and winds. The rich aroma of the freshly turned earth permeated his lungs.

All this was like the trees in the nearby orchard, their roots gripping the earth, as a farmer's powerful hands grab the soil to ascertain its condition.

Simply by leaning into a direction, he found he could move anywhere. Drifting to the farmyard, he was the house with its many rooms. His mind was the library protected and peopled with its shelves packed with books and thoughts. He imagined there was nothing that couldn't be known.

From the house to the oak that Daniel Jaeger had planted; he knew it was his branches that stretched broad and high, reaching up towards the sun, embracing all that circled his limbs. He couldn't tell how deep his roots penetrated but knew it was deeper than any other tree on the ranch.

Suddenly, words carried on the breeze revealed to him:

"...he shall be like a tree planted by the rivers of water ... his leaf also shall not wither; and whatsoever he doeth shall prosper."

And he knew he was this tree and that was what his grandfather wanted him to discover and understand so fully, because it would change the way he thought about himself.

For the first time, he knew he belonged. He would stay forever. He knew nothing could ever harm him again.

"Ah, you understand!" the rustling leaves pronounced. "You do understand, don't you?" They made sure he knew. And his supreme happiness was his acknowledgment.

But somewhere, something said this was enough. A pickup raced by on the road. Then his fingers and toes began to tingle, as though they had fallen asleep. His face felt warm, and he tried to shoo a mosquito that had landed on his arm.

Opening his eyes in the fading light of dusk, he saw his grandfather's satisfied face. He wanted more than anything to tell Gramps how it felt and what he had learned, but when he opened his mouth, no words would come.

"Now, I'm going to tell you something, Jesse. It's important that you understand. What you hold in thought determines who you really are. The thoughts you hold in your heart of hearts are you. If you dwell with sad ideas, you'll be unhappy. If you dwell in hate, you'll be bitter. But if ..." he searched the sky, "you dwell with good, virtuous ideas, you'll be powerful. You will be rich and have need of nothing else."

When Jesse was able to formulate words, his first question was, "Was I hypnotized?"

"Absolutely not! I don't know how to hypnotize." Sam stopped to think how to explain. "Jesse, it's no different from pulling a book down off the shelf in a library where thousands of people have written what they want you to read—what they want you to feel—either for instruction or entertainment. No, you were experiencing what has already been there—uniquely yours. I'm just allowing you to read, like the pages of a book, the thoughts of my experience so you can see what it's like.

"Some people drink to numb the senses to deaden their sensibilities. But this is unnecessary when we realize how to feel the power beyond these same sensitivities. Don't deaden them, explore what's behind them. That's what I'm teaching you. You're dealing with ideas!

"While I was in France, I learned that when I filled my thought with courage, then I became fearless and brave. I knew in my heart I couldn't be harmed. I glimpsed that by lifting my thought far beyond myself, I found the strength that was always mine, hidden safely deep inside. I became convinced nothing could hurt me, and nothing did. A paradox, perhaps, but nonetheless, my conviction."

As his grandfather spoke, Jesse realized that though it had become very dark and he could not see the farmhouse, he knew it was in the yard, so knowing was seeing.

"Gramps, I think I'm beginning to understand."

"Good. Good."

It seemed to Jesse that they sat in the darkness for hours.

"It's getting late." The old man interrupted his thoughts. "We'd best get back."

"Do we have to, Gramps?" How could he go about each day after what just happened? Jesse wondered.

"You will have many opportunities to apply what you're learning. But each situation will require a unique solution. You can't live in the solution; but you can live in the outcome. Nothing comes of living in a fantasy. You must resolve it. It may take some time. But it'll come."

Jesse was filling up with more questions, but knowing he couldn't convince his grandfather to stay there, he returned to asking about Will.

"What about the end of the war? When did you and Will come home?"

"Well, my lad, the war ended a year later, and I came home. But ..." The old man hesitated for a moment. "Will didn't make it."

The words shocked Jesse. He had imagined that he would soon hear the story of Will. He envisioned Will "larger than life." Someone who had done everything right and whom everyone couldn't help adoring. He was smart, kind, fearless, and loyal. Working hard, he didn't dream away his time.

"He was killed in the fall of 1918," Gramps continued. "It was during Pershing's drive into Argonne. We were grateful for the dry weather. The trenches were beginning to dry out, and the barley fields around us were ripe, though no one was there to harvest them. But we were still exhausted. Along with little food and the confines of the trenches, fatigue was our biggest enemy.

"Will was in the first group to go. When he climbed up the side of the trench, I yelled, 'Will, take care!' But he didn't turn around. I knew he heard me, but he wouldn't turn around. I wanted to see his face—one last time.

"After the commander gave us the go-ahead, we were the next to go. The area was secured within the hour. They told us we had made the difference—the war would turn. This lifted our men's spirits, but what did I care? The only thing on my mind was Will. I searched amid the smoky field, full of death, but I couldn't find him."

"Did ... did you ever see him again?" Jesse stumbled over the words, thinking of his grandfather's suffering.

"Later that night, back in camp, I searched the med tent for him. I asked the men who had scoured the field for bodies if they'd seen him, but no one had. Finally, another cart piled high with our dead was brought back. I didn't have to see Will—I knew he was there.

"I counted on Will to always be there, and now he was gone. He was my link to my ranch, to the Eastside, to Grace—to what was my life. And now he was gone." His voice cracked.

"When I came home, I planted a blood orange tree in the

middle of the fruit orchard as a memorial to my friend. It wasn't long before I got busy getting the ranch up and running again. The hard work forced me to stop feeling sorry for myself and dwelling on Will's absence. And besides, he no longer suffered, and he's with me always, now."

Picking up the rifle, the old man ran his fingers over the smooth wood handle and stood up.

"But that was many years ago, wasn't it?" he seemed to say to himself. Then he turned to Jesse. "It's time to turn in for the night."

Jesse could scarcely make out the outline of his grandfather's face, it was so dark, but there was no mistaking the affection in his voice.

"Jesse. Tonight, what you've learned, guard it fiercely! Be careful of sharing it, and don't let anyone take it from you."

Back in the yard, Jesse remembered the stone cross out in the orchard. Though only the two of them were on the ranch, he knew they were not alone. Now, he felt hundreds of soldiers standing behind the trees. He fought the pull to look over his shoulder. He knew that if he did turn, he would be giving into fear. And if he learned one thing tonight, it was the realization that no one could make him fearful unless he allowed it.

Later as Jesse prepared for bed, on his pillow he noticed a slip of paper with a verse written in his grandfather's clear, bold handwriting:

"...we look not at the things which are seen,
but at the things which are not seen:
for the things which are seen are temporal;
but the things which are not seen are eternal."

Folding the paper, he included it with other odds and ends he had been collecting to take home. Turning out the light, he climbed into bed.

Before settling down, he pulled back the curtains to reveal a backdrop of many stars. Captivated, he wanted to count them all.

Thinking of those killed in the war and how much they were missed, he now thought of the dead soldiers as these stars. Though they had fought and died, they were now untouched by anything. They brightly lit up the night sky for those below, seeming to sparkle in joy.

On the other side of the house, the old man searched the same night sky for two stars. Finding the double stars, Mizar and Alcor, he whispered a prayer and gradually felt Will's presence as he always did when he allowed it.

It was strange, this feeling of giving up a little of his life each day to Jesse. In the war, death permeated the very air and raised its ugly head at every turn, and yet each day, he grew less fearful. He remembered how, in training, they drilled the soldiers that they must always be brave for each other. His companions were as terror-stricken as he was, but they forced themselves to move in ways that denied it. And in this way, the fear evaporated for a time like the darkness to the dawn.

There was a time when his boys were children, for no apparent reason, he had suddenly grown very anxious about death. Trying to understand why, it dawned on him—it wasn't that he was afraid of what lay beyond or that he was terrified to remain behind. If Grace was gone, an essential part of him would follow her as it had Will. He would be faced with having to live his life fully for his sons, but to do this when his fullness no longer existed.

Then, his fears had come true with Grace's death. The fear of death was the separation from those he loved—he could not give his all, because a part of him disappeared with each loved one who passed on. Though the days following had been routine and empty without her, it was his love and duty that carried him forward. Raising the boys, farming, and the passage of time made the pain grow bearable, but it wouldn't erase the damage. What had his mother said when her elder brother was killed in another war? *The wound will heal, but the scar, never.*

Now, at the twilight of his life, he wasn't afraid; he hadn't been frightened when the doctor told him that his heart was slowly giving out. He wasn't surprised; this had begun with Grace's death. Coming to terms with what was to come, he hoped it wouldn't be the stars where he would catch up with Will and Grace. No. He wanted to meet them under the oak tree where he imagined they had waited for him these many years.

Still, he knew he had something to do before his heart gave out. He thought he had resolved it years ago, but it reared its head again. He had hoped that the decisions he had made years earlier would stay in the past, but he could see this was in vain. He knew that to earn his reunion under the oak, he would have to explain to Jesse why Dan was so angry.

It was almost too much to ask of him now. He sent out a prayer that this would be unnecessary. He drifted off, hoping that this cup might pass from him.

18

Stanza Liejos had appeared for the first time on the Eastside when she was seventeen. She was one of Moses' many daughters, or that's what Sam had finally concluded. To Hank Jamison, a shy widower who lived a few miles up the river, the appearance of this vivacious Mexican girl was the answer to his loneliness. They married, but after some bad years, they lost their land to the bank. Stanza persuaded Hank to ask Sam if he had any work, and before long they settled on Sam's ranch.

After Grace died, her sisters Kate and Ollie had pitched in to help with the Hunter boys when they could, but they had large families of their own to care for. So, Stanza happily became a full-time housekeeper.

As the boys grew older and there was little need for Stanza's constant help, she continued to clean and maintain the house. And as Hank aged, he gave up working in the fields and was given the job of gardener. Grateful to Sam, he meticulously tended the house's gardens, keeping them freshly planted year-round. Grace had made the flower garden her domain and, directed by Sam, Hank worked faithfully to keep it exactly as she had. The flowers were, in a sense, Sam's candles lit to her memory.

. . .

Downstairs in the library, Stanza found Sam sitting at the table with papers and books surrounding him.

"*Es* time to buy air conditioner," she said in her own particular style of mixed Spanish and English. She eyed the old man to see if he was listening. "*Es no bueno* for you too hot, every *año*. Dust too much. *Imposible* to clean up after."

She continued her cleaning, now swatting the air above the window seat, removing the delicate, Irish-lacelike spider web that had been woven overnight. Every time the same dialog and every time the same response—nothing.

"Move your books out in the yard. Same thing."

Humming a little tune, while dusting the windowsill, she noticed Jesse talking to her husband, who was outside trimming a rose bush. Jesse pointed to a plant nearby. When Hank nodded yes, Jesse picked a handful of white calla lilies and made for the road leading into the orchard, followed by Tex and Brownie. Catching sight of Stanza at the window, Hank shrugged his shoulders and then returned to his trimming.

"*Dios mia*, that boy grow more and more." She turned back to the old man. "He remind me of his papa."

"Yes, I imagine so." Neighboring ranchers had asked Sam to read some government paperwork on the mandatory retrofit of the river pumps and report his opinion as to how much it would cost. It was painfully dry reading, and Sam was determined to get through it this afternoon.

"*Donde* he go with flowers?" she asked.

"What is it?" Sam shuffled his papers. "What did you say?"

"I just say, I wonder where Jesse go with flowers."

Sam was glad Stanza had returned from Mexico; he had missed having her around. But he wished that she would leave him alone until he could figure out the retrofit issue. Knowing her good heart and genuine care for him, he gave in and joined her at the window, to catch Jesse before he disappeared with his handful of flowers. Then, hoping to resume his research in silence, the old man made a detour to the kitchen to get something to drink.

In a few moments, the hum of the vacuum cleaner drifting from upstairs ensured that Stanza would be busy away from the library. Returning to his desk, he finally became immersed in his reading.

. . . . .

At noon, Jesse and his grandfather sat at the kitchen table, picking at the tamales that Stanza had prepared.

"So, my boy, what've you been up to this morning?" He winked at Stanza. "Someone's been spying on you, and I've been told that you took a walk in the orchard with some flowers."

"Just took some flowers out to the grave."

"That was thoughtful, my lad."

"Gramps, I've been thinking a lot about Mollie and Joe. Whatever happened to them?"

Wiping his mouth with his handkerchief, the old man took a drink of his freshly made iced tea. Stanza peered over her shoulder at him as he swallowed hard and pressed his fist against his chest.

"Maybe *abuelo*, Grandfather, too tired to talk anymore." Stanza gave Jesse a warning look. "Too much sadness in that family. Why talk more?"

"It's all right, Stanza. It's important."

Summer 1918

The church members always made sure the graveyard was well-tended. The lawn had recently been neatly trimmed and edged around the protruding stones. As in town, so here, fences separated the families. Cottonwoods, eucalyptus, and black walnut trees supplied cool shade. Flowers left by visitors provided the only color aside from green. A small pond in the center supplied a raft of mallards with a place to swim.

Mollie sat on a stone bench across from Will's grave, which lay next to Letty's. The flowers lay in a basket on the ground at her feet.

"Dear Will, please watch out for Letty. Take care of her. Tell her how much I love and miss her."

The sun moved behind the oak tree giving welcome shade. Dividing the sweet peas in half, Mollie left one bunch on Letty's and the other on Will's grave. Then, taking a short walk, she searched for the spot where they had recently buried her father.

She thought about all the people buried beneath the stones. It didn't really matter how one lived one's life, nor how much they fought among themselves or how badly they frightened each other. They were all laid to rest side by side. She tried to picture Joe's stone and her stone next to each other. How poignant it was—like a poem from one of her books.

It was time to get back; she had not told her sister that she had left. Kate would be very worried.

Back on the horse, nearing the last turn before home, the shadows had begun to lengthen. Almost imperceptibly at first, then with gathering momentum, the all too familiar thick mental fog began to cloud her vision. This haze was what she had learned to dread most. Fearing that she might be lost to it forever, she made the decision to fight harder than ever before. She would think of something to make it go away. She needed to do something quickly if she was to push back the grayness that was beginning to overtake her.

Billy, a neighbor boy fishing down at the river, turned to wave at Mollie. At that moment she lost her hat to a breeze, which in turn caused her horse to spook, throwing her to the ground. Billy couldn't honestly say if he heard her neck crack or if he had imagined it, but he knew it was bad.

A few days later, Sam rode down a dusty road in the hills on an unpleasant mission—to find Joe and convince him that he must attend Mollie's funeral. Nearing the old place where the Pearsons had once operated their Mountain House, he passed the spot in the fence where years before, he and Will had gathered the stones for the fireplace of his own house.

A few miles farther, Sam found the road leading onto the property where he was told he might find Joe. A mile in, he spied a house. Two horses grazed on the weeds in the yard.

The door opened and a middle-aged man came out. "Private property. Can't ya read the sign?"

"I'm looking for my brother, Joe Hunter." Sam tipped his hat. "Do you know where I might ...?"

The man's eyebrows shot up. "Oh, him. Believe you'll find him down that road." He spat his tobacco in Sam's direction.

About a quarter of a mile down was what looked to be no better than a small shack amid an overgrown pasture. Jumping from his horse, Sam secured the reins to a tree. Cautiously he surveyed the area and approached the door. Arguing came from inside and then silence.

"Who's out there?"

"Your brother, Sam."

"Get the hell out of here!"

Sam pushed the door open with his boot. The cabin was dark. Empty bottles littered the floor. The air was acrid, smelling of rotten food. Joe was lying on a dirty mattress in a corner. His hair was matted and filthy, and he looked as though he hadn't shaved in weeks. Another man sat in the opposite corner with a bottle in his hand.

The man in the corner crawled to his feet. "Who are you?"

"Sam Hunter." He pointed to the form on the mattress. "That's my brother."

"Well, if this ... is going ... to be a family visit, I'll be leaving," the man slurred.

Sam brought an old crate close to the bed. Ignoring him, Joe took a drink from a jar. "What the hell do you do here all day?" Sam demanded.

"If you're going to lecture me, you can get out. I'm up here to get away from ..." Taking another drink, he blustered, "I don't care anymore!"

"Damn it, Joe, you have responsibilities. Family down on the Eastside needs you. You've got to clean yourself up and get down there."

"You're wrong! I got no responsibilities any longer." Joe wiped his beard with his filthy hand. "My child is dead due to my negligence, and my wife is dead due to my indifference. No one needs me ... and I ... don't need anyone."

"At least come down for the funeral?" Sam's voice grew angrier and louder. "Goddamn it, at least come down and show your respect for Mollie!"

Throwing the jar across the room, Joe screamed, "What the hell do I care now? Can't you see it doesn't matter anymore? Everyone has seen the truth. It was all just a lie. Wasn't it?"

His face turned red, as though it would explode. The spilled liquor spread broken pieces of the jar over the floor. Repulsed, Sam instinctively jumped up.

"I won't come. Leave! This hell is too hot for the likes of you." Joe's body spun toward the wall. Hiding his face, he sobbed into the dirty blanket. "Get out, I say!"

Sam could not believe Joe had sunk so low that he could live in this squalor. If he could only make Joe understand his great need to fight these demons and not give up. Liquor and self-pity would never make them go away. But, watching Joe's sobbing, he determined he had tried his best.

There was nothing more he could do. Out of his pocket he fished a silver dollar; he tossed it on the mattress before he left.

·   ·   ·

Because of the family feuds, Eliza insisted on a graveside service instead of a church funeral. Everyone knew that Joe would not attend, but custom insisted that a chair be reserved for him just the same. Aside from the flower-draped coffin, the empty seat drew the most whisperings.

Daisette Westland turned to her husband and said a little too loudly, "Well, at least to his credit being a rogue, he was a rogue to the end."

"I wonder what's to become of their place," her husband replied, not caring who heard. "I hear it's mortgaged pretty heavily."

Later, to their surprise, Billy—the boy who had seen Mollie's fatal fall— admitted how, during the funeral, Joe had ridden into the ranch and given him a silver dollar to point to the horse responsible for Mollie's death. Joe led the horse up to the hills, where he shot it in the head and then celebrated by drinking himself into a stupor.

A few days after Mollie's funeral, Sam was surprised to see Grace ride onto his ranch on horseback. Elizabeth sat in front of her, holding onto the saddle's horn.

"Hello there," he called out from the fruit orchard.

Puzzled, Grace scanned the area.

"I'm over here at the edge of the orchard," he called again.

"There you are. Hello."

"I'll meet you around on the porch."

She waved and walked her horse to the house.

As he walked through the fruit orchard, Sam picked an orange from the blood orange tree and brought it with him.

Grace handed him a bouquet of flowers wrapped in brown paper. "I brought these from my mother's garden."

He kissed her on the cheek and took the flowers. "Thank you. But don't you have it a little backwards? Do the women give men flowers in your city?"

Making as though she would playfully slap his face, she grabbed the flowers back. "Here, let me put them in some water for you."

In the kitchen, she arranged the flowers in a jar and left it on the kitchen table. Then, carrying two jars of tea, she returned to the chair under the oak where Sam was in the middle of teaching Elizabeth the poem "Who Killed Cock Robin?"

Falling into a chair, she watched them together. Soothingly, she rubbed the moisture from the glass across her forehead and neck. It felt wonderful to cool off a little and begin to relax.

Leaving Elizabeth to chase a chicken around the yard, Sam returned to Grace.

They both broke out in laughter when the chicken, having had enough, turned and began chasing her.

"I was thinking—"

"You wrote—" they said together.

"I'm sorry. Go ahead. What were you going to say?" he asked.

"You wrote me such thoughtful letters from France during the war. I loved to read them. They made me feel I was there with you. I know how difficult it must have been to be with Will when ..."

"Yes. Indeed, it was horrible." Sam looked down. He quickly found the empty chair next to Grace and tried to replace the memory with the one of Will sitting across from them now, smiling. That always made Sam feel better.

"It's strange, Sam, how we've never discussed Will's death."

Standing up, Sam paced back and forth pointing toward the fruit orchard. "When I was in the trenches, I saw nothing but barren fruit trees around me. I decided then that when I got home, I would have a fruit orchard. Then when Will was killed," he stopped and fished the orange out of his pocket, "I promised myself to plant a tree to his memory."

He offered her the orange that he had picked. Falling into his chair again, he closed his eyes. "I grew so tired of seeing death. I just wanted to see growth and life."

Taking the orange, she tenderly peeled it and handed it to him. Pulling it apart into sections, he stuck one in his mouth, chewing, and savoring the sweet juices. Giving her the other half, she took it and did the same. They finished the sweet red fruit in silence.

"What will become of Mollie and Joe's ranch?" she asked.

"Well, there's nothing much to do about it. The bank will auction it off, I suppose. He had it heavily mortgaged." He sighed. "I don't know what'll become of Joe. I can't believe one can live in such wretched conditions."

She nodded.

"You know he was the one who convinced my family to come here and farm. He seemed to have great promise with the land. But then ... he turned away from it. I don't understand. It's all right here under our noses, and yet people still can't see it."

Grace's eyes traveled around the farmyard, back at the house and out towards the wide-open fields. "Whatever it ultimately is, it's all the same thing, I'm sure." She sighed.

"Please come over to play," Elizabeth pleaded from the swing.

"In just a minute, dearest." Grace turned back to Sam. "The beauty here astounds me."

"There was a time when you didn't think so. Now you think a hen house and a stable full of manure is beautiful?"

She chuckled. "Oh, Sam. You know exactly what I mean."

"I'm curious. What is beauty to you?" he asked.

"Uhm." Slowly the thoughts came out. "I'm learning that sincerity ... honesty, they're beautiful because they are so rare."

The breeze stirred as it made its way through the oak tree. "Please come and push my swing," Elizabeth pleaded.

Sam could tell that Grace was relaxing and enjoying the solitude. He walked over and began pushing the swing.

As he and Elizabeth played, Grace admitted to herself that this was the place where she was the most content. The fields ripe for the harvest and the summer country sounds filled her with more peace than she had felt in years.

"Here, come back to me," she called to Sam. "There's so much I need to tell you. The time I was here, and you showed me the house and you kissed me in the library. I've kept that close to my heart. When I learned that you and Will had gone off to war, I prayed every night for your safety. I was so afraid that something might happen to you. And then to hear about Will ..." She stopped and stared at Sam.

"Sam. I've made some decisions ... I need to ask you something. Last time I was here, you—"

"Look who's here," Elizabeth cried out as Lou Landon drove into the yard.

19

Summer 1960

Jesse helped Stanza clear the table of the dinner dishes. Brushing past his grandfather, Jesse knew it had to be his imagination, but Gramps looked different. As Stanza began washing the dishes, Jesse tried to think in what way his grandfather had changed. And then it came to him. He didn't look as old.

Weeks ago, when he first arrived, he remembered how many lines were on his weathered face. But lately, it seemed his skin was not as weathered and appeared smoother.

The old man closed his eyes and swallowed hard, pressing his chest with his left hand, made into a fist. After a few moments, he grimaced as he took a deep breath and placed a white pill under his tongue. Stanza frowned as she watched him. Jesse wondered if she noticed some sort of change, too.

When Sam had retired from the fields, finally admitting to himself that his weakening heart and "turncoat" body could not keep

185

up with the intense work, he had not withdrawn entirely but kept his hands close to the land, on a smaller scale—working daily in the kitchen garden. Here he continued to watch the fruits of his labors blossom. After breakfast, he and Jesse could usually be found in the garden planting, weeding, and irrigating.

Since Jesse could first remember, his grandfather made a point to set aside an area near the summerhouse for Jesse to plant as he saw fit, with a little direction, naturally. And Jesse looked forward to it each summer. Something in the symmetry of the layout, divided in quarters by two gravel walks and enclosed by a picket fence, appealed to his hunger for order. Where the walkways intersected, Grace had a fountain placed for the birds to bathe. Four wooden benches surrounding the fountain made a place for pensive reflection while the sound of bubbling water soothed the air. A forlorn scarecrow stationed at the end of the east walk challenged the gossiping magpies to trespass.

When alone, Jesse worked in this quiet enclave with only the chattering birds and his silent thoughts as companions. The garden was small enough to manage but large enough to give him room to breathe; a place where he could break apart the soil's hardness around the plants. Pulling weeds as the sun's hot rays beat down acted as a catharsis, forcing anxieties to the surface, to evaporate in the cleansing breezes.

Learning that this had been his grandmother's place gave her a form somewhat. Though he would never know her, he still felt working in her garden that she would be pleased he was connecting to her in this way.

As Daniel Jaeger had cleared the land of brush and trees, marked the boundaries, laid out the fields, and called upon the river to give sustenance to his labors, so his grandfather had added the barns, planted the orchard, and built the house with the library inside. Each had added something of themselves to the land—a reminder—a journal of sorts to those who would come after. And yet there was more.

Grace had added her refinements by laying out the garden and designing the summerhouse built entirely to her wishes. To understand the garden was to glimpse that Grace had brought a remnant of the city with her. What more could be added or would come after his grandfather was no longer here?

Now here in the garden, Jesse had gotten an early start. Wiping the grit from the back of his neck with one hand, while batting away at the omni-present mosquitos with the other, kept him moving. Monitoring the water flowing down through the rows of peas and tomatoes, he stood ready to close the sluice gate before it flooded.

The click of the gate's latch announced his grandfather. Bearing two wedges of freshly baked orange spice cake, he spread out the little feast on the fountain bench.

"Here we are. Grace's cake made from the blood orange. From Will's tree."

In a few moments, the spice cake's pungent aroma enticed Jesse to break away from his work and join Gramps to eat.

"How's it taste, my boy?"

Jesse swallowed a forkful of his cake, licked his sticky fingers, and dried them on his jeans. "Really good!"

Impatient for the old man to notice and approve his work so far, he blurted out, "Gramps, am I tying the bean plants the right way to the support?" Then gesturing from the plants to the little canal, he asked, "Should I close the gate now?"

Carefully searching all corners of the garden, Sam nodded. "I think you're doing a fine job. All will turn out fine. And, yes, if I were you, I'd close the water gate soon."

His grandfather's rare praise emboldened Jesse to share something he'd been mulling over. "You know," he pointed to the little summerhouse, "we could plant a lot more tomatoes if that were torn down."

His grandfather's face seemed to lose its color. "Oh, no, that would never do." He shook his head as though Jesse had suggested installing a swimming pool and a snack bar. "Why, Grace had it built there—a place to rest, to escape from the heat and mosquitoes."

Picking up a few crumbs from his plate, Gramps savored the last.

"You know, my lad, that which lives in cycles is easily replaced. Tomatoes come every season. But that which people have left behind cannot be replaced. To rid ourselves of their gift, is to begin to destroy the very evidence of their existence."

He explained that he regarded the grounds laden with plants, fountain, building, and fences as a finished poem, serving their purpose perfectly. Any changes would be to tinker with completion. How could one improve perfection? He believed that if something was complete, its integrity was permanent.

"These gardens were carefully laid out," Gramps gestured to each corner, "and planted based on Grace's directions. She said it reminded her, on a smaller scale, of a park in the city that she frequently escaped to, when she missed the Eastside."

Noticing the water beginning to breach the rows, Jesse ran over to close the sluice gate.

"You see, my lad, she put a great deal of herself into it, and it has evidenced its worth many times over the years, proving that the original idea was perfect."

Jesse guessed his grandfather felt the same about his house. "What did people say when you kept building the house, Gramps?"

"Sorry?"

"I mean, because you weren't married?"

"Oh, I suppose I often felt like Noah must've when, without a cloud in the sky, he was commanded to build the ark to save his family and the animals from the rains. Initially, the people shook their heads, but soon their doubts were swallowed up by the floods."

He looked Jesse straight in the eye. "Don't worry too much about what people think. If you know you're right, trust your intuitions, and you'll not go so far off track that you can't retrace your steps easily."

At the fountain, Gramps washed the stickiness from his hands.

"My family said they never understood my reasons for building the house. Never wondered what I'd endured in the war. Never cared to know what this piece of earth means to me." He checked the sky for any signs of clouds, as the land could use some rain.

"I continued building the house then, for Grace as well. I had to believe somehow, she would return. You see, I had kept my promise."

The cake had been reduced to crumbs, and Jesse tossed them to the few birds that might brave the looming scarecrow.

The old man rubbed the back of his neck and looked critically at Jesse. "We could both use a haircut."

Oakton had changed very little over the decades. At the turn of the century, before the levees were built, the river overtook its banks and flooded the low land every winter. The area to the south of the river, as it made its gentle S turn heading further down the valley, was higher and escaped the periodic flooding. This piece of land, dotted with tall oaks and cottonwoods, was where the immigrants from the Civil War, after driving the native Indians away, had claimed as their own, branding it with their grid of streets.

Sam brought the Jeep to a stop across from the white clapboard church, whose steeple poked through the treetops. The front doors and windows were thrown wide open, allowing the breeze to mingle with the tranquil, holy air inside.

A clear soprano voice floated out to them bearing a simple hymn of praise. Sam sat back, smiled, and closed his eyes. Jesse thought he had never heard anything as sincere and joyous as this song.

"Gramps?"

The old man did not open his eyes. "Yes."

"Do you belong to this church?" Jesse swatted at a mosquito.

"Can't say I do. That is, at least I never signed my name to any roll." Without opening his eyes, he pointed in the direction of the cemetery. "But enough of my family is buried in there that, in a sense, it's already mine."

"You said your mother used to go to church. What about your dad? Was he religious?"

"Mother used to despair over getting Dad to church. He didn't like being indoors. But she badgered him every so often. He once told me that he believed 'the good Lord didn't know about names in a book.' He said, 'He only cares what a man's written in his heart.' Besides, he would tell my mother, 'God only counts those people in there who have changed because of it.'"

"How does being in a building change someone?"

"He told me that the test of a good church service is if a man walks out a little less worldly than he came in, then the world should reflect that wonder." Sam turned to Jesse. "Do you ever go to church at home, my lad?" He was curious if Lynn had allowed Jesse to grapple with the deeper things.

"Mom dropped me off a few times when I was little, but I stopped going."

"Why?"

"I don't know. I guess it had to do with Jack."

"Jack? What would he have to say about it?"

To hear Gramps say the name sounded so foreign. He decided he didn't like it.

"Just that I remember once in class, the Sunday school teacher made us write down the ten commandments on a piece of paper we cut out to look like two little stone tablets. The teacher told us that if we learned them by heart, she would reward us with a little Bible." Jesse took a deep breath; it hurt to recall how he felt back then. "I remember thinking that I would memorize one a day until I had them all."

"And did you?"

"I got the first one down, but then Jack found it on my dresser. He tore it up in little pieces." He had no intention of telling his grandfather anything about Jack; somehow it just slipped out.

"Why would he tear it up?" The old man's voice took on an edge.

"No reason." Jesse wanted to forget it.

"Why, Jess? Why would Jack care about something like that?"

"He told me that he didn't want any religious fanatics living in his house. Though I hadn't memorized them, the teacher still gave me the Bible. Eventually, Mom stopped taking me, and I hid the little Bible deep in my drawer."

The old man's face turned to stone. "At least you were able to hold onto what was of value," he said, as he turned the Jeep back into town.

Carefully they made their way down a rickety wooden sidewalk, which over the years had nearly been overtaken with dry rot. At a brick building where the International Order of Odd Fellows met upstairs, Jesse trailed his grandfather into the barbershop. Hanging up his hat, his grandfather nodded to the barbers and patrons.

"Well, stranger." Phil, the barber, looked up from his work. "Haven't seen you in a while. So, I guess you count yourself fortunate that you don't have any prune trees."

"Why's that, Phil?" Gramps winked at Jesse.

Phil winked as he brushed the sweat from his nose, juggling the scissors and comb. "I hear old Westy was testing a machine that'll turn all the prune trees into firewood. Word has it he's starting with his own orchard."

Everyone snickered with amusement.

"Well, actually, I think it works just fine," Sam said. "The more prunes it shakes on my side of the fence, the better. Hell, what I don't make on walnuts, I might make up on prunes." He nodded his approval to the others as he took a seat.

Settling in and flipping the pages of his *National Geographic*, Jesse chanced to glance up and catch his grandfather's reflection in the dusty mirror. His heart skipped a beat, when he noticed Gramps fiddling with his collar while beads of sweat slid from his temple. His chest seemed to move in and out more rapidly, and he looked a little strange, searching the room for what Jesse didn't know.

"Gramps, can I get you some water or something?" he whispered.

"It's too hot in here." Tossing the magazine aside, Sam jumped out of his chair. "Phil, we'll be back in a bit."

Stopping at the market a few doors away, they plunked down two quarters for two root beers and continued across the street, where at the river's edge they found a place to sit. Sipping from the bottle, Gramps stared into the river. After a few minutes, Jesse could tell he was beginning to breathe a little more normally.

Knowing his grandfather was better now, he let his mind wander, and before he knew it, he found himself mesmerized by the river's swiftness. The river's potential for evil sent shivers up his spine as he recalled the day he slid down its embankment. He envisioned how horrified Mollie must have been when she saw the limp form of her little girl laid at her feet. He could almost hear her shrieks of disbelief. What had Kate said, "It made everyone's blood curdle to hear her screams?"

Wiping the tears with the back of his hand, he soon found himself sniffling.

"Don't trouble with it, my lad. They no longer suffer."

Jesse blew his nose into the handkerchief his grandfather handed him.

"Do you want to hear how Grace and I came to be married?"

Jesse nodded.

20

Spring 1923

What was forecast to be a heavy downpour turned out to be nothing but a light shower that was almost not worth the effort. At least it was able to clear the air of the rough edges of dust and dryness, leaving the sweet scent of wet alfalfa in its wake. Through the rift of the clouds, rays of sunlight highlighted golden spots throughout the Eastside.

Sam had remained at the feed store swapping news with his neighbors, waiting for the rain to pass, when a tangible feeling of anxiousness seemed to grow in him. When the showers stopped, he was hoping to shake this feeling on the road home. But the uneasiness clung to him like the raindrops sticking to the cotton-wood trees, and he couldn't understand why.

Riding into his yard, he was disappointed to discover three other horses tied to the watering trough. Maybe this was the reason for how he felt. He was in no mood for visitors and couldn't imagine who had left their coats, hats, and a basket of food on the porch. If his mother had sent over another group of her church girls, he would send them packing, manners or no manners. He poked his head around the porch and called out, but to no response.

Then it occurred to him. Running across the yard to where the horses stood, he checked the saddle for its mark. Within moments, the laughter of children drifted in from the orchard. And then, a girl, a boy, and Grace appeared amid the golden sunrays.

It was so typical of Grace to burst into his life, unannounced and unexpected. Though in some respects, Sam had grown used to this, beginning with the first time she rounded the corner on the river road. He would never tire of the joy he felt when she came into view. And he could not complain because it seemed so natural, so like her, now to appear out of the blue. He never knew how long she would stay or what would cause her to fly back to the city.

Once gone again, she would leave him a fresh image of herself, one he could conjure up whenever he needed her nearby. Then, as the days turned into months and she didn't reappear, he wondered if because he conjured up her image too frequently, it may have faded or worn thin a bit. But, upon her return, he discovered that though the image he entertained comforted him and kept him company, the original far exceeded his poor rendering.

He made another discovery—it wasn't just the physical likeness he kept dear, but it was more of a presence of who she was, enhancing the one-dimensional image into three dimensions. It was always so hard to explain to himself. Too many women on the Eastside bore the heavy marks of their hard work on their crease-lined faces and stooped shoulders. They seemed to be pulled down, drawn towards some giant burden buried in the earth. But as the years unfolded, the lines around Grace's eyes and the soft lines around her lips defied gravity and added to her sparkle.

With each experience he learned she had been through, her character grew deeply, and with this growth came more beauty. She was like a flower that, refreshed after a hard rain, would always turn toward the light.

The little girl said something which made Grace light up and toss her head back with laughter. Spotting Sam first, the girl pointed to him.

The picture was perfect, Sam thought. Even the air took on a splendor sweeter than the scent of wet alfalfa.

Leaning down, Grace whispered something, and immediately the children took off running, but stopped shyly a few feet from him. The girl stuck out her hand to shake Sam's, and the boy, a little younger, prodded by the girl, did the same.

Sam bent down to make sure he could look them in the eyes. "My name is Sam Hunter. What's yours?"

"Lee," the boy mumbled and pointing to the girl, he proclaimed, "this is Elizabeth, my cousin."

"And who is your mother, Lee?" Sam asked.

"This is Ollie's son." Grace caught up to them.

"Oh, I see." And turning to Elizabeth, he sized her up. "And I know whose little girl this is. Elizabeth, you've certainly grown since I saw you last."

Feeling Grace's eyes on him, he realized his anxiety had instantly disappeared. "When did you come? How long will you stay?"

"I hope you don't mind we made ourselves at home." She smiled. "We took refuge on the porch until the rain stopped. We've had a pleasant walk in the back. Your fields are doing so well. And the back pond is still the same." Sam couldn't help noticing that she was trying to mask some nervousness.

Pointing to Lee, she said, "This one almost fell in and frightened the ducks away." The boy's face turned bright red.

"Lee, you and Elizabeth go on ahead. We'll meet you in the yard." Elizabeth pulled Lee with her, yelling at the birds who watched safely from the upper branches of a tree.

Grace wrapped her arm in Sam's. "To answer your question, I thought it was time that I came back to the Eastside for a while. And how long I stay depends."

Under the oak, they ate what Grace had brought, sliced beef

sandwiches, potato salad, and tomatoes so sweet they ate them like apples. After lunch, the children were given permission to explore the barn.

Allowing time for the familiar feeling of comfort and trust to again blossom between them, Sam and Grace continued to make small talk, catching up with the neighborhood gossip. When they both felt the trust was reestablished and the key clicked the lock open, Sam was the first to venture forth.

"Since you wrote to me about your divorce, I've heard from Kate that you bought a rooming house. How do you like being a landlady to a house full of college boys? They must all have a crush on you."

"Ha! Ha! College boys and their crushes. They keep me very busy, though. And that's good. It takes me away from the ... uh ... times I had with the divorce and all."

Picking up a tiny feather from the ground, Sam drew it across his face as he sat thinking about what an ordeal that must have been. Now that it was over, he cared little for the details, only interested if she still suffered from it.

"Was it difficult for you? I know there was talk ... I barely listened to it, but I wondered if ... it ... you're all right now. Aren't you?" He met her gaze.

"Gradually, I'm returning to myself, though I can't pretend that it wasn't difficult." She searched the yard, seeming to look for clues as to whether she should tell him the way it was for her.

"You see, I discovered what money Lou hadn't lost gambling, he threw away on drinking and," she brushed some dust from her dress, "on women. This had been going on for quite some time and I tried to keep it from our families. But when I couldn't pay our bills, he turned on me, blaming me." Noticing the sudden lift of her head, Sam felt she knew there would be no more hiding behind pride.

"We lost our apartment; we were forced to move around staying with friends until eventually there was no place to go."

"Why didn't you come home?"

"Home?" She took a deep breath.

"To be with those that would take care of you?"

"Sam, at that point I wasn't sure what home was or what it meant. I was so troubled with where I found myself. All I could think about was getting away as far as I could. Here was the last place I wanted to be." She shook her head. "I couldn't bring myself to return in defeat."

"Defeat?"

"Yes. I had left to pursue a life apart from this. I couldn't come back without something to show for my years. So, I moved across the bay and bought an old house near the university. Mother surprised me by leaving me some money she had put aside from the sale of her place near the Springs before she died. Fortunately, she left it in a way that Lou couldn't get to it. I guess she knew more about Lou than I thought she did." She glanced over at the river and the hills beyond.

"Then I returned to teaching. You know, once I had my own house, I felt my life was beginning to return to normalcy. Independence, for me, was imperative. Going back to teaching and being a divorced woman was a humbling experience; quite a different life than I had expected."

So many questions came to Sam, but he would not ask, now. To break this moment when he could clearly see she was confessing for absolution, he would do nothing but wait and hope it would draw them closer together.

"It was a chance for me to start over." She took a sip of iced tea. "I love teaching. The students need me and appreciate me. To heal, I had to go back to what … I guess, in a sense, I had to retrace the path I had started upon.

"You know me. I must do things my way. And I desperately needed to regain my confidence. This is something I need right now. I gave up too much to Lou."

Two mourning doves postured on a branch above. Smiling, she asked, "Did you know they mate for life?"

"Yes. Of course." He added, "And they never venture far from their home."

"I should have known."

She stood a little abruptly, as though to stretch and relieve the tension that had crept up during her admission. "How many wonderful times we had here." She seemed to search the shade for something that she knew was not there.

On the serpentine oak branch above, the doves bobbing and weaving in their mating ritual led Sam's thoughts to the cycles of life. When the leaves dried and withered, there was no cause for alarm; they followed an unhampered plan of renewal. The buds of new growth brought new life, without fail. Even fruit when it fell to the ground held promise. The seeds brought forth another, replacing what had been lost. Weren't people the same? When troubles present themselves, don't they ripen us, revealing the seeds for new growth?

As the breeze played with Grace's hair, he was enthralled by her loveliness. And his heart sank with the growing awareness that she would never be his. After all these years, he hadn't given up hope that she might make this her home. But he was beginning to understand that the pain it was causing both, in this gentle tug of war, was not kind. And for it to cease, he would have to forfeit to win. Perhaps his hanging on was causing her to suffer more, and that was something he could not abide.

Now, faced with the unthinkable, he realized that this was what she, in her own awkward way, was trying to tell him this afternoon. He couldn't believe he had been so dull, blinded by his own desires. She knew that the ranch had always been hers for the taking, and yet now free to return, she didn't—but chose to begin her new life away. How blind he had been. And how he would suffer for his selfishness.

. . .

When the children had enough of exploring the barn, they took to the swing that hung from the lowest of the oak branches. Taking turns, they pushed one another higher and higher.

How like these children she, Will, and Sam were once, Grace thought—innocent and free, aware of nothing but themselves. She had left for more opportunities and a broader view of the world. Her brother left to escape disappointment, to fight for a cause, and to come of age. But why had Sam ever left? What made him leave this to go fight in a war he once said was not his? Why would he leave the land he was such a part of? She could never picture the man without his land. One might as well pluck up the cherished oak tree, as if that were possible, and plant it in some desert.

How was she going to let Sam know why she had come this afternoon? She had tried to tell him that day she was here with Lou but had missed the chance. Her mother had made her promise never to marry Sam; she couldn't bear to think of another suffering daughter with another cruel Hunter. Grace was tired of leading Sam on—she must let him know what she had decided; it could not go on like this any longer.

Grace searched for the right words. "Sam, I have a confession—"

But Sam's attention was suddenly taken by the sight of one of his workmen galloping his horse into the yard. The man jumped from his horse and ran across the yard.

"What is it?" Sam asked, meeting him halfway.

"Señor ... we ... need help. Jose is hurt."

Sam, wasting no time, jumped on his horse, and yelled over his shoulder, "I'll return shortly. Please stay."

"Yes, of course." She got to her feet. "Should I come?" she shouted back. "Perhaps I can be of help."

"No. I shouldn't be long."

Grace shooed the children into the library where they could read picture books before they went down for a short nap. While she waited for Sam to return, she gathered up the picnic leftovers. On her way to the kitchen, she heard a kitten mewing in distress. She followed its meowing down the stairs, where near the cellar door, she found the kitten that somehow had ventured too far. Kneeling to pick it up, she noticed a piece of wood attached to the house that looked like it had writing carved into it.

Brushing off the cobwebs and dust, she squinted to make out what was written. Pondering the message and realizing this was the exact sign she needed, she would wait no longer. She bounded up the stairs and headed towards the orchard.

Sam shouted to a man to bring a large steel rod from the nearby tractor. Realizing what Sam was planning, two others rolled a large rock to the fallen tree. Sam and another threw their weight onto the rod and using it as a lever, raised the trunk enough that Jose's companions pulled him free. Checking him carefully, Sam was relieved to find his leg wasn't broken, although painfully bruised.

Reaching down to scoop up his hat, Sam noticed Grace coming down the road from the orchard. Grace, the one who always appeared unexpectedly. And thinking nothing of it now and suspecting no alarm in her sudden appearance, he made his way towards her.

"It's the funniest damn thing," he called. "They were taking their siesta when the dead tree decided to give way. Of course, it's so old, and the roots were saturated ..."

Grace couldn't make out his words. She couldn't remember a time when she loved him more. He was everything she had hoped for. He was everything she had crossed the river and the hills in search of.

Though tears began to fill her eyes, she was smiling, and still he harbored no suspicions. He could only wonder how she could be so beautiful right now, at this moment. All the love he had for her, all the love he forced himself to believe would never be returned, swept him like a river flooding its banks, and there was nothing he could do to stop it.

Pulling her to him, he held her tightly with a love that had been years in the making. He kissed the tears from her face and then kissed her wet lips.

Suddenly, aware that they were not alone in this moment of

theirs, this moment that had taken years to perfect, but were sharing it with field hands, he smiled shyly. Amid the workers' smiles, Sam took Grace's hand and led her back to the house he had built for her.

And that summer, thirteen years after they had met, they married under the oak tree, with an empty chair reserved for Will.

21

Summer 1960

Jesse and Sam returned to the front porch for a well-earned rest after sweeping out the stalls and combing down the horses. Jesse felt the horses all seemed to enjoy it except Max, who, when it looked as though they might approach, seemed to dare them to try, so they left him alone. Next on the list, Sam planned to clean and oil the saddles, but when the heat and flies became too much, he decided they would take a break.

Jesse watched his grandfather stir a third spoonful of sugar into his iced tea. After the excess settled to the bottom, his grandfather took a sip and smacked his lips. "Just the way I like it." Smiling, he told Jesse, "You know, Mother told us she could tell a true Southerner by whether he took his tea sweetened or unsweetened."

Jesse glanced from his unsweetened iced tea to his grandfather's. "What kind of tea does a Southerner like?"

Sam studied his grandson as though Jesse had just asked on which side of the river Eastside was. "Why, sweetened, of course!" And then, remembering breakfast, he winked. "And they don't put sugar on their grits, either!"

"Gramps. I can't help it. They're like Cream of Wheat." Jesse snickered.

"I'm of no mind to go back to the tack room until it cools down. I'll ride to Westy's. I need to hand off some research I've been doing. Come along?"

Sinking further into the porch chair with the book he had found in the library, which he discovered was Sam's when he was a boy, he weighed his choices. He had begun to delve into *The Adventures of King Arthur*. "Gramps, if you don't mind, I think I'll stay here."

"All right. But don't sit all day. Get out and get your blood moving."

A little while later, Jesse had second thoughts—maybe he should have gone with his grandfather. With every paragraph he read, he'd have to go back and re-read it, and he found himself growing more restless and couldn't figure out why. There was a point in the story where King Arthur was thrown by a black horse, when Jesse realized Max had gotten under his skin. He had to do something about that.

He would like to surprise Gramps, when he returned, by having Max brushed down. He thought if he tried slow and steady, maybe Max would allow him to get near enough to do that.

Lugging the carryall brush box from the tack room, Jesse tiptoed towards Max. He peeked around a corner and caught a glimpse of Max staring out at the yard as though he was working out how he would escape at the first opportunity. Suddenly the gelding's ears flicked back. Swinging his head around, he stared at Jesse, who had the distinct impression he was being sized up. After a moment or two, the horse snorted and shook his head back and forth. If Jesse didn't know better, he would swear that Max had just dismissed him as not worth the bother of a pesky fly. And then to make certain Jesse got the point, the gelding resumed his contemplation of the yard.

Jesse wondered what it would be like to ride a horse like Max— a ride that you weren't sure how it would end—either swept off your saddle by a low-lying branch or in a mutual understanding that, though the rider was in control, Max had the power. Jesse was more inclined to believe that the opposite might be more accurate—Max would not relinquish control nor exchange his power. How would his uncle convince a horse to surrender to his dominion? What was it that made a horse give in to the rider? His grandfather's horses had always been good-natured and friendly. But this one was a mystery.

Jesse decided he would wait no longer. He would prove to this beast that he was just the person to brush him down whether the stupid horse wanted it or not. Swallowing hard, he tiptoed to the stall door. As he went for the latch, the gelding with no warning kicked the lower door.

Max almost seemed to sport a look of satisfaction, though Jesse knew that was impossible; still he studied the horse to make sure. Returning the carryall to the tack room, he decided to put plenty of distance between the stable and himself.

The porch with another book didn't appeal, so he ventured towards the orchard. Here, the irrigation process was in full swing. A few days earlier, a worker had created "checks" by dragging an implement behind the tractor. This piece of equipment had large steel discs or plates fixed so that it gathered the soil leaving an inverted V, about four feet wide and three feet high. These checks would hold the water within each section, allowing it to seep deep to the tree's roots.

Every few years, Sam surveyed the orchard to map the changing contours of the land caused by the harvest, winds, and rain, as well as with irrigation. The checks followed the contours and were essential for the even distribution of the water.

On the orchard road, Jesse spotted four workers working and talking, swiftly moving through the trees inspecting the checks. When the water had stood long enough in a section, a worker would cause a break in the check, allowing the water to rush into the next portion. But because it took some time for the water to fill in and saturate the area, their primary job was to investigate the checks for any evidence of leaks.

Looking alike and dressed alike in worn blue jeans, sweat-stained blue work shirts, and mud-encrusted cowboy boots, Jesse guessed they were the sons of Guillermo, his grandfather's fore-man. Each wore a uniquely styled broad-brimmed hat. Like sentinels, with shovels slung over their shoulders, they marched back and forth with melodic chatting and laughter, keeping an eye on everything.

A few yards ahead, where a trickle of water began, one fellow ran over to work on the rift before it grew too large of a breech to repair. Leaving their companion to his task, the three continued on.

Tapping down the last shovel full of dirt, the fellow leaned against his shovel to rest and, seeing Jesse, waved him over. Jesse was surprised to find a boy hardly older than himself. Touching the brim of his pampas hat, the boy grinned, revealing a front tooth encased in gold.

Smiling even more, he revealed two more gold teeth. "*Como se llama?*"

"Uhm." Jesse guessed it was his name he was after. "I'm Jesse."

"*Me llamo* Felipe Diego," the boy said quickly, extending his hand.

"I'm sorry. What did you say?"

"Felipe Diego. Felipe Diego," he repeated, jabbing his thumb at his chest before extending his hand again.

"Oh. Hi!" Jesse shook his hand. "Um, do you like—"

Felipe shook his head, laughing. "*No hablo ingles, amigo.*" He gave Jesse a lookover, examining his clean clothes. Then he glanced at his own muddy clothes and broke out laughing.

Jesse didn't understand the joke but smiled anyway.

Felipe pulled a pack of papers from his pocket and a little sack from another. In a smooth motion, he sprinkled in some tobacco, rolled it to the size of a thin, short pencil, licked the edges of the paper, and stuck the paper tube between his lips. Almost by sleight of hand, he pulled a match from somewhere. After drawing it quickly across his thigh, it burst into flame, and with this he lit his cigarette.

Jesse's eyes widened more.

Sucking in deeply, Felipe seemed to savor the experience. Exhaling a gray puff of a cloud, he held it out to Jesse.

"Oh. No." Jesse's hand pushed it away. "I don't smoke ..."

Felipe seemed perplexed.

All right. What the heck, Jesse thought. *Maybe just this once.*

Grabbing the cigarette, he stuck it between his lips and, copying Felipe, took a deep breath. Immediately, as though he had been hit in the stomach, he gasped for air. He tried hard to breathe but choking and coughing was all he could muster. His throat burned so much, it felt like he'd swallowed the match instead.

Felipe burst out in deep guffaw and took the cigarette from him. Back in the corner of his mouth, it bobbed up and down, keeping time with his chuckles. Jesse couldn't decide what hurt more—the burning in his throat or Felipe's laughter.

Felipe flung his thermos at him.

Grateful for the gesture, he quickly took a mouthful, but it went down his windpipe, which started his coughing fit all over again. Felipe grabbed the thermos and took a swig, but it seemed more water spilled down his chin and soaked his shirt than made it down his throat. Brushing his sleeve across his lips, he re-offered the water.

Jesse waved no; he had finally gotten some air.

"*Felipe, venido aquí, rápidamente!*" His companions called out for help, where they were hurriedly filling in a breach that was quickly growing larger.

Felipe tossed the shovel over his shoulder, tipped his hat, and smiled coolly. "*Adios, amigo.*" He ran to rejoin the others, leaving the smell of his cigarette lingering behind.

Felipe was just a kid his own age, Jesse said to himself. *He was just trying to be friendly, and here I am a fool. He's probably over there telling them how ridiculous the gringo looked when his face turned different colors.* Looking for an escape, he took off in the opposite direction.

Nonetheless, he couldn't get Felipe out of his mind. He had to admit Felipe and his brothers belonged here more than he did. This wasn't fair, he judged. This was his grandfather's ranch, not theirs. They were only hired hands. Granted, they knew how to do what was needed— and he didn't, of course.

How would Felipe be treated at Jesse's school, he wondered? He knew the popular kids would sneak out to the parking lot, and led by Felipe, would practice hand-rolling a cigarette, and then lighting it by rubbing a match on their jeans. And Jesse was certain the girls would oooh and aaah over his unbuttoned shirt.

But what was Felipe's appeal to Jesse? Then it came to him. Felipe wasn't afraid. He was sure of himself.

He was tired of just observing. He wanted to join in with the workers—to work, to laugh and joke with them, to belong. He tried to imagine how it would feel to be slapped on his back in friendship. They would nod their approval when the team captains argued, trying to get Jesse on their team. And the looks of admiration they would bestow on him for having broken in Max, while smoking his own hand-rolled cigarette.

Absorbed in wanting to escape, without intending to go in this direction, he found himself at the old stone cross. Felipe and his companions' occasional bursts of laughter and bantering echoed through the orchard. With more water rising quickly around the stone and more laughter flying through the trees, an eeriness overtook the orchard.

Back at the house, Jesse rummaged through the icebox for drinks and slapped together a sandwich from last night's supper. Then he went upstairs to get a pad of paper and some drawing pencils. Stuffing everything in his backpack, he made his way through the yard and out onto the road.

A few miles towards town, he came to a narrow road that led into the Three Sisters' Place. The frontage of this ranch bordered on the river road, but the bulk of the property extended far back.

Behind it, adjoining the river, existed a narrow strip of land called "the bend" because of the turn the river took on its southward flow. This land, bordering the river, thick with tall cottonwood trees, wild blackberries, and sumac, was like a jungle. Two small meadows, ablaze with bright yellow mustard flowers, lined the river. The smaller of these two meadows was where Jesse headed.

About halfway down the road, he passed what remained of the three sisters' old house. Most of the paint had long since peeled off the structure, with the remainder in tatters.

He continued down the road farther into the property. Here in the bend, in the middle of overgrown vines hanging from thickly clustered trees, the road narrowed into a dirt path, barely passable for walking or horseback riding.

At the path's end stood a simple little cottage. Last summer, when Jesse had explored this area and discovered the cottage empty, his father had told him Moses had lived there for a while. He explained that Amanda had allowed Moses to live there in exchange for a little handyman work when she needed it. Not many even knew of its existence.

Last year, Jesse had found the cottage dry and sturdy; it would make a good place to escape to. He was so pleased to have a place of his own that he told no one about it. Sometimes, when his father worked on the Three Sisters' Place, it seemed he would often forget that Jesse was there, which gave Jesse the opportunity to explore the meadow on his own.

Pushing the door open, he peeked in to be sure that nothing had snuck inside. He left the door open to allow the breeze to clear out the musty smell. Behind the door was half a broom. He swept a little to tidy up but was careful not to get too near a wasps' nest he had noticed under an eave.

Satisfied, he sat down and began rummaging through his backpack.

With the melody of the birds' chattering in the nearby cottonwoods, he ate his lunch. A jackrabbit surprised him by stopping at the porch for a second before skipping on its way. He made a good choice to come here today, he decided. It felt good sitting there, protected by the river on one side and the meadow on the other; knowing that no one really knew about this place gave him solace.

After lunch, he brought his paper and pencils down to the river's edge onto the sandbar. Spotting an area across the river where he thought a grove of tall cottonwoods swaying in the breeze would make a good picture, he sat down and began to sketch. As he added the finishing touches to his drawing, he grew drowsy. He stretched out on the warm sand and began to doze but was startled when a twig snapped.

A sleek doe and her fawn had slid down the sandy bluff and onto the sandbar. Catching the scent of someone near, the doe hesitated, while the fawn instinctively moved to her other side. Discovering the intruder, she watched Jesse for a few moments, before deciding she would continue down to the water to sip. Then, as quickly and gracefully as they arrived, she turned and led her offspring to disappear above the embankment.

Marveling at the grace in her movements, what impressed him most was her courageous stance. Requiring no permission, she seemed not to doubt her right to be there. The river was there to supply drink; what could she doubt? Then Jesse wondered, was she granting him permission to occupy what a man may own, but she alone possessed?

As soon as they left, he picked up his pencil and sketched from memory the two creatures into his drawing.

With his drawing now complete, he looked around before climbing back up the bluff to the cottage. How wonderful it was to be here alone and yet now being reminded, not completely alone, sharing the bend with creatures graceful and unseen. Checking his watch, he decided he should get back. He had not told his grandfather where he would be.

He was packing his things up when he heard a horse sneeze. His heart sank, as he walked onto the porch and looked towards the path. Relieved and a little puzzled, he saw his grandfather riding slowly on the path. Sitting astride Nair, the old man held the reins loosely in one hand, and with the other he shoved the branches away from his face. Surveying the thicket and the growth around him, he seemed lost in thought.

Glancing up, he saw Jesse. "Ah. There you are. I thought I might find you out here."

"You did?"

"You didn't think I knew about this place?"

Jesse shrugged his shoulders.

"This was one of Dan and Colton's favorite places when they were about your age. Especially while the old patriarch lived here."

Slowly dismounting, Gramps looped the horse's reins around the porch's post. His eyes twinkled. "Going to invite me in?"

A bit embarrassed, Jesse showed him in. "Here, Gramps. Sit here and I'll get you some water."

Judging one of the chairs strong enough, the old man lowered himself in. He scanned the interior. "It's been a long time since I've been out here. It doesn't seem to have changed much, though." He picked up the drawing.

"I drew this a few minutes ago down at the sandbar." Jesse offered a cup from his thermos. "Two deer came out to the river for a drink, and I added them in. What d'ya think?"

"Yes. It's fine."

The old man took a sip of water. He was thinking of an earlier time, of being here with his sons, as youngsters. Many hours they'd spent hunting and exploring the bend. Back then, he thought hunting was very important, but now he had no interest in it.

"So, you like it out here?"

Jesse nodded. "This is the first time I've been out here this summer."

"Like you, the boys enjoyed being here, too. Your dad would come here more and more to be by himself to escape."

Examining Jesse's drawing, he said, "He would often draw or write about his experiences, in this solitude. After his mother died, this place would become a haven for your dad."

"Was my dad ..." Jesse's voiced trailed off.

Speaking in a steely tone, Gramps explained. "He took his mother's illness and death very hard. Wouldn't be comforted. He clammed up. Wouldn't talk about it. I couldn't get through to him to help. He preferred to be alone." He looked back at Jesse. His voice softened.

"I watched him carefully, and I decided to allow him to deal with his grief in his own way. At first, I forbade him to come out here. But later, I relented. I thought he needed to be alone to heal and that this was as good a place as any to accomplish it, despite the three sisters nearby. So, you see this was a special place for someone else before you."

"Dad used to write and draw, too! Mom said she wasn't the artistic type. She said I must've gotten that from Dad," Jesse said.

"Why couldn't he tell me that he used to write and draw? Why doesn't he talk to me? Sometimes, I feel like I'm nobody. You tell me I'm like him, and still, he doesn't talk to me. It's like I'm not part of any family."

Jesse's words sliced his grandfather in two. In one respect, he was glad the boy was voicing his feelings; Sam wouldn't let himself think Jesse could be like Dan in that respect. But on the other hand, it cut him to the quick to think his grandson felt as though he belonged nowhere.

"Your dad does care for you in his own way. It's just that ... well, it's just that he's lost a few people in his life. Remember that once he was much like you and loved the same things as you. And, my boy, you're a Hunter!"

The old man traced the sketch lines of Jesse's drawing with his finger, desperate that Jesse understood. "Why don't we take a walk down to the sandbar? I'd like to revisit the place that inspired such a fine drawing."

He carefully followed his grandson down the short incline where they found a log to sit on. Together they watched the river. Occasionally, the sky was interrupted with a flock of blackbirds sailing overhead to settle in the cottonwood trees across the river before exploding forth to repeat their exercise.

"You know, Jesse, being a parent, a dad, a mother, is a solemn business. There is much that we must teach our children. And then if we've done our job decently, we often discover that we've learned even more."

"What do you mean, you learn? You're an adult," Jesse said, frowning. "You don't have to learn. You can do what you want."

"Not necessarily. Learning continues. You'll know what I mean when you have children of your own."

Jesse skipped a rock over the river's surface.

"I tried to teach the boys to feel every moment as it occurred. To be aware of all that they experience. To savor it. Draw from each experience the embedded lesson. There's always something to learn, even if the lesson is to just enjoy the moment. And during challenging times, don't slink away; face them. They make us grow. Remember what I taught you after the rifle practice. Sometimes we must dig in deep to get their lesson. But don't worry."

He pointed across the river. "We'll always get safely to the other side if we aren't afraid."

Jesse was silent. What was his lesson to learn from living with Jack? What was the lesson in watching his mother suffer?

"Earlier today, I watched the workers in the orchard," Jesse finally said. "There was a guy, Guillermo's son; he said his name was Felipe. He was my age, and yet I felt like a little kid. They were having fun, working, talking, and laughing. Gosh, Gramps. Sometimes, I feel so alone. Like I'm not good enough."

"You are good enough. Why, you … you're like a wonderful story in the making. You are learning, growing."

"But why don't I feel good enough?"

"Because your story consists of many, many layers, but you're hearing it read by a reader who can't understand it. You mustn't judge yourself by the reader, but by what you have to offer."

"What do you mean?"

"Just that you shouldn't judge yourself by how others in their ignorance treat you."

"But what do I have to offer?" Jesse wondered.

"Much, my boy. And this will be revealed, in time. Don't forget, most troubles sharpen us, though they're hard lessons." Squinting into the sun to watch the blackbirds, he continued, "But we eventually gain. Gaining, that is, in the same measure as we lose fear."

Then as though it just came to him in a flash, Gramps slapped his hand against his thigh. "Never give up the ranch! No one can take it from you."

A portion of the embankment fell to be swept down river.

"The ranch?" Jesse exclaimed in surprise.

"Yes. The answer is in those two words. The ranch. What you learn here will ensure your safety."

He didn't feel like he could argue with that. He loved being here. Feeling very safe with his grandfather nearby, he didn't want to leave.

"Gramps. You think I'm like Dad?"

"Yes. My boy. You are very much like your father was at your age."

"How?"

"Oh ... your father was thoughtful." It hurt to think of Dan as he was when a child, so distant from what he was now. Oh, how he'd give up the rest of his life if he could just go back and undo it all. But this was an old refrain and he had accepted things as they had become long ago. "As I said, he loved to draw and write. He was very close to his mother. And like you, it hurt him terribly to see her suffer."

Jesse stared at the old man.

Enveloped by his grandfather's soothing voice, his concern about everything disappeared like the darkness before the light. Closing his eyes, he let his grandfather's words, like the river breeze, roll over him softly.

22

Fall 1940

The pop of gunfire startled a flock of blackbirds out of the trees. Escaping like a black undulating cloud, they flew swiftly over the river where a cottonwood absorbed them. Even the crickets pocketed their warm air song for a few moments. The gunfire also drew Moses out of his house holding a shotgun. A few months earlier, some high school kids stalking jackrabbits had ventured upon the cottage and, assuming it was deserted, used it for target practice. Being met with returning fire, they high-tailed it back to town.

"*Hola*, who goes there?" he yelled.

"Moses! Moses! It's your *amigo*, Colton," the visitor shouted. Over his shoulder were two jackrabbits. Though only fourteen years old, he was acclaimed as the best marksman on the Eastside.

Dodging the colorful sheets and shirts waving in the breeze, he made his way to Moses. Colt's two pointers, Jules and Jamie, followed, whining and jumping up, trying to sniff the rabbits. Moses' dog joined the two.

"*Aqui*, Moses. For you," Colt said proudly. "I just shot 'em a minute ago."

Moses accepted one of the rabbits, lifted it far above the dogs, and hung it on a nail in the wall. Colton set his rifle and backpack down before plopping down on the porch.

"*Gracias*, Colt. I have it tonight. Nothing no better than fried rabbit," Moses said. "See anything more in bend there to hunt?"

Colton took out a hand-rolled cigarette, lit it, and blew a smoke ring out over the yard. "Naw. But I got my eye out for pheasant. Mother likes pheasant, and I'd like to bring one home if I can find one."

"How *es usted* mama?"

Colton's smile faded as he shook his head. "Not so good. Dad is awfully worried about her. She says she's okay. But I know better because she's always in bed. And when family comes visiting, they leave crying."

Moses searched the road near the bend. "Where brother?"

"Dan came over with me, but he stopped in at the house. We were walking by when old maid Amanda came out and called to him. She had some chore or something for him to do. I broke out of there. Those old ladies give me the creeps. Seems to me they sit there all day like spiders in a web. Dad said he'd meet us here; he had things to do in town."

Moses shook his head in disappointment. "I told Dan no go there. He *no bueno* be there."

"Hey, what's the problem with those old maids, anyway? I mean, I don't care. But why the fuss? Aren't they related to Mother in some way? Why should we stay away from them?"

"*Cuando lo siento*, so sorry, your mama. You need help your papa. Tell Dan leave the sisters alone. No reason be there. Too young."

Shrugging his shoulders, Colt announced, "I'm going in for a swim. It's mighty hot. I'm going to die if I don't cool off. Hey, Moses. Don't let Dad know I had a smoke. Okay? Thinks I'm too young."

Moses nodded as he took the rabbit off the nail and disappeared inside the cottage.

Colton slid down the embankment with Jules and Jamie

following. Generally, the river was off-limits, being too swift for swimming, but here on this stretch where the water flowed shallow over the sandbar, Sam gave in to the boys.

Colton kicked off his boots and socks, slid out of his jeans, and slipped off his shirt. Throwing his hat to the side, he checked both ways before slipping out of his underwear. Then, flying across the hot sand, he dove into the river.

"Come on, Jules, Jamie. It feels great!"

The dogs howled and darted back and forth on the bar, lapping at the water.

In the middle of skinning the rabbit, Moses was again startled by his dog's barking. Dan trudged along; a pack slung over his shoulder. He seemed to be talking to himself. Moses waved.

"Hello, Moses. Colton here yet?"

"Swim in river." He looked the boy over. "What are you doing at the house?"

"Old lady Amanda had something for me to do."

"Stay away from them!"

"They're just lonely, that's all."

"No good for you to be there." Moses shook his head.

"Why? I don't know what the big deal is. What makes you say that?" Dan stared at Moses, waiting for an answer.

"Never mind. No go there."

"Fine! I'm going down to the river."

Dan found his brother splashing about the river with his dogs dashing back and forth the length of the sandbar.

"Hey, Dan, you finally made it. The old witches let you go. They didn't eat you for lunch." Colton laughed out loud.

Trying to ignore him, Dan pulled out his drawing tools to capture the scene. Colton continued jumping up and down in the river, trying to catch his eye. Still Dan pretended to ignore him.

"Hey, Brother." Colton stood up. "Come on in. It'll do you good. It's too hot out there."

"Nope. Just want to draw."

"Come on. What're you afraid of?"

"Leave me alone. Not afraid of anything. Besides, you know Dad says how dangerous the river can be."

"Hell, Dan. Not here. Dad says it's okay." Colton grabbed a stick floating by and threw it out to the dogs, who wrestled for it.

Trying to get a rise, he looked at Dan again. "You know, come to think of it, you're afraid a lot."

"Am not."

"Are so!"

"God damn it, Colt! Just leave me alone."

Dashing out of the river, Colton plopped down next to him. "I'm going to tell Dad you cussed."

"I'll tell Dad you smoke."

Colton shook his head, sending water everywhere.

"For crying out loud, Colt!" Dan moved his things out of the way as Colton leaned over to examine the drawing.

"What're you drawing?"

"Nothing."

"Come on. What is it?"

"Just drawing the other side of the river." He pointed exasperated. "Over there with the cottonwoods."

"Hey, looks pretty good."

Dan studied Colton, wondering if he could trust his brother with a question. Something they had not broached before.

"What? What is it?" asked Colton.

"Nothing!"

"Come on, what is it?"

"Well, you said I was afraid of things."

"Yeah. So what?"

"Well. I am afraid. I'm afraid for Mother. I know Dad is worried about her, and old maid Amanda said—"

"Hell, I don't care what those old windbags have to say. And you shouldn't either if you know what's good for you. You know, Dad doesn't think it's a good idea—"

The cracking of a branch up on the bluff behind them made them stop.

"Come on up, boys," Sam said, "and get something to eat. I brought some lunch."

After lunch, on Moses' porch, Dan wrote rapidly in his journal while his brother cleaned his rifle nearby. Moses, gently rocking back and forth, dozed. Between the drags of his cigarette, Sam intently studied Dan.

"What're you writing?" he asked.

"A poem."

"About what?"

"Well. If you must know. It's about death."

"Hmm, dark subject for a poem, eh? Why not write about the bend or the meadow? A little cheerier, don't you think?"

"I don't feel like writing about something cheery." Dan dodged his father's stare.

"Son. What is it? What's bothering you?"

"No use talking about it."

"Try, son. What is it?"

"Okay. What about Mother?" Dan blurted out. His strained voice showed Sam how tired he was of asking and not getting answers, while pretending nothing was wrong.

Sam searched the meadow as if the answer might come from one of the wild plants. How could he tell his boys that he himself was very troubled and could hardly admit to himself how ill she was becoming?

"I don't know, Dan. We just must have faith and know that all will be all right. We can't give in to it. And we certainly can't let your mother know how concerned—"

"Cousin Amanda said that when bad things happen to people it's punishment from God and—"

"Don't ever say that again." Sam threw his cigarette down and jumped to his feet, nearly overturning his chair. "What a horrible thing for that woman to tell you."

He turned to the now awake Moses. "Can you believe this?"

Then his tone changed as he said to Dan, "Your mother's a good person. She doesn't deserve any suffering. Those idle women don't know what they're talking about."

As his father paced back and forth, Colton's eyes grew wide. His dad was very rarely so worked up.

"That's it! I don't ever want to catch you talking to those women again. Do you hear me? I can't have it. I've put up with just about all that I can put up with."

"No, you're wrong, Dad. They're only trying to help. They're only trying to explain how things are. They say Mother was wrong, that she shouldn't have let it happen. They say it's not their fault. That it's Mother's fault that—"

"That's enough. Don't say another word. So, help me God, not one more word from you!"

Dan shouted back, "All you say is, 'Be strong, be patient.' But it doesn't help. I need to know why. If you can't tell me, then there's no use. I'm leaving!" He jumped from the porch and onto the path, leaving his things behind.

It took all the strength Sam had to keep from running after him. He wanted nothing more than to confess that he was also scared and angry at the same time. That he couldn't stand to see Grace suffer and that he didn't know what he was going to do if she ... He couldn't bring himself to even think of the word. But he had to be strong for his sons and for himself.

"Want me to go after him, Dad?"

"No, let him go. I don't know what to tell him anymore." Then he quickly changed his mind. "Yes, Colt, go after him, just follow him. Make sure he heads home."

Sam lit another cigarette.

"You know, *mi amigo*," Moses said, "This will all pass. You *bueno hombre. Bueno* papa. Dan and Colt, *bueno*. Will be okay. Difficult time now. No one used to losing their—"

"God damn it, Moses!" Sam flicked his cigarette into the dirt path. "I'm not going to lose her. I waited so damn long for her. They need her. I need her. She's got to get well."

He had had enough. He wanted to get away from the three sisters' place. Climbing on his horse, he hesitated before riding out. Staring at the river, he decided. "The boys aren't going to be allowed here, Moses. I'm sorry. I don't want those miserable old women pouncing on them."

Before turning his horse to the path, he added, "They've already ruined one life. I'm not going to allow them to ruin another."

Summer 1960

A speedboat racing around the sandbar jarred Jesse as his grandfather's deep voice slowed and then paused.

"Well, my boy, I'll give you a ride home before the dogs send out a search party for us."

Sitting behind Nair's wide rump as they jogged along, Jesse listened to Gramps whistle a familiar Southern tune. At some point in the ride, Jesse noticed much to his wonder that the old man's neck had very few wrinkles. His skin seemed almost smooth.

That night, Jesse slept fitfully, tossing, and turning with a dream. During a strong storm, as he watched the deer on the sandbar, Moses came down from his cottage. Though Jesse had never seen Moses, he knew it had to be him because of the staff he held. Moses paid no attention to him but continued his way down to the river's edge.

Jesse watched the old patriarch as he stood and lifted his staff. Instantly, the wind grew fierce and worked hard, cutting a path in the river's strong current. Once the river had parted, Moses walked across. Jesse noticed that the deer followed him into the rift to the other side. There, Moses stood on a large rock and, like a statue, waited silently.

Curious to discover what kept the water parted, Jesse approached the river, but when he reached the edge, the two sides began to rejoin. When he backed away, the two sides would part. It was as though the river had an intelligence of its own and, like Moses, was patiently waiting for something or someone.

Next, he found himself sitting on the log with paper and pencils sketching out Moses walking through the split in the water. But then another strong gust blew the paper away. It appeared the wind forbade him to record what he saw. With that, he turned to see a young man, whom he recognized, from the photograph on the mantel, as his grandfather, walk directly toward the opening in the river.

Sam did not look in Jesse's direction, though he seemed to know he was there. Suddenly, Jesse realized his grandfather was to follow Moses' path through the river. When his grandfather got halfway across, something pushed Jesse to go to his aid. But as he approached the river's edge, the river instantly swallowed the old man.

Jesse quickly realized, with a horrible guilt, that he had prevented his grandfather from safely reaching the other side where Moses had waited.

He awoke in panic, bearing the weight for a terrible loss.

23

The next night, a slamming door woke Jesse from a sound sleep. Struggling to get his bearings, he guessed Jack had stormed out of the house again, and Jesse was grateful he wasn't headed to his room. But hearing his grandfather downstairs, he breathed a sigh of relief and pulled the sheet over his head. Almost dozing off, the scent of burning filled his nose.

He jumped out of bed and ran to the window to search for clues. In the south sky, above the top of the orchards, he saw an orange glow.

"Gramps. What's going on?" he yelled down.

"Smells like fire," his grandfather called up. "Let's go out and see."

. . .

A mile down the road, from the middle of the orchard, smoke billowed into a thick cloud. The flames illuminating the cloud made it look like a giant Chinese lantern.

As they wheeled into the driveway, fears were confirmed when they saw Max Martin's house engulfed in flames.

"Good God." Gramps shook his head. "What a pity. Poor, poor Max! What a pity."

Maneuvering around a half-dozen pickups and as many cars that had beat him, he pulled over. Car doors opened and slammed shut as neighbors ran toward the conflagration.

PJ Heeg moved towards Sam. "Just awful, isn't it?"

"What can be done?" Sam kicked a rock nearby.

"Nothing! It's too late. It was just a dry stack of kindling."

A woman's scream rose above the fire's roar. "Has anyone seen Max?" she cried hysterically. "Where's Max? I say!"

Phil the barber yelled out. "We searched high and low when we got here. But no trace—"

"You don't suppose he's—no—it just can't be." Daisette burst into sobs.

Within moments, the realization hit that Max Martin must be trapped in the house. Driving in to offer help, they had not expected to helplessly stand by, witnessing their friend's death. A hush descended on the crowd as they solemnly watched the house give in to the flames.

Recalling the night that he, Grace, and Will had met in the library, Sam had to accept that this too was being taken from him. Once again, he watched as a link to the past was being severed. Despite the roar of the fire, he forced his hands deep into his pockets to ward off the early morning chill.

A few moments later, hushed murmurings floated along the night air. Then, beginning at the edge of the group, like the fire that spread quickly from one end to another, a cheer.

As though coming out from behind the curtain after a stunning performance to meet his audience, Max Martin was led out by Daisette, hand in hand. She had discovered him around the side of the barn, alone and in shock, wearing a bathrobe hastily tied around his middle, his face blackened with soot. His eyes, wide in wonder, seemed to ask why everyone was here.

Westy grabbed his hand. "Max, we're so sorry. But we sure are glad to find you all right."

"What do you think caused it?" someone asked, once the group settled down.

Max searched the familiar faces, feeling obligated to say something, yet each time he opened his mouth, no words came. Then he caught sight of where the house once stood.

"It's ... it's empty," he cried out before collapsing on a nearby box.

Leaning on his grandfather, Jesse listened to the whispers. These neighbors had witnessed the swift destruction of what had been standing for as long as they could remember. These landmarks were their touchstone to an era when their fathers and grandfathers were still farming. As events in their life forced them to move forward, they had to turn from the familiar things of the past to face the present. And for these reasons, it was also their fire.

With nothing left to see, most made their way back to their cars. Shuffling past Max, they offered their condolences and assistance.

Riding home in sleepy silence as the sun's first rays faintly edged over the Buttes, Jesse poked his head around the windshield, letting the wind blow the soreness from his eyes. He cast a glance at the river, which continued to flow down its path, and he knew the farmers would soon turn their tractors out in the fields to begin the day's work.

What had happened on the Eastside early this morning affected the life of everyone nearby, and yet, the sun would rise, the river would continue its journey through the valley, and the fields would yield their growth. Life had a way of bursting forth, despite these tragedies, forcing those who remained to press forward.

A few days later, Jesse and his grandfather drove into town to pick up some groceries.

"Here now," Jesse overheard his grandfather instruct the clerk.

"I want you to credit Max Martin's account for two months' worth of groceries. Just bill my account." He glanced left and right. "And make sure no one knows about it, either."

"Gramps?" Jesse asked, once outside. "Why did you do that?"

"When a neighbor is in need, it wouldn't be right not to do everything I can.

For the remainder of that summer, Jesse gained an important lesson, witnessing the generosity of the people on the Eastside. The neighbors banded together and converted a small bunkhouse into a comfortable little house for Max. Jesse's grandfather pitched in by promising a few pieces of old furniture that had been gathering dust in the old grain barn. As the fire had belonged to everyone, not only to Max, so had the conversion of the bunkhouse. With the rebuilding complete, they settled in to embrace the healing.

Finally, everything on the ranch was almost back to normal. The only thing missing was the once grand symbol, an elegant monument to another life, another era. But even this was not really lost. The neighbors' memories "rebuilt" the house in a way. Their reminiscences outshone the original structure as they shared how beautiful and grand the house and grounds once were. Kept alive and embellished in their minds, the mansion surpassed its original glory more than if it had been fully restored.

Jesse glimpsed that when something disappears it ceases to be hampered by its original limits. This, he realized, is also what makes the beginning of a legend.

24

Like Grace before him, Colton had followed his desires, at an early age, to explore the attractions away from the Eastside. And, like his mother, having discovered that the allurements beyond the river did not satisfy, he returned and established himself among the familiar surroundings. He brought with him his bride, Lil, a renewed love for the land, and a promise to his father to always remain nearby. He and Lil lived with their three daughters farther up the road from the home place, near the county line.

Though this was a crucial time in overseeing the irrigation of his rice crop, Colton had set aside a few days to help his father. Not used to being without her two older sisters, who were traveling with their mother, Leeney was anxious to be with her cousin. After his episode with Felipe, Jesse also missed the company of someone his own age and was eager to see Leeney as well.

Each year when they met, they spent the first few days sharing what happened during the school year—comparing teachers and friends. Then, as the weeks flew by and they had once again reestablished the bond of trust, they talked about their own personal realms and thoughts they would have found difficult to share with others.

At the end of each summer when they said their goodbyes, Jesse would taunt her, "You can choose your friends, but you're stuck with your relatives." They would laugh and make faces at each other, but on the train, he would feel the void no other one his age could fill. She was more than a friend; she was someone he understood, and because she was a Hunter, they shared a family history whose bond grew deeper every year. And because he trusted her, he felt comfortable not holding back.

During the school year, trying to recapture their summer companionship, he poured himself into long letters describing his classes and the kids around him. But re-reading these accounts, he would toss them away. What is pen to paper, when he had felt his feet securely grounded in his grandfather's ranch? A letter was a thin piece of paper with squiggles of blue ink when compared to the vastness of the land and the flowing river. He might as well try to interest a cowboy in a merry-go-round horse as to attempt to recapture summers on the ranch while he lived with his mother and Jack. For his and Leeney's relationship to work, they had to be together on the ranch to share.

One hot July morning, Leeney and Jesse were finishing breakfast while Gramps and Colton discussed the plans for the day.

I think I'll look in on old man DeJarnett," Colton decided. "My rice harvester is falling apart. I don't think I can make it last another season. I hear DeJarnett has one to sell. Do you want to come along, Dad?"

The old man blew the steam from his coffee. "No, thanks. I need to go into town." Eyeing the youngsters, he said, "I'm sure you two can keep yourselves busy."

After breakfast, Jesse and Leeney drifted out to the stable.

"Have you seen the new gelding?" Jesse asked.

"Nope. But Dad's warned me to stay clear. He's to work him a little before he would even consider letting us give him a try."

At the stall, the horse and the two cousins exchanged glances.

"I tried to brush him the other day, but he has a mind of his own."

"He looks okay to me," Leeney said. "He's certainly a beauty. I want to be here when Dad gives him a piece of his mind."

"I'll be sure to be around to see that." Jesse remembering how Max had instilled him with such fear, he changed the subject. "Gramps showed me how to shoot one of his rifles a few weeks back."

He pointed to the other side of the barn where he had set up the tin cans during target practice. "Come on. I'll show you the one we used."

Back at the house, knowing the cabinet was always kept locked, still he jiggled the door just in case. Pointing out the rifle, he said, "That's the one. It's a lot heavier than it looks, and it kicks back. In fact, if Gramps hadn't supported me, I would have been knocked—"

"Shhh." Leeney put her finger to her lips.

They crept closer to the open window, where they strained to hear.

"... a little concerned," Colton was saying. "Dad seems to be slowing down quite a bit lately. Dan should be here to help. Have you noticed anything recently?"

"Sure." Hank wiped his brow with his stained handkerchief. "Even Stanza has seen a difference, 'specially lately. The old man shouldn't be doing all that he does around here. But I can't tell him to slow down or do it for him." He chuckled. "I'm not a young colt myself."

Jesse had to admit that Gramps did seem different this summer. That day at the river, he'd had to rest on a log to catch his breath before slipping a pill under his tongue. And then there was the time at the barber's shop, where he had broken out in a sweat. And at lunch, a few days ago, Stanza seemed worried when she saw him make a fist against his chest. To know that others were seeing it caused Jesse more concern.

"I caught up with Dan yesterday." Colton's voice turned a little gravelly. "He was with one of those good-for-nothing friends of his. Anyway, I told him the old man wasn't looking right."

"What did he say?"

"Same old thing. Put up some damn argument. Still, I told him he'd be wise to come home to help Dad."

Suddenly, Colton looked over his shoulder toward the window. Jesse and Leeney quickly moved back into the shadow.

"Not to mention the care of his son. A boy needs his father."

A boy needs his father ... a boy needs his father, thought Jesse. *What about the father ... doesn't he need his son?*

Hank stuffed his handkerchief back in his pocket. "Can't imagine Dan liking that. What did he say then?"

"That he'd spare a day or two to help around." Colton lowered his voice. "And he'd be a great help for Dad, if he'd stay sober." He sighed. "I suppose he'll come." Shielding his eyes from the late morning sun, he checked the road. "Well, I'd best be off. You take care of yourself."

Hank tipped his hat and returned to his pruning as Colton disappeared around the corner of the barn.

Leeney gave Jesse's arm a squeeze. "I'm sorry. We shouldn't have eavesdropped."

"Don't worry, Leeney. It's okay. Nothing's changed much." There was that burning sensation again in his eyes. It always seemed to surprise him when the subject of his dad came up. But he knew that just because he buried his feelings below a stone of disappointment, this didn't make them go away.

"Hey, listen." He grabbed Leeney's hand. "Let's go see the five brothers."

"The five who?" Leeney tagged along.

"There're five roosters that live out in the orchard. I've named them the five brothers."

"Where?"

"Out by the grain barn."

"Where's that?"

"You must've been out there. It's near the old grave."

"Grave?"

Jesse cocked his head. "You've been here before, right?"

"Smart-ass."

"There's an old stone cross where a man is buried."

She looked in the direction of the orchard. "Okay. Now I know you're making this all up!"

"Nope. Wait 'til you see it."

Now that the orchard was covered in water from the irrigation, he checked for the best path. They began their hike on top of one of the small checks in the general direction of the grain barn. But after a while, Jesse realized that he might as well be walking a maze; this was leading them farther away from their goal.

He looked around to get his bearings. "Hmm. I don't want to go all the way back and start over. Besides, I'm not sure which check would get us there. We'll just have to wade through the water. Take off your shoes and roll up your pants."

"I don't want to get all muddy."

"I swear you're beginning to sound more like a mall girl every day."

"A mall girl?" Bending over, she untied her shoes, complaining under her breath. With her shoes flung over her shoulder, she thrust one foot into the water and let it sink into the oozing mud below. "Yuk!" she cried out. With her foot stuck deep, she began to lose her balance, but plunging the other one in, she regained it. Trudging through the muddy water, she made disgusted faces and made sure Jesse saw them.

After fifteen minutes, they made it to the barn, wet and muddy.

"Is this it? This old building?" Leeney seemed unimpressed.

"Yep. Wait till you see inside. There's so much stuff. You won't believe it."

He tugged at the heavy door. Dozens of birds inside rustled and flew around, opposed to the disturbance of their quiet sanctuary.

Leeney stood back. "This is creepy, Jesse. I don't like it."

"Shhh!" He looked around as though checking for someone. "We have to wait a minute for it to calm down." On previous visits to the barn, he had paused at the door, convinced that he should wait for permission to enter.

Finally, he could feel the peacefulness return. "They're giving us permission."

"Who's giving permission?" Leeney began backing away. "What's in there anyway?" She stared at Jesse, who calmly waited. "Okay. That's it. I want to go back."

"Leeney. Wait." He grabbed her arm. "Listen. The memories are giving us permission to be their guests. We must be very quiet to enter."

"Memories are giving us ..." She screwed up her face. "And just who are these—"

"They're what's left of the people that've died. And to those that believe, their memories can be read."

"To those that believe ..." she repeated.

Once the birds had settled down, Jesse slipped through the door. Having no other choice, she reluctantly followed. "It doesn't look too scary," she whispered to herself.

Jesse wondered if she would see it as he always did when he ventured in. To him, the interior seemed like a sacred old church where many had come to rest and cast off burdens from things that at one time were so essential. Dusty sunlight penetrated through the spaces between the weathered boards, giving the space a golden luminosity.

Thinking of the relatives, long dead, who once made the Eastside their home, Jesse wondered each time he visited here— did they miss the things they left behind?

"Look at this!" Jesse pointed out. "This is the stuff that Gramps is giving to Mr. Martin."

"What does he want with it?"

"His house just burned down. You must've heard about that huge mansion down the road."

She nodded.

"Anyway, Gramps is waiting for the orchard to dry so they can get a truck back here to load it up."

"Oh. Look at this desk!" Leeney wiped the dust away and started poking around in the drawers and pigeonholes.

Jesse found a steamer trunk with its corners gnawed away and its lock hanging loose. Rummaging through it, he felt he was trespassing in a private crypt. He wondered what he would think if someone went poking through his things. But he guessed that if he were dead, he would no longer need them, so he wouldn't mind. At least, there wasn't much he would be able to do about it.

Leeney had discovered, in a hidden drawer, a packet of letters tied together with a black ribbon. She was struggling with the knot when Jesse called out, "Hey, come here and see what I found."

She tossed the packet on top of a box and ran over. Jesse had discovered the edge of a battered green journal, hidden under a stack of clothes. He sat down in a chair nearby. "It looks like Gramps' handwriting."

Carefully turning the yellowed pages, he found each one full of that unmistakable, ordered writing. "How strange!" he said. "Gramps has been telling me about our family and the ranch. And here it is. It's written down."

His voice was somber as he began to read aloud:

> I can barely accept that Grace is gone, lost to me.
> And now, I have two boys to raise, on my own.
> They are my comfort. They shall keep my mind from my grief.

Reading their grandfather's words, revealing his uncertainties and fears, made the cousins very serious. As in a church, though the music is uplifting and the interior serene, without the writings, the faithful cannot be touched. Until Jesse began to read what his grandfather had been thinking, he had only been able to guess what Grace's death really meant to him. Now he could begin to feel it from his grandfather's heart.

It had seemed to Jesse that Gramps had all the answers to life's questions. That he had always lived here next to the river, witness to all that happened around him, and providing help to those that needed it. Providing a home to those who would accept it. Asking little in return but to observe his crops grow, watch his livestock prosper, and to be left alone to live under the open sky.

He was like a … what was he like? Jesse pondered.

He was like the ranch! Is that what Gramps meant at the river when he warned Jesse never to forget those two words—the ranch?

Leeney gently took the book. She carefully turned the brittle pages, stopping every now and then to read aloud:

> *Today, Kate and her family came over to see us. They helped with the walnut harvest a little and then we had dinner outside. After dinner, before she left, Dan hugged Kate good-bye and began crying. He told her that she reminded him of his mother. And that he missed her so much. When I looked through my tears, I saw that she too had tears streaming down her face landing like a benediction on Dan. Sometimes, it is just too hard …*

"I wonder if we should even be reading his journal," Jesse said slowly.

"You know, I think it's all right." Leeney tried her best. "Because all this happened so many years ago."

Their consciences weakly vindicated, they continued to read, stopping at various entries with dates clearly noted at the top of each page.

"Wait, listen to this. Gramps writes more about our dads."

> *Now that the boys are down for the night, I can relax and sit undisturbed in my library. They are good boys. They miss their mother tremendously. Today, I found them out in the bend. Dan was on the porch with his pencils and*

sketchpad. Colton was hiking through the growth, hunting for rabbits.

The artist broods and mourns too much. But what can I do? I miss their mother as well. How can I heal him when I'm searching for healing? Can one teach when the subject hasn't been learned?

Then Leeney turned a few more pages to another entry written a few months later:

The boys and I enjoyed a full summer day. Oh Lord, how I remember the days of my youth. It reminds me of those carefree times when Grace, Will, and I spent many days fishing and hunting.

We worked so hard this morning that I promised the boys we would break in the afternoon, when the heat became too unbearable. We rode to the pond where the fishing was good. We caught five trout and feasted on them for supper.

It was so warm tonight; the boys and I ate outside under the oak. After supper, we lay back and let the dogs lick the plates clean. We studied the evening sky and took our time watching the setting sun paint its colors.

As the stars began to shine, I pointed out the constellations to the boys. At one point, there was silence and then Dan asked, "Pa, if my eyes were sharp enough could I see to forever?"

"Yes, I suppose you could," I answered.

"Would I be able to see Ma?" he asked.

I had to think about that. It was a while before I could respond. "When you study the night sky, let those stars that you see remind you of those that have gone on before us. And the stars not quite as bright as the others are for those that will follow. So, you see, when you search the evening sky, your dear mother is never far from us, always watching over us."

They fell quiet for a while. Then I decided it was the right time to give them my gift, the one that I had been saving.

Leeney's voice seemed to float softly somewhere above Jesse, as he closed his eyes attempting to see what he was hearing about:

"Look there," I said, as I pointed up to the sky.

"Where?" Dan asked.

"Up there, at the handle of the Big Dipper. See it?"

"Yes, Pa. I see it now."

"Boys, most of the things I can give you will perish. But there is one thing I can give you that won't." They looked at me with questioning eyes.

"I give you the most wondrous and priceless gift I can this night. Tonight, I give each of you a star.

"There, the second one down is called Merak; that one is yours," I said to Dan. "And next to it on the other side, that star is called Phecda." I gestured to Colton. "It is yours. Up from that one, on the edge where the handle joins to the bowl, is Megrez. That one is mine, and there, next to it, but farther out on the handle, notice the brightest—that is called Alioth. That one is your mother's.

"See how brilliantly that one shines? We each have a star close together. Our stars will never move away from each other. It has been set in place from the beginning to last forever." They were quiet and I wondered if they understood.

"What about the first star? What's its name?" Dan asked me.

I told him, "Dubhe is its name."

Then he asked, "Who does that belong to?"

"There are many stars in the vastness of the dome above us." I could only bring myself to say, "Each belongs to someone. I have told you which ones belong to us. That is enough for now."

"I can't read this anymore." She sniffled and looked for something to wipe her nose.

Jesse wished he could sit here for as long as possible. The picture of the night sky, the stars, and a father with his sons, giving them the eternal gift of stars, was awe-inspiring. How could he go back?

"Jesse." Reluctantly, he opened his eyes. Leeney carefully handed the book to him. And he read the next passage aloud:

> *I took the boys up in the hill country today. We rode past the old Mountain House, and I told them it once belonged to their mother's family. Then we rode farther to the Rock Cliff Falls Ranch where Joe lives. After checking on the cattle, we had our lunch on a large outcrop of stone ...*

Turning to one of the last entries in the old volume, Jesse spotted something. "Listen to this!" He read:

> *I still cannot believe that Amanda and her sisters would fill Dan's head full of lies as they did. I wonder what they thought they might benefit from it. I suppose in their wickedness they believed they might also turn Dan and Colton against me. But they little realize that is impossible. I have raised my boys on truth and have never resorted to lies.*
>
> *And yet, I am concerned about Dan. He has changed since that time. He is not as gentle as he once was. I am confused. Is he just going through a growing-up process, or have their lies filled his mind full of doubts? Only time will prove.*
>
> *I pray that someday, he will understand why we did what we did. I hope that he will come to me for the truth and not to those heartless old maids, who have already woven their lies on others before him.*

"Is that it? Is there anything else?" Leeney asked.

"No. That's it." Glancing up from the journal, he stared at the puzzlement growing on Leeney's face.

"I wonder what he was talking about. What could Amanda have said?" Leeney spoke softly, thoughtfully.

"We've read too much. We've imposed on the memories too long. They've almost given us too much," Jesse said, though he couldn't understand why he had put it that way. He almost felt as though some power had set those words in his mouth.

He gently returned the book into the trunk, and they made their way quietly out of the barn.

Passing by the stone cross, they stopped. "This is the grave?" Leeney read the dates and name. "Do you really think someone is buried here?"

The stagnant water from the irrigation surrounded the cross, making it more sinister looking.

"Now, I'm more convinced than ever," Jesse said solemnly before breaking out into a race to the house. Every few yards, he glanced over his shoulder to see how far behind she was. But he knew she had no idea he was more interested in seeing how much distance he was placing between himself and the cross.

The cousins remained uncharacteristically silent as they walked toward the house. The world they had entered through their grandfather's journals was one for which they had not been prepared.

They didn't realize that when a storyteller relates his tale in person, he edits and changes it on the fly, taking his cues from his listeners' responses. In a sense, he is giving them the story based on a mutual pact. He is leading them through the garden, and the listeners are willingly following him, delighting in the unfolding wonders.

But to read a journal, to read someone's personal confessions, is to force open the lock of the gate and directly enter the garden, without any guide to caution as to what may be found. Often this path is rough or barely passable to the trekker. These words need to be parsed out to avoid overwhelming or troubling the sightseer.

25

Approaching the yard, Jesse noticed his uncle and his grand-father chuckling while another man was busy working on a gate. In the shadows of the oak, Felipe Diego and his three companions watched. Quickly rolling a cigarette, Felipe stuffed it in his mouth and then noticing Jesse, he nodded.

There was something strangely familiar about the man pounding nails. Suddenly, Jesse's stomach felt as though he had swallowed a dozen butterflies. It was his dad!

For his dad to materialize suddenly didn't make sense. Where had he been? Why today? He guessed it didn't really matter—the fact was he was here. But Jesse was in the middle of the summer; his dad was the last person he expected to see. But then that was Dan, like the north wind, appearing and disappearing without warning.

Jesse had grown used to being with only Gramps. That he might have to go with his dad and miss his grandfather's story would fill him with disappointment. Still, he was glad to see his dad had finally decided to come see him.

Besides, wasn't his grandfather's story finished? Or was it?

After reading the journals, he wondered. He had some unanswered questions. But maybe it didn't matter now. Gramps had
given him so much.

Dan had aged this past year; that was the first thing Jesse noticed. His father's chiseled looks were often his only brightness,
and, in a sense, they seemed to be fading. The color gray seemed
to be dominant. Gray circles under his eyes, gray hair peeking out
from the sideburns, and cheeks taking on a gray hue. Jesse
guessed this must be the result of too much "working up north."

But what Gramps had written in his journal about Dan as a
sensitive young boy provided Jesse with another image. Once,
this young Dan liked to read, write, and draw. He liked to work
in the barn on engines and would fish at the pond. And this was
the man he wanted to see.

Trailing behind Leeney, he felt as though his legs would buckle
underneath him. Emerging from Leeney's shadow, he took a few
steps in his dad's direction and tried to wave. But Dan seemed to
have no peripheral vision. The business of replacing slats of wood
onto the frame of the gate appeared to require as much con-
centration as splitting diamonds.

Where a smile should have been, Dan's lips tightly held a few
nails. He continued to hammer fiercely as though he was killing
bugs—bugs that would overtake him if he slowed down or
stopped.

"Hey, Dad." He poked out his hand. "I was worried you might
not come." His voice cracked. "Will you be staying here now?"

Dan's vision seemed nailed to the wood. "Oh. Hello there," he
mumbled. Miraculously, not one nail fell from his lips. Then, as
though some invisible hand forced him, his head turned towards
Jesse. But the greeting was like a response to someone who had
returned from an errand empty-handed.

Then with two swings of the hammer, he concentrated on
sinking the last nail into the slat. "I'm only here for a couple of
days." He fished a cigarette out of his pocket and, spitting out the
nails, stuck it between his lips. Like Felipe, he struck a match on
his jeans and lit it.

"When I'm done here," a cloud of smoke drifted Jesse's way, "I've got to get back to work on the interstate." He gave Colton an accusing look. "Been repairing the gate. Colton drove the god-damn tractor through it."

"Come on, Dan. I didn't do it on purpose." Colton glanced from Dan to Jesse and back to Dan.

Dan shot up, tossing the hammer at Colton's feet. "Try to be more careful next time."

And like two rams on a mountain road, the brothers stared each other down.

"Tell your father about the little house in the bend." Gramps tried to diffuse the tension.

Leeney moved towards Jesse. "What little house?" she asked.

Following the shadows on the ground up to his father, Jesse said, "Remember you told me last summer about the house that Moses lived in?"

At the mention of the house, Dan glared at Colton and the old man.

"I've … cleaned it up and … I … spend time out there, some-times." Jesse stumbled on. "The last time I was out there, a doe and her fawn came onto the sandbar."

Dan sucked on the stub of his cigarette until the smoldering ring reached his lips. He flicked the remains over the fence, where it landed in a puddle of water, sizzling.

"You've no business down near that river," he said, glancing from his brother to the old man. "It's too dangerous. Stay away from there."

Turning on his heel, Dan joined Felipe Diego and his compan-ions, who quickly jumped to attention.

Fighting back the burning feeling growing in his throat and beginning to rise to his eyes, Jesse clenched his teeth.

Colton shook his head. "Hey, young man, why don't you give the twin here another driving lesson?" Colton pushed Leeney toward the Jeep.

Jesse stood paralyzed, not knowing what to do. He felt he was the center of attention—everyone waited on him. He was back on the basketball court with the ball coming his way. He wished he could sprout wings and fly over the oak tree. But instead, he forced himself to move.

Dan kept his eyes on Jesse and Leeney as they shuffled to the Jeep.

Trying to forget his dad's presence, he hopped into the mud-encrusted Jeep and motioned to Leeney to take the driver's seat.

"Remember what we did last time?" Jesse whispered out of the side of his mouth.

Leeney shook her head.

"Okay. It's easy enough. Every limb has a job. Left hand on the wheel. Right hand on the ignition. Left foot down on the clutch. Right foot on the gas." Jesse couldn't help noticing that Dan shook his head. He corrected himself. "Check the gear shift. In neutral?"

"Yep."

"Good. Now start the engine. Slip it into first gear. A little off the clutch and little on the gas."

Concentrating on his directions, she navigated across the yard and over to the gate where the Jeep sputtered to a stop.

"You'll have to back up away from the gate," Colton motioned them back, "so I can open it." Gramps seemed amused.

Jesse nodded at his uncle. "Okay, Leeney. Start it up again. Okay? Good. Now take your foot off the gas. *Goooood*. Now press the clutch down to the floor. No, not that one. That's the brake. With your left foot, press the pedal all the way down. Now give it a little gas."

The engine revved.

Jesse wished his dad would stop staring. "Okay. Good. But now let off the gas a little."

Out of the corner of his eye, he noticed his dad was making gestures that he couldn't understand. Leeney waited for the next instructions. But receiving none, she ground the gear until she found one.

"Now let the clutch out just a little and press the gas pedal at the same time." Jesse mimed the movements to Leeney. The engine started to sputter.

"You'll have to rev it up a little. Give it some more gas."

Leeney revved up the engine. "Good. Now just let off the clutch." Jesse instructed.

When her foot accidentally slipped off the clutch, her reflex was to slam the accelerator all the way down with the other. The instant Jesse realized what had happened, his mouth opened with words formed but no sound. He threw his hands in front of his face as slats of wood flew by. On the other side, the Jeep sputtered to a stall. Jesse counted the moments of painful silence and was somewhat relieved when Colton broke it with a whoop of laughter.

Gramps choked back his laughter, with tears rolling down his cheeks. Felipe Diego and the other three failed to hide their amusement.

"Good Lord," the old man yelled over to Dan. "Almost beats the day you backed the tractor through the barn wall and into the ditch."

"Oh my God, Leeney. It was supposed to be in reverse," Jesse yelled when he regained his voice. He glimpsed his dad, looking as though he might explode.

"For Chrissakes!" Dan threw his cigarette on the ground. Jesse's butterflies instantly tripled.

"That's it!" His dad ran towards them. "Get out of the goddamn Jeep now! The both of you!"

They leaped out and would have stood at attention if they hadn't been shaking so much. And yet, Colton calmly motioned them to get back into the Jeep.

Dan strode up to his brother and stood in his face. "Just a goddamned minute, here. They're not going anywhere!"

All amusement faded from Colton's face. "She's my daughter. And I said she can get in the Jeep." And, he added, "Don't be an ass! You heard Dad. You've done worse, and no harm came of it. Let them go!"

Dan backed up about a foot, gave his brother a contemptible look, and spat, narrowly missing Colton's boot. Again, like two rams on a mountain pass, each dared the other to make the first move. When Dan did an about-face and headed towards the house, Leeney and Jesse were unsure as to what they should do.

Colton motioned. "Just be careful and be sure to stop at the gates now."

"I can't do it." Leeney shook her head, refusing to get back into the Jeep. "I don't want to drive anymore."

"Leeney." Her dad waved her on. "It's all right."

"No. I can't."

Jesse pushed her into the driver's seat. "Come on. You can do it. You must do it."

With her dad nodding and waving his support, she un-enthusiastically started the engine. The Jeep stalled and sputtered once. But with Jesse's coaxing, she worked the pedals and used the correct gears to keep moving down the road.

Achieving some distance from the yard, the air feathered all traces of tension from their faces, and as the ride began to smooth out, they began to relax. Leeney concentrated on the road, while Jesse gathered dirt clods from the floorboards and threw them into the ditch near the road.

Leeney stole a glance at him from the corner of her eye. "Jesse. I'm sorry."

"About what?"

"About embarrassing you in front of Uncle Dan."

He threw another dirt clod and watched it explode on the trunk of a tree. "Don't worry about it. Doesn't matter."

"Yes. It does matter."

"Well, even if it did, nothing can be done about it. Every summer I come up here to be with him, and every summer even when he's here, he's somewhere else. He's so … I don't know why … but he's so damn mad at something. I mean if I lived here all the time, I'd be happy."

"You know," she offered, "Dad says he's just mad that things haven't turned out the way he wanted them."

"Well. Welcome to the club." Jesse threw another dirt clod, but it missed the target. "Things haven't turned out exactly the way I wanted either. But here I am, and there he is, and," looking over his shoulder, he added, "here's the orchard between us."

"Jesse. What if—" Leeney tried to ask.

"Look, there's nothing to be said. It's too late. That's the problem." He gave her shoulder a squeeze. "I appreciate your thoughts. I don't want to talk about it anymore."

She bit her lip. "You can talk to me, you know. You can tell me anything you want. It might help."

The last thing he wanted to do was burden Leeney with his home life.

"Dad says that your stepfather isn't the nicest person on earth." Jesse gave her a disgusted look.

"Leeney, what's it like to have your dad give you a hug and tell you he loves you? What's it like to have him here?"

She didn't answer, but the tears welling up in her eyes were beginning to obscure her vision. She hit a pothole, and they both bounced in their seats.

"Whoa!" Jesse held on. "Are you okay? Do you want me to drive?"

"Nope! I'm fine." She brushed her face clear. "What about your step—"

"He's not my stepfather! He's Jack. Just plain old asshole Jack!" Leeney burst into more tears.

"Look, I'm sorry," he said. "I didn't mean to get so worked up. I guess it's just seeing Dad and all. Let's just try to forget about this and enjoy the ride. Where do you want to go?"

"I don't know." She glanced at him. "Jesse?"

"I said forget about it." He winked and smiled. "Where shall we go?"

"I guess the pond."

"Okay. Let's take a shortcut." He pointed to a spot near the road where two worn spots veered off into the field. "Turn over here. You can cut through the field."

Bringing the Jeep to a stop, she examined the ground. "It's not dry enough. Too muddy." She nodded to a clump of trees in the distance. "I think we should go on the road around over there."

"Come on, just turn here," Jesse persisted. "It's fine really."

"Look, it's too wet."

"Just do it, Leeney. It's starting to dry. Can't you tell? Just trust me!"

Shrugging her shoulders, she made a funny face before throwing it into first. Turning off the road, they slugged ahead about five yards before the Jeep was trapped. She pressed down harder on the gas. The tires spun, but the more gas she gave it, the more the Jeep stayed in one place.

"Shit. Shit. Shit." Jesse looked around, not sure what to do now. He pictured himself hiking back into the yard to tell his dad. And that visual was not appealing. "I'm going to get out and push. When I shout, you step on the gas."

He jumped out of his seat, and his boots disappeared in the muck. He clomped slowly around to the back and pushing against the back with all the strength he could muster, he yelled, "Okay. Hit the gas!"

He pushed as hard as he could, while the wheels spun, but the Jeep stayed put.

"Forget it!" he yelled above the engine's gunning. "Leeney, forget it!" He waved to get her attention.

As he came around the side, she broke out in peals of laughter.

"What's so damned funny?"

"Oh, my Gawd! You should see your face."

Jesse glanced into the side mirror and then spat some mud at her.

"Okay. So that didn't work. Now what?" She waited for the next suggestion.

He wiped mud from his face. "Well. It's obvious."

She searched around her.

"You'll have to walk back and get my dad to come help us."

Her mouth dropped open. "Kidding? Right?" she said, raising her eyebrows as high as they could go.

The question was answered with a silent, grim face.

"You've got to be nuts. Did you forget how mad Uncle Dan was? No way am I going back there. You made me go through the—"

"Come on, Leen … please?"

"No!" She sat still, hands locked on the steering wheel.

"All right, I'll go. But if I don't come back soon, drag the river for me."

. . .

A half an hour later, Jesse trudged into the yard. Dan and Gramps were loading Dan's pickup with the surveying tools.

"Jess, what happened?" His grandfather checked Jesse's muddy face and looked over his shoulder. "Where's Leeney?"

"We just got stuck. That's all."

"What do you mean, you got stuck?" His dad shook his head. "Can't you see they're irrigating out there? What the hell happened?"

"I wanted Leeney to take a shortcut to the pond, so we cut across the first field. I thought it was dry, but then—"

"Never mind," Dan spat out. "I get the picture."

"Go ahead, Dan," Gramps said, relieved. "I'll wait while you pull them out."

. . .

Side by side on the tractor, father and son began their ride in silence. Searching for something, anything, to say, Jesse had to shout to be heard above the diesel engine. "Dad?"

Dan took a drag from a cigarette that Jesse had decided could be permanently glued to his lips. "What is it?"

"Where've you been?"

"Like I said, working on the interstate."

"How long will you be here?"

"Depends."

"On what?"

"When I can get away."

"Dad?"

"What is it?"

"Gramps told me you used to draw when you were a kid."

Dan slowly turned to Jesse and stared.

"Well, I was just wondering ... do you still have the pictures? I'd like to see them."

"Of course not." Dan pushed a low-lying branch away from his face. "Why the hell would I keep such ..."

Jesse wasn't sure, but he thought he saw his father's shoulders sag a little.

"Listen." Dan took a deep breath and turned towards him. "There's too much work to be done to waste time with childish drawings. The quicker you learn that there is work to be done around here, the better. You're at the age where you can't just play all day. Don't let your grandfather fill your head with a lot of dreamy bullshit. The sooner you learn that life is work, the better off you'll be. Dreams are for old women!"

When they passed by the stone cross, Jesse glanced from it to Dan, but his dad was too busy lighting another cigarette to notice it.

"Whose decision was it to leave the road?"

"Um. Mine."

"Christ!" Dan said, shaking his head.

As they got closer to the muddy field, Leeney waved. "Uncle Dan, I'm sorry," she yelled over.

"Never mind." He gave a half-smile and tossed his cigarette away. "I guess I have nothing better to do than repair gates and pull yokels out of mud."

He pulled a heavy chain from the box under the tractor seat and handed one end to Jesse. "Here, fasten this onto the Jeep's back bumper, then wait in the Jeep."

After securing his end, Jesse climbed back into the driver's seat and waited while Dan fastened his to the front of the tractor.

Throwing the tractor in gear, he slowly backed it up until the chain was taut. Then with a tug, the tractor effortlessly pulled the Jeep onto the road. Throwing the tractor into neutral, Dan motioned to them to start the jeep. While he unhooked the chain and stuffed it back into the box, Jesse tried to start the engine, but it just made a clicking sound.

"I don't have all day," Dan yelled.

Jesse frowned, speaking quietly. "How could the battery be dead?" Leeney did a poor job of hiding a guilty look.

"Don't tell me you were playing the radio this whole time?" Jesse was incredulous.

"I had to do something while I was waiting," she whispered.

"What's going on?" Dan shouted.

"The battery's dead," he shouted to his dad. "She was listening to the radio."

Dan rolled his eyes and mouthed something they decided was best unheard. Throwing the tractor back into gear, he guided it back to the Jeep.

He threw the chain down to Jesse. "Same fire drill."

Dan didn't stay long after dinner, saying he had to meet some friends in town.

After the dishes were done, Jesse and Leeney climbed upstairs to get ready for bed.

While Jesse brushed his teeth, Colton sat on the side of the bathtub.

"I have something that you can look forward to tomorrow. But it's a surprise," Colton announced.

"Really?" Jesse spat out the toothpaste. "What is it?"

"Well, then, it wouldn't be a surprise if I told you, would it? Just look forward to it as you fall asleep tonight."

Later, before the cousins turned out the lights, his uncle returned to tuck them in upstairs on the sleeping porch.

"I've got a big day planned tomorrow." He jabbed at Jesse and his daughter to make room for him where he stretched out.

"Uncle, what was it like to be a boy growing up here?" Jesse asked.

Listening to the crickets and the occasional hooting of an owl in the tree, Colton sighed. "Gosh, let's see ... well, make no mistake about it, life was hard. A farming life is hard work. But it's different than anywhere else. You make your own hours; you make your own decisions."

"But didn't you go away for a while? Didn't you see if there was something else to do?"

"Yep. I did, kiddo. But you know a piece of it is, if you go out looking for satisfaction, you'll be disappointed if you don't find it inside you first. I soon realized that nothing beats a life in the great outdoors." Colton examined the two. "Okay. Maybe that's exaggerating a bit. But the Eastside is magical to me. It has history. When I drive down the road, every ranch reminds me of someone, of family. There are so many memories here. It's a part of me."

"Is that what made you come back?"

"I suppose to a degree. Yes. But it's also ... I don't know. Hard to describe. We're all in it together. I guess that's it. Though we all seem to be working separately, you look over at the neighbors' fields, and you realize we're all in it together. We're plowing the same earth, hoping, expecting the same things."

"Gramps says his family was big. Do you remember them?"

"Yeah. They were big. They used to come to help each other with the harvest. You see, farmers feel differently about themselves. They feel insulated. Kind of like no one else really understands what they must do. Not everything was so automated then. All the cousins helped. While we worked, we played games.

"Maybe it has to do with faith." He was quiet for a minute. "I don't know. I never really had to put it into words before. But maybe that's it. You must have faith, and that sets you apart from those that don't."

Jesse thought it strange that like his dad, Colton had never mentioned Grace before. And here Jesse was learning all about her life from his grandfather. "Was your mom religious?"

"I don't know that Mother was an overly religious person. She would tell us Bible stories, so I guess she must've been familiar with the Bible. But I don't remember much about what she believed in. I can tell you that she had faith in Dad and the ranch. And that made her happier than any sermon.

"I know how I feel," Colton went on. "To me, God is as large as the universe, unfathomable, huge. You can't get that into a little church. I prefer thinking about him through his creation—the country and nature. That's probably the closest I come to understanding his order."

Jesse liked the idea of God too big to fit inside a church.

"What was she like?"

"Mother?" Taking a deep breath, Colton searched the stars. "You know, I remember her, but not really as a person, more like a presence … I remember her tenderness." His voice seemed to take on a lighter, ethereal tone. "I remember her singing. She loved to sing, and she loved to laugh."

Turning away from the stars to Jesse, his voice turned normal. "But, Jesse, it was so long ago I can't really picture her with me. I just know she was around me.

"But Dad was the one. He was always there. Through thick and thin, we could always count on him. No matter where you had been, you could count on driving up the river road and turning into the ranch, and he'd be there. He was the strength of the family. He never let us down."

Interesting. That's how Jesse felt about his grandfather, but he hadn't thought of it in those exact words—until after he had read his journals. But the lingering, beneath-the-surface question always remained.

"What was my dad like?"

Smiling at Jesse, Colton sighed a little. "You know, your dad was a good kid. He was a great older brother. He was athletic, artistic, and quite a thinker. You never knew what he was thinking about, but you knew it was deep. Kind of like the river, eh? Some people don't grow up easily. He couldn't just accept life. He was always thinking of some way to fight it."

"Fight it?"

"Oh, I don't know really. I guess he was always trying to figure it out. If he couldn't figure it out, he got mad."

Colton glanced over to Leeney, who was snoring.

"Don't worry about plowing through gates or getting stuck in mud." He got up to leave. "I can't count how many times your grandfather had to pull your dad and me out of many muddy fields."

"Really?"

"You bet. Just enjoy yourself. Don't worry about the little things. I know we didn't," he said, messing up Jesse's hair.

He gave his sleeping daughter a kiss on the forehead.

"Look forward to tomorrow."

.   .   .

As Jesse began to doze, he caught bits of conversation drifting up from the porch below.

"Dad, I'm worried about you. I think you're trying to do too much here. Dan should be here to help you."

"Nonsense. I'm fine," Gramps said firmly.

"Even Hank can tell that you shouldn't be here alone."

"It's all right," the old man said. "It'll be all right."

"Dammit, Dad, you're not a young man anymore. You need help."

"How are Lil and the girls? Has Lil had any luck?"

"Changing the subject doesn't help, Dad. But as you mentioned it, yes. Lil says the girls are having a great time." He sighed. "She's been searching and came up with—"

"Shhh. The kids are upstairs. They'll hear."

Colton looked up. "Nah, Dad. I left them asleep."

"But have they discovered anything?"

"Yes. I've been trying to think of ways to—."

"Just spit it out," Gramps ordered. "It's been too many years. What did Lil find?"

"She's been dead five years, Dad."

Jesse, now wide awake, rolled gently out of bed and crept towards the side of the porch to hear.

"Five years. That long? I had hoped ...what about her son? Any word on—"

"No. There's no trace," Colton said.

Jesse heard his grandfather's chair begin rocking.

"No trace, huh? That's a fact? No trace," Gramps repeated, sounding sad about whatever had happened. "Well, then. That settles it. I'll go into town tomorrow and meet with Rutledge, my lawyer to have a codicil ..."

But those were the last words they spoke on that subject after the floorboard under Jesse creaked.

.   .   .

About midnight, Jesse was awakened when his father came home. In his drowsy state, three voices intertwined, and though at first, he couldn't tell for sure, it sounded like an argument was in progress.

Creeping halfway down the backstairs, Jesse could hear his father.

"Goddammit, leave me alone—"

"Dan. What's wrong with you? It's time for you to be strong and be responsible for your son," Colton said.

"Don't ... don't tell me what to do. You ... you who even had the chance to leave. You're so stup—you even came back."

"Here now, stop this talk," Gramps insisted. "I won't hear of it."

"Listen, old man. You lecture me about being a father when you're the one that took my son away from me. I've done exactly as you've wanted. And ... and look ... where it's gotten me!"

"You don't even know what you're saying. You're drunk."

"Yeah. Well, I may be drunk. But I know how I feel. I don't care what the hell you do with this place. Leave it to the devil—"

"Dan, my boy. You can't mean that. You know what this ranch has meant to us all, especially to your mother."

"Don't speak to me of Mother," Dan spat back. "Besides, Jesse ... doesn't need me. You look after him. You've interfered before and ruined ... Old man, you've never learned. Stop interfering with me! It's too late!"

He began his slow ascent up the stairs. Jesse quickly escaped to the porch.

Missing the last stair before the landing, Dan nearly tumbled backward. Gaining his balance, he leaned into the next one, made it upstairs, and disappeared into the darkness of his own room. And when he slammed his door, the entire house seemed to groan.

26

W ell, if you ask me," his dad's gravelly voice jolted Jesse wide awake even though it was not quite sunup, "I think a man'd be wasting his time."

Jesse wondered if Leeney had gone downstairs for breakfast. But a quick check showed she was still curled up on the other side of the porch, snoring.

"A man can't just plant the front section," Dan continued. "He'd never get his money out of that land until the entire place is sunk in trees!" Sometimes, when uncertain, Dan gave himself away by speaking in the third person.

"Yes, Dan. But that's just the problem." Colton's tone betrayed his annoyance. "That piece floods every winter, and the water sits for too long. And the trees being dormant, the roots'll rot for sure. That's why everyone on the river sticks to row crops for the back side."

"Why, if that's true," Dan spat out, "what about the west side of the river? They're planted in trees. They don't seem the worse—"

"That's because the land is much higher on that side. It doesn't flood," Colton said. "You know that!"

Jesse pictured the scene downstairs: Gramps would continue to eat his breakfast, allowing his sons to debate the issues before settling the matter.

"Well," Dan continued, "that doesn't make a damn bit of sense to plant such a small section. It wouldn't be worth the—"

"No, your brother is right." The old man had decided. "It'd be foolish planting it entirely. We've augered the holes in the front piece. We'll leave it at that."

"Dad, I think we should re-survey the entire place, anyway," Colton said.

"I believe so. The trees'll be delivered in a few days. Then we'll start planting."

The silence was tangible. Even though Jesse was separated from his dad by a floor, he could feel the electricity.

"Now, Dad, you're certain you don't need me today?" Colton asked. "I don't mind coming along."

"No, with Dan's help here and Felipe Diego and his crew, we'll finish up today."

With the scuffing of a chair, a dish tossed in the sink, and the banging of the screen door, Jesse knew his dad had left.

An hour later when the cousins came downstairs, they found Colton, whistling a tune, dishing out bacon, potatoes, fried eggs, and stacked hotcakes onto plates for them. Reserving a plate for himself, he pulled up a chair, and began his second breakfast of the day.

Jesse picked at his eggs and barely touched his hotcakes. Here his dad and Colton were only a few years apart. They had the same parents and were raised in the same place. And yet they couldn't have been more different than summer and winter.

"Dad," Leeney said, "I heard you talking about the Three Sisters' Place. Will we be able to help?"

"You bet. We'll need all the help we can muster. It takes many hands to get them in. In a few days, everything will be all ready to go."

Colton watched Jesse pick at his breakfast. "Well, I'm here to make good on my promise of last night." He pointed a stiff slice of bacon at Jesse, before popping it in his mouth. "Have you ridden Max yet?"

"Excuse me?" Jesse was sure he had heard wrong.

"Max! Have you ridden him yet?"

"No. Gramps told me to stay away from him."

"He did, did he?"

"He said he was a little wild, and he didn't trust him yet." Jesse had an uncomfortable feeling this could be leading to his surprise.

"I've worked him a little over the past few days," Colton said. "I don't see any reason for concern. He just needs to be ridden more. And I want you to start."

Jesse choked on his milk. "I don't ... I ... Uncle, I don't want to. Besides, Gramps said—"

His uncle waved another slice of bacon in Jesse's face, then tossed it in his mouth. "Enough of that!" He pounded the table, and the plates danced. "Go fetch the fishing equipment, and I'll meet you over at the stables after I've cleaned up this mess again," he leaned down to look his daughter eye to eye, "for the city risers."

Jesse led Nair out of the stall past Max. He knew Max sensed something was up. Securing Nair to the side bar near the stables, Jesse came over to the trough to wait. Though the trough didn't need more water, he turned the spigot anyway. In a few moments, Leeney followed with Dan's horse, Nilam. Joining Jesse at the trough to wait, she turned the water off.

"Well, well, well," she teased.

"Well, well, what?" he shot back, ignoring her gaze.

"Well. Here we are, two horses and three riders."

Jesse ignored her.

"So. Are you going to bring Max out?" She prodded him.

"Oh. Yeah. I forgot about him."

"You forgot about him?" She smirked.

"Sorta, kinda."

"You're afraid?"

"No! Okay, sorta kinda. But I don't know why I need to ride Max. He's not ready to be ridden. It's going against what Gramps said."

"I drove the Jeep yesterday when everyone was watching," Leeney reminded him. "Didn't want to, but I did. Not to mention that I drove through the gate in front of everyone. And I shouldn't have to remind you that we got stuck in the mud and had to have Uncle Dan pull us out. I think you can ride a stupid horse. Dad knows what he's doing."

He splashed some trough water at her and then shot her daggers before trudging back into the stable.

In his stall, the gelding snorted and gave Jesse the evil eye.

"Come on. Please." Jesse hesitated at the stall door and began pleading. "Now you'll be a good guy, won't you?" The gelding's eyes grew round, and his ears lay flat as he backed away.

"Do you need help in there?" Leeney called.

"No," he said, feeling as trapped as Max. "I've got it." It was either face this animal or his uncle. He couldn't quite decide which was harder, as the familiar butterflies began to stir.

Mindful of Max's uncertainty, Jesse scooted around Max's rear. Continuing to talk softly, he came around to the front and began to stroke his neck. Then ever so gently, he slid the lead rope over Max's head and moved the halter around into his neck. The horse seemed concerned, but to Jesse's surprise still allowed him to place the halter around his nose and fasten it. Maybe Max was going to let him think he would cooperate. Sort of allow Jesse to let his guard down. Keeping this in mind, Jesse maintained his caution.

In a few minutes, he led the prancing gelding out to the trough past Nair and Nilam. The other horses seemed unimpressed with this new addition. If they could have understood that Max was here as payment for a debt, they probably would have snubbed him further, and perhaps he wouldn't be so high-minded. But as it was, they pretended to ignore him. As Jesse led Max to the trough, the horse quieted and stood calmly for Leeney when she grabbed the lead rope.

Jesse returned to the barn for the fishing poles and baskets and then returned to wait for his uncle and to calm his butterflies.

Impatiently, Nair pawed the ground. Max glanced over at her and then resumed his now strangely quiet wait.

"He's a beauty," Leeney said.

Jesse could sense that Max was sizing him up again, evidently smelling his wavering courage. He tried to bluff by returning the gelding's stare. He told himself that once his uncle caught sight of Max all saddled up beside his shaking nephew, he'd realize his poor judgment and switch horses.

In a few moments, Colton marched across the yard followed by the dogs. Rubbing his hands together, he studied the cousins. "Are we ready?" he asked somewhat rhetorically.

"Would it really matter if I said I wasn't?" Jesse asked, certain that Colton would release him from his growing anxiety.

"Here now. None of that." He examined Jesse from head to toe. "Come with me."

Jesse's heart skipped a beat.

"Come on, you can help me with the saddles. And you, little girl, bring the blankets, bridles, and halters."

In the tack room, Jesse dusted off his father's saddle before carrying it out. On his way out with a second saddle, he was shocked to see his uncle throw his grandfather's black leather saddle onto the reluctant gelding.

"Uncle, that's Gramps' special saddle!" Obviously, his uncle wasn't paying attention. Only his grandfather used the saddle Moses had given him.

His uncle slapped Max's flank to assure him who was in charge. Max jumped a little and pulled Leeney dangerously close.

"Hold on, Leeney!" Colton told his daughter.

"You betcha!" He resumed his reasoning with Jesse. "Nothing

but the best. You've got to show him who's in command here. How do you expect him to let you be in charge if you saddle him with anything less? Besides, look at him. He knows how handsome he looks with the black saddle and how good it looks with his dark mane and tail. Look at Nair and Nilam. They're so damned envious; they won't even give him the time of day."

He pointed to the other mare. "Leeney?"

"Yes, Daddy."

"Saddle up Nair!" Then he added, "You, young man, lead Nilam over here and don't forget the fishing gear."

Except for the crunch of the gravel beneath their boots and the grunts from his uncle as he strained to make sure the saddle was secure and tight, silence prevailed. Jesse desperately tried to break it with a protest, but his mouth was so dry, his tongue stuck to the roof of his mouth.

Glancing around, Colton seemed to take inventory, and then pointed to the gate. "Jesse, lead him over there. We'll mount on the other side." He watched Jesse, then smiling big, said, "I don't think he has an appetite for gates, but I'm taking no chances."

Any other time Jesse would have laughed at the joke, but humor couldn't dissolve his tension. The gelding danced around nervously. Jesse pulled on the reins, but Max tugged away, his eyes large.

On the other side of the gate, they stopped to mount. Colton screwed his hat on tight.

"Okay, now here's the plan. We're gonna start out slow. We'll just walk a bit. We need to get him used to who you are and the surroundings."

Jesse liked the sound of it, but as he tried to settle into the saddle, the dogs following them began barking. Nervously, Max danced to the right and to the left, clearly upset they were behind him.

"Here now! Get away from there." Colton waved the dogs away. With the dogs at a safe distance and in his line of vision, Max seemed to like that better.

"Okay. Let's go!" his uncle commanded.

Jesse squeezed his legs against Max's sides, and he trotted forward a little too uncertainly.

"Let up now," his uncle cautioned.

Jesse relaxed a bit. "Come on, boy. It's okay now."

Colton was on Nair to his right, and Leeney rode Nilam a little ahead and to the left. Jesse felt a bit captive and imagined Max did as well, which soothed him a little. Captive or not, Jesse could feel the immense power of the horse beneath him.

Max began to hesitate, slowing to a walk.

"Hold the reins a little looser," his uncle barked out. "Now, give him a little more squeeze." The gelding picked up the trot again.

"Listen." Colton shook his head at Jesse. "If I were the goddamn horse and had eyes in the back of my head, from the look on your face I'd have no doubt as to who's in control. Let alone the smell of your fear. You can do better than that! Sit up! Don't let him sense any fear. A horse is smart as hell. You know all this! You've ridden long enough. They know what you're feeling. Be careful what you think. Focus on confidence. Then you will control the situation. Understand?"

Jesse heard nothing but unconnected words shooting from his uncle's mouth. He was too busy visualizing Max galloping through the trees while he dodged the low-hanging branches.

"Understand?" Colton repeated.

"What?"

"What I just said."

Jesse guessed the answer should be in the affirmative.

"Who's in control?" Colton commanded like the Marine drill sergeant he once was.

"I am?" his reluctant recruit responded.

"I don't think so. Let's hear it again."

"I'm in control."

"Well, then. Believe it!"

Though Jesse nodded, he couldn't begin to explain his fear

even to himself; he was now at the mercy of this powerful 1,100-pound beast. It wasn't more than a dozen yards before Max seized the opportunity that both the horse and rider realized was inevitable. The gelding bolted forward and sideways in one move. Jesse slipped to his side but managed to grab the saddle horn and pull himself upright, just as they entered the orchard, breaking into a full gallop.

"Well, I'll be a son of a ...." Colton exclaimed. "Pull back, Jesse! Pull back!"

It was all Jesse could do to stay on. Max continued to veer dangerously close to the trees. Coming up to a low-lying branch, Jesse ducked just in time. Before he knew it, they were headed for another branch. Realizing Max deliberately galloped to the trees to punish his rider's charade of courage made him even more frustrated and helpless. Though he could duck to avoid the branches whizzing past, still the leaves left his face stinging.

With every jarring bounce, his tail bone slammed against the saddle, sending bolts of pain up his spine. And fighting hard to keep his legs around the beast as they flew through the orchard, his leg muscles were beginning to cramp.

Ducking another branch, he lost his grip on the reins. Quickly, he wrapped himself around the gelding's hot, prickly neck. Trying to cut Max off, Colton raced up to his left side. But Max immediately veered right, throwing Jesse off balance. Again, Colton prodded his horse so he could make a second lunge for the reins, but he missed.

With the nagging thought of how much longer he could hold on, the answer came when they broke free of the orchard. But only for a split moment did Jesse believe this was deliverance; no sooner had he felt relief than directly ahead lay the irrigation canal. Realizing Max had no intention of stopping, Jesse knew that once they hit the other side of the canal, he would explode like a dirt clod when he hit the ground.

"Gramps!" he cried out.

It was all he could do to hold on until Max slid to an abrupt stop at the canal's edge. Jesse couldn't believe he had not jumped. "Thank you. Thank you. Thank you." he whispered to the air.

The gelding looked back at the approaching riders, and then to the canal. The next thing Jesse knew, Max slid down into the canal, and then down a way, he stopped in the middle, deciding this was as good as any, and plunged his head in to drink.

Now shivering from shock, Jesse could barely make his hands grab for the reins. "You stupid horse!" he shouted through his tears.

Colton pounded up to the edge followed by Leeney, both splashed with mud. To see them covered in polka dots of mud would have been comical at any other time. But Jesse could muster no humor. He shouldn't have been forced to ride Max, and yet he had wanted so badly to prove that he wasn't a coward.

"Are you all right?" Colton's voice betrayed his concern. "Hum. A few scrapes on your neck and face." He took stock. "Nothing serious."

"Uncle, I tried," Jesse pleaded, and losing his temper, he shouted, "I told you this was a mistake. Gramps said not to ride him!"

"Calm down now. No harm done, really." Sliding from his horse, Colton grabbed the reins and led Max out of the canal.

Examining the soaked saddle, Colton shook his head. "Dad's going to be madder than hell."

After they rubbed Max down and dried the saddle with the blankets they had brought for the pond, his uncle proclaimed, "Perhaps it's wiser if I rode him."

A half an hour later, after everything had been dried off and repacked, Jesse was relieved to be on Nair and back on their road, content to lag behind.

If only he could be more like Colton. He was in awe that his uncle was unafraid to ride Max after what the horse had put him through. He never seemed to be concerned about anything. Sitting high and straight in the saddle, Colton remained Jesse's hero.

He imagined living here full-time, riding in the fields with nothing but fresh air and the sounds of the birds. It just felt right and free. He knew that goldfish grow to the size of their habitat, and he felt he could easily do the same. He imagined expanding to the ranch's boundaries.

And yet, there were no boundaries here—just wide-open spaces with the Buttes on one side and the river and foothills on the other. And even then, the fences couldn't keep you in. The entire countryside was free. Mobs of mallards flying from the pond unfettered as the air that supported their flight. It all made so much sense. Everything seemed perfect.

Jesse picked up the cadence a little. and catching up, they allowed the horses to break into a gentle gallop.

"Dad. Did Gramps ever ride like this?" Leeney yelled over.

"You betcha," he shouted back. "He and Mother were fine riders."

"Did you ride with them?" Jesse shouted over.

"I recall riding up front with Dad. Must've been very young. I guess Dan rode with Mother."

Turning to the cousins, Colton said, "Something has just occurred to me. Get up!" His uncle shouted to the horse.

Breaking away, Colton led Max into a full gallop onto the path next to the corn field.

Prodding her horse to catch up, Leeney yelled over, "Come on, let's follow!"

It took little to convince Nair to move out.

Down the road, Colton veered right, directly into the next field of alfalfa, and from there, cut a diagonal path to the irrigation canal.

The horse and rider gained flat-out speed. Yards from the canal's edge, Colton leaned forward slightly, signaling the gelding his intentions. To force a horse to jump without knowing its capabilities or character was foolish and dangerous. Jesse knew his uncle was well-versed with horses, and yet he had insisted Jesse start out with Max. Was his uncle making another mistake now? Perhaps Jesse had confused his uncle's bravery for foolishness. He wondered if there was a difference. When Colton and Max effortlessly followed an invisible arc high over the canal, landing safely on the other side, he realized his uncle was neither foolish nor mistaken, just intuitive and brave.

Colton slowed Max down and brought him back to the road. Stroking his neck, he spoke into his ear. As Jesse and Leeney worked to catch up, Colton struck past them, this time towards the fence. And to the cousins' astonishment, the horse and rider sailed over the fence. Floating back down to the ground, Colton pulled Max down to trot, then gave him an appreciative pat on the neck as they circled around to the road.

Jesse and Leeney broke into a gallop to catch up. Maneuvering through the open gate where Colton and Max had sailed over, they reached the pair.

"You're a good old boy now." Colton patted him. "Aren't you? We knew it all along. That's just what you wanted."

"Oh, Daddy! You could've been hurt."

Colton smiled. The horse seemed to nod.

"Darling girl, I have been ridin' like that since well before your age. I know exactly what I'm doing. Besides, I thought he was familiar. This boy was trained for this. I don't think Dad knew that when he agreed to take Max. That's why he's so high-strung. Makes sense, now."

Is this man afraid of anything? Jesse asked himself.

27

Allowing the horses to cool down, they walked the rest of the way to the pond.

Cattails and wild berries around the perimeter limited access to the west side, where the land gradually dipped down to meet the stream. Thick grass in the shade provided a comfortable place for those who came to cast their lines or escape from work for a bit.

To the right of this clearing was a sturdy oak tree. Its roots drank deeply from the marshy ground, and its tangled branches hung over the water, creating shade.

Leeney threw the basket out near the edge along with a blanket. And while she laid out their lunch, Jesse finished brushing Nair down. Soon, Leeney walked upstream with her fishing pole and gear. Colton flopped down and surveyed the area.

A black crow squawked its gossip to another nearby, while a ground squirrel chattered away on a rock safely on the other side. All the country sounds seemed to converge at the pond.

"Some mornings before our work began, I would sneak out of the house to ride out here," Colton said. It was as though the place forced his memories to the surface.

"My horses were all much like Max. Your grandfather always saved the wild ones for me." Watching Leeney move upstream, Colton yelled over, "You take care, little girl."

"Yes, Dad! Of course." She waved back.

Colton turned to Jesse. "I would plant myself right there on that rock so I could watch the sun peek over the hills, sweeping away the darkness. And then I wouldn't leave until the sun dried the dew from the grass and I had my catch for breakfast." He paused a moment, then added, "Jesse. You're awfully quiet."

"Just thinking." Jesse studied the ground.

"About what?"

"Aren't you afraid of anything?"

"I don't know that I'm not afraid. I don't know that anyone is completely without fear."

"But you weren't afraid of Max."

"That's different. I'm not afraid of things I know about."

Jesse felt confused and shook his head.

"I mean you've got to meet your fears, head on," his uncle said. "You can't run away from them. Each time you run away, they grow bigger. But each time you face them down, you become bigger."

"But what are you afraid of? You said no man is completely without fear."

"I don't give it much thought, Jesse. But now that you've asked … I'm not afraid of anything that can be done to me. That I can do something about. But I guess I am afraid of losing those I love. That would devastate me. That I have no control over. I guess no one does, do they?"

Jesse shrugged, remaining silent.

The sound of a rattle, very near Leeney, ripped through the air. Colton sat up sharply. "Leeney?"

"Daddy? It's … it's … a rattler."

"Where?" Colton jumped up.

"It's right … in front of me … on a rock. I … I almost … stepped … on it."

"Keep still. Don't move."

Slowly, Colton made his way towards her.

"OK, honey, now just back away, slowly. It's okay."

"Daddy. I'm scared." Colton had reached her.

"Listen to me. It's okay. If you just back away slowly, you won't provoke him."

As Leeney stepped back, the snake uncoiled and extended its head in her direction, hissing.

"Daddy," she whispered.

"Shhhh. Just back away."

Slowly, she inched herself back while Colton came to take her place. Jesse was amazed when his uncle squatted down within striking distance. The rattler moved its head up and down, almost seeming to size up Colton's intentions.

"Now listen here, buddy. We mean you no harm. But this is our place, today. You can have it another day. But today it is ours. Understand?"

Colton continued to stare at the snake. The snake bobbed its his head. And then within a moment it shrank back and slid away until it disappeared into the grass.

Colton stood up and checked to make sure no others lingered. Then, he returned to Jesse and Leeney.

"It's okay now. He won't bother us anymore."

Jesse shook himself, incredulous. "How could you do that?"

"Hell. He didn't mean us any harm. He just wanted to sun himself. And we needed to come to an understanding. That's all."

"But he could've bit you."

"Ah. But you see he didn't. He could've, but he didn't. I've heard it said that creatures attack fear. Having no fear confuses them, and they leave.

"Jesse, this is what gave Max the advantage. You gave him his victory."

Jesse felt a shiver down his spine. "What about those things that you don't have control over?"

"You can and will be afraid until you find a way to control

them. Young man, we're Hunters." Colton scanned the area around them, as though searching for all the Hunters, though no longer alive, who would back him up if asked. "To be in this family is not to let anyone control you. Believe me, that's our destiny.

"Our family came from Scotland generations ago from the highlands. They were fierce warriors. And when they weren't fighting, they were adventurers," Colton continued. "Wanderers, fighters, seekers, workers. Hunters are fiercely independent, and that can get us into trouble."

"Why?"

"Because we'll never give up while there's anyone trying to take away our independence. It's the independence in us that keeps us seeking and maintaining our independence." Colton leaned toward him. "We don't like to be controlled. That's your destiny."

Here it was again—not liking to be controlled. That's the way he felt when he was at home. Jack was so controlling that it seemed he would breathe for his mother if allowed. His mother might have put up with it. But Jesse wouldn't, and with this realization he was beginning to understand what Colton was telling him.

He could see now that he shouldn't show Jack any fear; he wouldn't make it easy for Jack. And he would always fight Jack because he would never give up who he was, not for him, not for anyone. He was a Hunter, as his uncle was explaining.

When the sun began to lengthen the shadows and they had their fill of fishing, they packed their gear to leave.

"Well, my boy," his uncle asked, "with all that you've learned today, do you feel ready to try Max one more time?"

With all he had learned this afternoon, he still didn't feel ready.

"Don't worry, he knows who's in control and won't try anything funny," Colton said. "Besides, now he knows me. He wouldn't dare."

The gelding looked over at Jesse, as though he understood English.

Jesse looked to Leeney for support and wondered if he was the only one that the butterflies pestered. Maybe his uncle was right, the gelding would be calmer now. Maybe he could show Colton he could overcome his fear. After all, Colton had dispatched a poisonous snake just by not being afraid.

"I guess I'll try if you think so. But just a slow walk." He mounted Max.

Together, all three began their walk along the dirt path.

"Daddy, the corn looks just about ready to harvest."

"Yep. Just about. Then we'll be out here to help—"

It sounded like a rifle or a car backfiring. Whatever it was, it flushed a flock of blackbirds from the cornstalks near Jesse and Max. Spooked, Max made a beeline towards a service road at the edge of the field. Jesse had no time to even adjust and could barely hold on.

"Dammit. What now?" Colton shook his head.

Disappearing into the rows of stalks, Jesse had no idea where they were going. He tried to pull back on the reins, willing the horse to stop. Through clenched teeth, he sucked in air. The saddle began to slip a bit, and he instinctively tightened his legs around Max's girth making him fly faster between the rows.

Suddenly, somewhere in the middle of the field, a man yelled out, "Whoa there! I say whoa!"

Jesse couldn't see or tell who it was; he still had his eyes closed. Whoever it was, he was glad that someone was there who would stop Max.

The gelding emerged into a large, barren circle, where it abruptly dodged the man who lunged for the reins. A few yards behind the man lay another irrigation canal. Before Jesse could process all that had happened, was happening, and would happen, he found himself leaning down as Colton had done, inadvertently conceding to Max an agreement to jump.

With this, Max headed full speed towards the canal, where he stretched out to sail over the water, landing them both unharmed on the other side.

Working to get his breathing under control, Jesse almost lost it again when he saw his dad.

And before he could form the words to ask why his dad was there, Dan had jumped over the narrow canal and grabbed the reins, yelling, "Who in the hell gave you permission to ride this horse?"

"Dad. I ... didn't fall ... off!" Jesse was surprised and exhilarated. "Dad, I jumped ... the horse ... over the ... canal and I stayed on." He could barely force the words out as he fought to catch his breath.

"Where's your uncle?" Dan demanded, searching all directions.

"I was so afraid at first, Dad, but I stayed on. Uncle said I could do it, and I did."

In a moment, two riders came ripping through the cornstalks.

"Here you are!" Colton said as they came into the clearing. Catching his breath, he seemed unaware of Dan holding Max's reins. "The goddamned gelding has a mind of his ... How did you get to the other side of the canal? Don't tell me you jumped?"

As though Dan had suddenly morphed from a cornstalk, Colton asked, "Dan? What the hell are you doing over here? I thought you were with Dad."

Dan looked as though he would explode. "Never mind why I'm here," he spat back. "You ... you should know better!"

"Know better? What's to know? I'm teaching Jesse here how to master this horse."

"To ride?" Dan hissed.

"Yes. Something you could be doing."

Dan was speechless.

"So, Dan. What in the hell are you doing out here?" Colton asked. "Are you following us?"

"Colton. I don't owe you a damn thing!" Without another word, he turned on his heel, climbed into his pickup, and drove down the road in a cloud of dust.

. . .

That evening at supper, Colton cleared his throat. He gave Leeney and Jesse a wink.

"Well, Dad, you can expect to be short some corn around the alkali spot."

The old man continued to soak up the gravy with his bread. "Oh? And why is that?"

"Well, Jesse had quite an adventure this afternoon with Max."

"Max?" Gramps stared hard at Jesse. "You were riding Max? That's how you got your face scraped up?" He frowned, pausing to study the three.

"No one was to ride him. I thought that was—"

"Dad, I insisted." Colton tried to make light of the incident. "It all came out all right. Jesse here mastered Max with a little help from Leeney and me. Max is a jumper, Dad. I think he won't give you any more cause for concern."

"Maybe so. But I'm still not happy my wish went unheeded."

Preparing to leave later that evening, Colton threw the fish they had caught in the back of his pickup. And Leeney tossed in a muddy ball of clothes.

"So long, partner," Colton told Jesse. "We had a great time today. You did a wonderful job with Max. I think you showed him how it works. But remember, it's about fear. A horse smells fear, as do people. And if you're not careful, they'll take advantage of it."

Colton started the pickup and turned it into the road where it disappeared into the evening.

Jesse remained on the porch after Gramps went indoors. He scanned the sky that was turning from the reds into the deep blues of twilight. It occurred to him: If he could look up to the stars, could Grace and Will look down on him?

Then he felt an impulse to see for himself which stars his grandfather had referred to in his journal. In the middle of the clear sky, all the stars sparkled; it was difficult to pinpoint where the Big Dipper was. But allowing his eyes to adjust and carefully scan the northern sky, he caught the dipper's shape. He traced the outline, stopping at each star to determine which one was his grandfather's.

After locating Grace's bright star, he found the next one, the star that he had read was his grandfather's. It was bright as well. And for reasons he couldn't understand, he began to tear up.

"Hey, my lad." His grandfather startled him. "What's the matter? Seems to me that you had quite a day."

Jesse quickly brushed the tears from his face. "I wish I were more like Uncle Colton. He's not afraid of anything. Is that why Dad doesn't like me?" The words tumbled over one another.

The old man searched the sky, as if waiting for an answer, then took a seat beside Jesse.

"You do have the courage. It comes from inside. You're discovering every day that you've always had it. Didn't you just tell us at the dinner table that you stayed on Max the second time and how proud you were to do it? As far as your father ... well ... you've done no wrong. Like I said before, he was a lot like you when he was your age," he whispered as he stood up, "before ..."

"Before what, Gramps?"

His grandfather turned to go. "What?" As he took a deep breath, his eyes rested on one star, or so it appeared to Jesse.

"You said, 'before.' What did you—"

"Oh. I didn't realize I said anything."

"Gramps?"

"I've got to finish the dishes."

. . .

Later that night, lying in bed, Jesse felt more alone than ever before. Something was happening around him, and he wasn't sure what it was. But he felt left out and couldn't figure out a way to even ask Gramps about it. It was as though a question lingered in the air, and rather than answering it, everyone was denying the question existed.

Still sore and tired from the day's ride, he fell into a light doze.

He tossed and turned and wished he could fall asleep. The fan in the corner was powerless to cool the air and could only move the stillness from one corner to the other. Dripping in sweat, in a fitful drowsiness, he pictured himself alone in the clearing in the corn field. At least, he felt he was alone. But he could hear voices coming from the field, though he couldn't see anyone.

Then, with the painful loneliness too much to bear, something made him look above, where the deep blue dome was illuminated with thousands upon thousands of bright stars.

And this blue darkness with pinpoints of light was all there was. Nothing else existed. And he felt the stars were sparkling just for him. Then he wondered if he had a star of his own, and if he did, where it might be.

28

Just after sunrise, Lil pulled her car into the yard, setting off Brownie and Tex, who barked and ran circles around it, frightening the chickens. Even the horses poked their heads over the stall doors seemingly to see if any of this would ultimately involve them.

Four car doors opened and slammed shut.

"I want to see Gramps first," Steph said.

"I haven't seen him all summer," Shay yelled, pushing her out of the way.

"Gramps, Gramps. We're here," Leeney shouted, elbowing past them.

"Girls, please quiet down," their mother commanded. "You're much too wild this morning. Goodness, you even have the dogs upset. Now, now, Brownie, Tex, shhhh ... it's okay."

Racing up the porch steps, Steph burst into the kitchen. "Gramps! How are you? It's been too—"

"Gramps!" Shay caught up. "I heard about Bella's foal. I'm sorry."

At the sight of his granddaughters, his face lit up. Pulling a chair from the table, he was instantly surrounded.

"I heard you have a new horse," Steph said. "Can we ride it?"

"Well, as a matter of—"

"His name is Max, right?" Shay butted in. "But Dad says we can't jump him."

He gazed from one to another and then back again to each, listening to their chatter, as his face showed many expressions.

Lil forced her way past the dogs into the kitchen. "I'm sorry, Dad. They're wild this morning." She plunked down in a chair.

"Don't worry about me. I've managed worse. I can handle three beautiful girls."

Lil got up and poured herself a cup of coffee. "I'm standing over here, where it's safe and a little quieter."

Upstairs, still lying in bed, Jesse tried to remember if he had known they would be here today. He thought Shay, Steph, and his aunt weren't due back from their travels for at least another few days.

By the time he made his way down the back stairs, the initial outburst had dipped a few decibels. The girls sat around the table chattering and eating breakfast. His grandfather and Lil stood near the sink, deep in conversation.

Shay caught Jesse hesitating at the back stairs. "Hey, twin. How've you been? Surprised to see us?"

"More like surprised to hear us!" Steph commented.

"Why are you guys here? I didn't think you'd be back so soon."

Lil broke away from Gramps to give Jesse a hug. "How about it? Ready to spend the day with these women?"

Though the early morning quiet was almost a religious experience to him, and their wildness had done away with that, Jesse was still pleased they were here. He had forgotten how much he missed them.

Leeney motioned to him. "Sit next to me."

He scooted in next to her and picked up a piece of toast. Lil refilled her coffee, shot him a smile, and went back to the corner of the room to resume her conversation with his grandfather.

"We just got back from St. Louis," Shay said. "And Gramps wanted to surprise you by inviting us out."

"Why?" Jesse was puzzled.

"When Gramps found out we had come home earlier, he invited us out to help plant the trees on the Three Sisters' Place," Steph said.

"Today? But my dad isn't here. And what about Uncle Colton?"

"Daddy and Uncle Dan are on our place working on some machinery. But Gramps said we could do it ourselves," Shay added.

"With Mother's help!" Leeney said.

Lil went to the sink to begin washing dishes while their grandfather prepared to head out.

"When you're finished with breakfast," he said at the door, "meet me in the yard for assignments. Don't take too long. The day's a-wasting!"

The girls bolted for the door, leaving Jesse munching on his toast.

Gramps called over his shoulder, "You'd better catch up, my lad."

Then to Lil, he winked. "You'd better hurry, too. All the good jobs will be taken."

She picked up the dish towel. "It doesn't matter what I do now. It's just good to be home."

In the yard, the small crew of field hands had been waiting. Jesse nodded to Felipe Deigo, who nodded back.

Taking his place as captain of this small battalion, Gramps pulled a piece of paper from his pocket and studied it, looking up occasionally to check his crew. His lips moved silently as he reviewed his list.

"Tsk, tsk, hmm, that won't do." He took out a stubby pencil from his front pocket and crossed out something.

As though inspecting his troops for vital work, as he had done since he first began farming, he cleared his throat. "All right, I've made a few changes, and I think I've covered everything.

"Shay, my dear," he pointed his pencil in her direction, "you have no problem with reverse gear around fences, do you?"

A burst of laughter as Shay and Steph pointed at the twins. "We heard about that one all the way in St. Louis!" Shay elbowed Steph.

"If not, you are to drive the watering truck," Gramps said.

"And what's my assignment in all this?" Lil joined them. "And what's so funny? The twins look sheepish."

"Something about reverse gears," Shay said.

"Ah." Her mother chuckled.

"If you will, you can drive the truck loaded with the fertilizer. Steph, you'll throw the fertilizer out to the trees once they're planted. Okay?"

He turned from his list to Jesse and Leeney. "You'll bring up the rear. Once the trees are planted, you water them."

Having their assignments, they jumped in the vehicles to leave, while Gramps joined Felipe and his crew, explaining their tasks.

In front of the old house at the three sisters' place, the group formed a half-circle around Gramps, waiting for final instructions.

"All right now. We have a lot of work to do today. We can have fun, but we must work together to get most of it done. And it's important that we work in an orderly fashion. No one is to get ahead of anyone else."

Steph interrupted. "What about the holes for the trees? Are we going to do that?"

"No. But thanks for the concern."

The orchard had been rolled smooth to facilitate the planting. A few days earlier, following Dan's survey where stakes marked the spots, Felipe and his crew had finished augering holes.

The process opened with the first field hand in the lead, assigned to drive the flatbed truck stacked with new trees. Felipe, walking beside it, pulled a tree off the truck and carefully placed it in a hole. His partner followed, unwrapping the burlap around the root ball, and gently working to break the roots apart. Marching behind, the next worker used his shovel to fill in the hole around the young tree.

Second to the last in this work parade, Lil drove the Ford as

Steph sprinkled a shovelful of fertilizer around the base of the tree. Picking up the rear, Shay drove the watering truck while Leeney, balanced on the running board, controlled the water spigot. Jesse walked alongside pointing the hose at the base of each tree.

As they began, Gramps rode Nair alongside, making sure all proceeded according to plan. Once he was convinced that everyone was doing correctly what needed to be done, he rode ahead.

Riding up to a rise, close to where the road disappeared into the bend, Sam reined in Nair and watched with peace and contentment that his land was being planted by his family. It was always a great joy to watch the orderly, harmonious activity of those that worked the land. And to see his family following these patterns gave him immense satisfaction.

He believed, though he would never tell anyone, that others benefiting from his labors ensured him a kind of immortality. And therefore, as he grew old, he had no great fear of death, because he believed he would continue to live on to his family, in evidence of what he would leave behind.

Jesse looked up from his job to see his grandfather riding toward him. Approaching the truck, Gramps smiled at him. For just a fraction of a moment, Jesse saw reflected in his sparkling blue eyes the clouds and the land.

Examining the newly planted orchard, his grandfather seemed to take everything in, even to encompass Jesse, as well. Without a word passing between them, eloquently and profoundly, he communicated distinctly: *I may plant, but you'll have to harvest because I won't be here to see it.*

When both hands of his pocket watch pointed north, Gramps blew a whistle he had fished from his pocket.

Shay threw the truck into neutral. Lil stepped on the brakes. Felipe Diego and his work crew stood up and stretched their arms, legs, and stiff backs.

"We'll meet over at the yard. Stanza has lunch all set out," Gramps announced.

At the yard, they found that Stanza and Hank had spread canvas cloths under the shade of a tree, where once again, the house's garden waited to play host to a luncheon.

And, precisely an hour later, prodded by the old man, hats in hand, the workers reluctantly returned to the emerging orchard.

"Oh, Gramps," Shay pleaded, "can't we finish tomorrow?"

"No. What is set out to do today must be done today."

"Gramps," Steph whined. "It's too hot."

"Have the twins spray you with water. That should do the trick."

"I'm too full and too tired," Leeney complained.

"You'll work it off in no time at all," their grandfather explained.

"Gramps, you have an answer for everyone," Jesse interjected.

"Or so it seems." Gramps smiled.

Only little more than half the area remained to be planted, and it looked as though they would finish by the end of day. The space was filling in with saplings and beginning to look like a miniature orchard. By mid-afternoon, the air turned unbearably hot and very dry.

From her perch on the side of the truck, Leeney groaned, "Lord, I'm so hot. I can't take this anymore."

Jesse, tired of her complaining, turned the hose on her, nearly washing her off the running board.

She screamed in surprise and glared at him. Then, looking at her dripping self, she said, "Do it again!"

Before long, the whole operation had come to a halt, and one by one everyone received a blast of water from Jesse's hose.

Towards the end of the day, with the sun just above the hills, a slight cooling breeze moved their way. Gramps decided enough had been done. He blew his whistle again, this time signaling that the day could end.

Lil yelled over, "But we're not done yet."

"It's all right," the old man said. "Felipe and his crew can finish up tomorrow.

"Stanza and Hank left dinner in the clearing for us." He pointed towards the north. "In the middle of our new orchard."

Stanza had set out steaks to grill, with a huge pot of homemade baked beans that she had prepared the night before. Hank brought fresh cucumbers, tomatoes, and onions he had picked from the kitchen garden that morning. Stanza had tossed them in a wooden bowl for a salad. And she made sure freshly baked bread over-filled a basket.

As Gramps put the steaks on the grill, Colton's pickup turned into the road. Parked next to the house, he hiked out to the campfire.

"Hey, Dad." Leeney said. "I thought you were busy with Uncle Dan."

"We finished up and I knew you all were down here. The saplings look great." He surveyed the once barren field.

Jesse looked behind his uncle, and then verbalized the question that had been on his mind all day. "Where's my dad?"

"Oh, son. Well, uh ... he said he was feeling tired, so I left him there to rest." Colton moved closer to the grill. Rubbing his hands together, he took a sniff and smiled.

As dark descended, Lil and the girls went back to the ranch to clean up. Colton and Gramps spread out canvases and sleeping bags around the campfire. Exhausted from the work of a hard day, but strangely exhilarated, Jesse joined them, as they searched the August sky for shooting stars.

When the girls returned, they quickly claimed their space by throwing out their sleeping bags.

"You all did a tremendous job today." Gramps spoke softly. "You should be very proud of yourselves." Searching their tired faces, he asked, "Do you know why you can be so proud?"

"Because we worked so hard?" Jesse asked.

"It's more than that. Because we created a work of art today."

"Planting trees is a work of art?" Shay asked.

"It is. I looked up the definition this morning. Let me see if I have it right … 'human effort to imitate the work of nature.' Well, if planting trees isn't supplementing the work of nature, then I don't know what art is."

Lil chuckled. "What do you know? I never thought I was artistic."

"But it's even more than that, because we all learned something today."

Steph took the bait. "What did I learn? All I did was shovel horse sh… manure around a tree."

"Yes. I know it may seem small. But you see the process is just as important as the result."

Shay sat up in surprise. "I don't understand. Isn't planting the trees the most important? Soon you'll have an orchard that'll yield a money crop."

"No, my dear. How you get there is just as important."

"That doesn't make sense," Shay said.

"Why doesn't it make sense, Shay?" Gramps questioned.

"Well, take for instance a painting. It's not important?"

"No. I didn't say that. I would say how it got to be painted is as important as the picture."

"Why? What does it matter if in the end you have something to show for your work?" Shay argued.

"Okay. Fair enough. Answer this. Is there anything wrong with having a million dollars in your pocket?"

"Nope! Just think of what I could buy."

"What if you cheated someone to get it?"

"Oh." Shay hugged her knees.

"See, it is important how you got the money." Gramps explained, "Though the artist presents his idea through his art, how he accomplishes the process is just as much a part of the art and is shown through his creation. But most forget about that element. They only look for the result.

"Painting or art is merely an imitation of the work of nature. At least that's what the dictionary says. True art is already created by the universe. You can't create the glorious sunset. You can only capture your view of it. Man just imitates. We can only translate what's there—what exists. How we do this is almost more important than the result because the process is our unique contribution. We create the process."

"You mean it's important to consider what the artist was thinking?" Lil wondered out loud.

Gramps nodded. "Also, what was his day like? What life problems was he working to resolve while completing his art? This will inevitably show in his art.

"So, you've all created a future orchard," he added. "Many will look upon it for years to come, but you have already left an invisible record of how it happened. Though most won't see our activity today when they see the trees and enjoy the harvest, nonetheless something important came before. Be proud that you have given to the earth your labor. You'll find that what you did today will return to you many times over, and—"

"I think," Jesse spoke up, "I understand a little, Gramps, but—"

"Wow!" Shay pointed directly overhead. "Up there! Did you see it?"

"What? What?" Steph sprang to her feet.

"I saw it! A shooting star!" Leeney was awed. "It was huge. Did you see it? Gramps, it was like a small tear in the darkness letting the light behind shine through."

"Ah," the old man murmured something to himself.

They all became silent as they searched the sky for another shooting star.

Gramps pointed to the north sky. "Colton, point out some of the constellations for the kids."

"Hell. Let's see. It's been so many years. Okay. Hmm ... Let's see ... Toward the north, there near the horizon. You must look low, just above the tops of the cottonwoods, and a little to the right is the Big Dipper. Or Ursa Major. Those are the stars that Dad gave to us as boys. Remember, Dad?"

"I certainly do. The brightest one is your mother's." He couldn't resist going on, "Now follow the pan of the Big Dipper further up and a little to the right. That is Orion, the hunter. We've always liked that one for obvious reasons."

"What's the story of Orion, Dad?" Steph asked.

Colton scratched his head. "Dad, isn't it in Greek mythology, that—"

"Orion was a great hunter." The old man took over. "And Artemis, the moon goddess, fell in love with him and forgot her duties, leaving the night sky dark. Her twin brother, Apollo, watched Orion swimming far out to sea. With the bow and arrow, Apollo challenged his sister to hit what looked like a mere dot. Artemis shot the arrow that killed Orion. When his body washed up on shore, she grieved so much she placed his body in the sky, together with his hunting dogs."

Gramps stared at the constellation and added wistfully, "What greater memorial than to live with the stars in the summer sky."

"What's below him?" Lil asked.

"It's a rabbit called Lepus, the hare," Colton answered. "And over there is Perseus, the hero." He paused, as though trying to remember.

"Perseus was to kill the gorgon, Medusa, one of three sisters that were so ugly that one glance of them would turn the person to stone," Gramps said. "When he cut off her head, the winged horse Pegasus sprang from her blood."

"I've forgotten so much of what you used to tell us about the stars, Dad. It's been so many years." Colton leaned back on his arms and stared straight above.

Jesse stretched out with his hands locked behind his head, trying to imagine where the sky ended. "It's so beautiful out here. I'm glad this place belongs to you, Gramps, and not the three sisters. Did they leave it to you."

He shook his head and chuckled. "No. No. They certainly

didn't leave it to me or anyone for that matter. They would be surprised to know how it all turned out. What would they think to see us all out here surrounded by a new orchard?"

"Dad, tell the kids how you came to have this place," Colton urged.

"Oh, goodness," the old man said. "That is a story. Are you sure you want to hear it? Perhaps, though, it is important to tell."

The dark form of the three sisters' farmhouse sat as a silent witness.

"They were the Lungreen girls," he began. "The eldest was Amanda, the next Hattie, and the youngest was Polly. They were cousins of Grace and about her age. I don't think they were as ugly as the gorgon that Perseus had to kill, though.

"At one time, Polly lived in San Francisco where she met a man and became engaged. But he broke it off. And, oh, my goodness, Hattie and Amanda were so loyal and fierce. They were a hard duo. They vowed no man was worth the grief that Polly was enduring. So they promised never to marry, but live on the land their father had left them.

"Phil, the barber, told me they wasted their time making that pact among themselves. He said there wasn't enough prime river land or cash in the bank that could entice a self-respecting man to marry into that family."

That brought a chuckle from Colton.

"Over the years they persuaded others to help them, promising that they'd be remembered in their wills." The old man shook his head sadly. "Poor Will was one of those who took them at their word.

"When Polly, the last sister, died, the town was not surprised to learn they left the ranch to no one. It was sold at auction. Everyone tried to discover who would bid on it. It had been a difficult year for us, and money was scarce. But what we most feared happened."

"What was that?" Jesse asked.

"An investor from outside came to bid on the land. Folks here on the Eastside all believe the responsibilities of ownership are in working the land ourselves. The river gives the water, and the sun gives the energy, but nothing comes of it until our sweat and labor infuse the soil with life. We don't want to compete with the farming cooperatives, with a board of owners and a manager on the payroll.

"Anyway, as it turned out, the man and I were the only ones bidding on the property. Every bid I made, he bid higher. We all knew his resources were deep, and I thought I was going to lose. When I had to give up bidding, everyone stared at him. Just before the gavel came down for the third time, do you know what he did?"

The cousins were hanging on to his every word. "What, Gramps? What happened?"

"He glanced around, smiled at me, and before walking out said he didn't belong here. I couldn't believe it myself."

"Wow." Leeney's eyes were big in the firelight.

"That's a wonderful story, Gramps." Shay got up and hugged her grandfather.

"I'm glad you think so. The sisters wouldn't allow the fields to lie fallow for a season. This depleted the soil. And now my desire is to bring peace to this land by planting trees."

"And now," Lil told them, "I think it's time to get some sleep."

After listening to the story and understanding their place in its record, the four cousins settled down into the sleeping bags around the dying campfire, pleased with their contribution. One by one, they counted the shooting stars in the immense August sky, as they fell asleep, surrounded by their grandfather's gift to the land.

29

W hen their grandfather declared that their hard work planting the orchard should be rewarded, the cousins decided
to spend the next afternoon at the pond.

Jesse lay on a granite outcrop at the edge of the stream,
loosely holding the fishing pole, fighting the drowsiness brought
on by little sleep under the stars the night before and the gentle,
warm breeze here. Nearby, sitting against the tree, Steph seemed
oblivious to the heat. She was deep in an old mystery she had
found in their grandfather's library. And Leeney stretched out
on the grass near the pond's edge, ignoring the fishing pole on
the ground next to her. Her fingertips strummed the water's
surface.

Shay anxiously wrote in the journal she had begun on their
St. Louis trip. Lil had become interested in researching the
family history and had allowed Shay in on her findings. Now,
Shay jotted down bits of information she recalled her mother
telling her, trying to make sense of all the pieces.

She looked up from her writing. "Hey, Jesse!"

His chin slipped from his hand as he awoke with a jolt. Checking his fishing pole, he saw nothing nibbling.

"Leeney said you saw a lot of Gramps' things in some barn?"

Jesse's heart sank. Why had Leeney shared what they had found? That was their secret. "Naw. Not really. There's nothing …" He tried to convince her.

"Yeah." Leeney spoke up. "We did see old clothes and other stuff. We even read some journals—"

"Leeney!" Jesse shouted.

Her eyes shot wide open. "It's just a barn with a bunch of old stuff that Gramps doesn't even seem to care about."

Shay looked from her sister to Jesse. "Really? Journals? What kind of journals?"

"Just stuff that Gramps wrote about the family. Jesse said Gramps has been telling him the story of the family—"

"Leeney. I'm telling you!"

The corners of Shay's mouth rose a little. "You must've read some good stuff to get such a rise out of Jess."

Jesse shot her a look that spoke his warning.

"Nothing. Really," Leeney said, trying to back-pedal. "Shay, it's not worth it. Listen, when we were there, we felt awful reading the journals and decided that it was not really ours to read." Shay didn't look as though she was going to relent. "Besides, it's hot, dirty, and smelly out there."

"Let me be the judge of that." Shay got up, gathered her things together. "Come on. Let's go see them."

Jesse stood up. "No. Wait a minute. We can't."

"And why not?" Shay said.

"Because it's not right. That's why. All that stuff belongs to Gramps. You can't go read his journals. That's like opening someone's mail. It's illegal!"

Steph, closing her book, listened intently to the argument.

Shay shook her head and jabbed her finger at his chest. "Listen. I've got as much right to read them as you do. That's not—"

"No! We can't go." He pushed her hand away.

She stared at him for a moment. "Okay. You're right. We shouldn't be snooping in Gramps' journals. But this is important. Mother's been pursuing something about the family. There might be a clue in the journals. It would really help Mother. Besides, if you go along, I'll let you in on a secret."

He shook his head. He couldn't imagine his grandfather approving of the four of them rooting through his writings. Especially where he wrote his most personal feelings at the time he grieved for his wife. "I don't care! Not worth it!"

"Oh yes, it is!"

"Call her bluff." Leeney sidled up to Jesse.

He studied the look on Shay's face. "Okay. What secret?"

"Well, something that's really big. You'll be very surprised. In fact, if we all go there, I'll let everyone in on it. But you mustn't tell Mother that I've told you."

Leeney began to look a little interested. She nodded to her older sister. "Count me in."

Jesse gave her a dirty look. "Traitor!"

"Come on, Jess," Leeney said. "What's the harm?"

Though she could not reel in Jesse just yet, Shay had landed Steph and Leeney. Patiently she tugged on his line a little bit more. "Besides, if you don't take us there, Leeney knows where it is. She'll take us. Won't you?"

"That's not fair, Shay," Steph spoke up. "It should be all or none. If Jesse doesn't agree, then we shouldn't go."

All eyes were on him.

"I'm not going to help you." He tried again.

"Have it your way! Come on, girls, let's go solve a mystery."

Steph and Leeney obediently followed their sister. Watching them march down the road, heading towards the place he believed was so holy, he felt helpless to stop them. The barn to him was no different than the museums he visited during school. It was stuff that connected one age to another, and that people wanted to look at, and where the guards told you not touch to anything because you might spoil it. The barn was private. Only those who could feel the past should be allowed the privilege of being there—he had tried to make her understand.

Jesse grew to believe that once things were touched by those who couldn't appreciate them, the objects mysteriously lost their link to the past. To disturb these things destroyed the only real link. There was only one thing he could do now. He had to protect it. He ran to catch up to them.

Approaching the grain barn, Jesse sensed how silent and vulnerable it stood. Suddenly, he shivered, intuiting that the barn was the place where all the mysteries would be revealed, whether he wished it or not.

Dashing ahead of them, he beat the girls to the door. "You know, I'm only doing this because I want to make sure you don't mess anything up."

Hesitating, he waited for the birds inside to quiet down, so he could complete his ritual of asking for permission.

Quick on his heels, Shay shoved him aside and tugged on the door. "What're you waiting for?"

"Shay. Stop! You must ask permission," he insisted.

She looked around. "Get out of my way."

Once inside, she slowly walked around taking inventory of the boxes and things piled on the floor. As though consulting a mental treasure map, she seemed to be following certain steps.

"What *are* you looking for?" Leeney asked.

"She's not looking for anything," Jesse said. "It's only a game. She doesn't know anything."

"Come on, Shay," Steph said, waving the cobwebs away from her face. "It's too hot in here. Let's go back to the pond."

"All right. All right, I'll tell you. But you can't tell anyone about this. If you do, you're dead!"

She pointed at Jesse. "Are you ready for this?"

"Ready for nothing, you mean."

"Are you?"

"Yes. For God's sake, cut the dramatics," he said. "Just tell us."

"We have an aunt."

The four stared at each other.

"Yeah. Right. Told you there was nothing." Jesse glared. "My mother and Aunt Lil didn't have any brothers or sisters, and we all know that Dad and Uncle Colton don't have a sister. Go figure."

He felt a degree of relief that this was just a game she was playing. Still, the strange feeling of the barn's vulnerability and its holding some sort of mystery persisted in haunting him.

"I'm telling you; Dad and Uncle Dan had a sister."

"Really? Where does she live? In another dimension? Oh, I get it. This is the Twilight Zone, right?" he asked Steph.

"It's true. Really!" Shay insisted. "Listen, I was shocked when Mother first shared it. But I was sworn to secrecy and promised not to say. That's why Mother went to St. Louis. We were trying to find her."

"Then why are you telling us?"

"Because I need your help so Mother can get more information."

"Okay. If she's not in another dimension, where is she, if she exists? What's her name?"

"We didn't find her."

"Aha!" He threw up his arms and turned towards the door, trying to will them into following him out.

"But we know her name."

"I still don't believe you." Jesse spoke firmly, even though the sneaking feeling that there might be something to this lingered in his mind. There was the night he overheard Colton and his grandfather speak about Lil's find and something about a woman being dead. And there was the nagging question about something the three sisters had done that affected his dad.

Shay opened a box, searching through loose papers, while Steph moved uncomfortably about, shoving some things around.

Leeney looked at Jesse and nodded toward the trunk that contained their grandfather's journals. She mouthed the words, "Jesse, over there."

Creeping over, he closed it up.

Shay shot up like a cat after a mouse. "Hey, what're you doing?"

Spotting a packet of letters sitting on top of a box nearby, Shay and Jesse dashed for them. Getting to them first, Jesse grabbed the packet. He dodged Shay's flailing arms as she tried to knock them from his grasp. He held them high above her head. She punched him in the stomach, and when he doubled over, she caught them in midair.

"Shay. That hurts." He sucked in shallow gulps of air.

While she worked to loosen the knot in the ribbon, Jesse knocked the bundle from her hand. Letters spilled over the floor like a deck of cards. Quickly he fell on his hands and knees, trying to scoop them up, but Shay was able to grab two before he lunged towards her.

"Touch me and I'll kick you where it really hurts," she warned him as she scanned the contents.

Jesse backed up a safe distance. "Give 'em back, Shay. Give 'em back now!" he shouted.

She danced around waving the letter. "This is it! What luck. This was written by Elizabeth."

By this time, Jesse felt defeated and was surprised to find himself curious as to what she had found.

"Here, read this one." Shay tossed one to Steph.

Leeney leaned over Steph's shoulder as she began to read:

> *You have filled my head with nothing but lies. I refuse to live with someone who would have lied to me these many years. I am going to where the people love me enough to tell the truth.*

They stood motionless as though someone had knocked the air out of all of them. To discover something they weren't sure really existed was a shock in itself. But to read the angry words this person wrote made them shiver.

"It's true. Now d'ya believe me?" Shay whispered.

"That doesn't mean anything. That letter could be from anyone called Elizabeth," Steph said. "If Dad had a sister, why weren't we told?"

Something was familiar about the name, Jesse thought. He had heard it before. But where? It had to be from his grandfather. Then it hit him—she was Kate's daughter. Oh my God! They thought Elizabeth was Grace's daughter. That was the big mystery? The muscles in his shoulders relaxed. But he felt sorry that his aunt had misunderstood and had traveled all the way back to St. Louis to track down someone who they thought was …

"Listen, there's a mistake," he said calmly. "I can explain."

"You know something about this?" Shay squinted at him. "You told me you knew nothing."

"Well, sorta. But you've got it all wrong. Elizabeth was Kate's daughter, not Grace's. Gramps has been telling me the story. He told me that when Grace came to visit, she would bring her niece Elizabeth with her." He waited for them to agree and leave the barn in disappointment.

In the ensuing few moments of silence, Shay seemed to weigh all that her mother had told her. "No. You've misunderstood. She was Grace's daughter. Gramps told Mom."

"I don't believe you." Jesse was smug and confident. "You have no proof."

"Okay. Calm down. I'll tell you the story." She looked around as though checking for someone who might have secretly sneaked in. "Grace had a daughter who ran away many years ago and has never spoken to the family since. One of the reasons we made a trip to St. Louis was to see if we could find her or to see if she's still alive."

"Not true," Jesse sang out.

"Still. Mother told me. What do you think Mother and Gramps have been discussing since we came back?"

"But this makes no sense. He's been telling me the story of the ranch." Jesse's voice grew more emotional. "He never said any-thing about a daughter."

"Hey." She checked the door. "Keep your voice down. Don't

get mad at me. Besides, she wasn't Gramp's daughter. She was Grace's."

Jesse couldn't believe his ears. This was blasphemous to his grandfather's story. He wouldn't listen to this. "What a lie. Shay!"

Leeney came over and gave him a hug.

"Say what you will, but it's true." Shay was unrelenting.

With a glance at Jesse, Steph turned to Shay. "Jesse's pretty upset. This is strange news. Maybe we should take it slower."

"Who was Elizabeth's father?" Steph asked.

"Grace had an affair with another man before she married the Landon guy."

This was all wrong. "You expect me to believe that not only Gramps wasn't this Elizabeth whatever's father, but Grace's first husband wasn't even the dad?" Tears came to his eyes. "But this doesn't make sense. Why would Gramps keep this from—"

From the timbers high above, a barn owl swooped down after a mouse in the corner.

"What the hell was that?" Shay demanded.

"It's just an owl, Shay," Steph announced.

"Mother can come out here and look for more information. This place gives me the creeps," Shay said. "I've found what I was after, and I'm tired of trying to convince you of the truth." She grabbed the letter from Steph. "Come on, Steph. Let's get outta here."

Jesse stood speechless. His head was spinning.

"Jesse. I'm sorry they made such a mess of things," Leeney said, surveying the open boxes.

"This is weird, Leeney. What does this all mean? Why didn't Gramps tell me about this? He's told me every detail already. He hasn't left anything out."

Leeney seemed not to hear him. "You must admit this is exciting. I mean, you think you know all about your family, and then everything changes."

She waited for him to agree. "I'm going back. Coming?"

He shook his head. "Just leave me alone."

"Well, then, later." She ran to catch up to her sisters.

Jesse stared out the door, watching the trees wave their branches to his cousins on their way to the house.

Scanning the barn's interior, he spied on the floor the black ribbon that for years had held together the packet of letters containing the secret of Grace's daughter. Absentmindedly, he picked it up. Leaning against the doorway, he wove the ribbon back and forth through his fingers, thinking about what his cousins had said.

He thought of leaving, but if he returned to the house, his cousins might taunt him. Aimlessly, he walked amid the boxes and randomly searched through the contents. What he hoped to find was unclear. But he felt led to continue for reasons he couldn't explain. He would have liked to discover something that proved Elizabeth was merely Kate's daughter and they were all wrong. He would have liked to prove anything contrary to their story so this pit in his stomach would go away.

He was drawn back to the box containing his grandfather's journals. Pulling a journal out, he sat down and carefully turned the pages, all filled with the old man's strong hand. This was one he and Leeney had not read. A few words jumped off a page at him, and he began to read. The more he read, the more alarmingly ill he grew. His face felt chilled, while the tears welled up, burning his eyes. His shaking hands turned page after page, reading deeper and deeper.

The farther he read, the easier it became for the captive, the secret, to unloose itself till, totally free, it confronted the boy face to face.

There it was in his grandfather's bold, clear handwriting. There was no getting away from it or around it. His mind reeled, and he felt as though his head would explode. Now he understood what Gramps had been trying to tell him. And knew why he couldn't. He now began to understand why his father was so cold and distant.

Attempting to force all of what he read to go away, he tried to concentrate on the sound of the field crickets and their steady song—anything that would take his mind from what his grandfather had written. Why hadn't he followed his cousins to the house?

What was it Gramps had made him think about that night when they went target shooting? He must think about something good and powerful. He must breathe in deeply the smell of the freshly turned, rich black soil. He must think about the trees in the orchard and how deeply their roots dug securely into the ground. He must think about the river that continued to flow throughout the years, unaffected by anything that happened near its banks. But he couldn't concentrate. Desperately he prayed for any peace to come to him.

He was not prepared for what he had read and couldn't understand, believing Gramps had told him everything. The time he had spent with his grandfather didn't matter now. Life at home with his mother and Jack was unbearable, horrible.

He had counted on the world Gramps had created for him through his stories, and now it was disappearing. What else had Gramps left out? How could he preach about the importance of being truthful when he himself had not been?

Jesse brushed away the salty tears on his cheek. Forcing himself to his feet, he walked around the boxes, looking at the mess his cousins had made.

"This place was ... holy," he said aloud. It held memories of others for safekeeping—others long gone. This was where others had left their things. *This place wasn't supposed to be about me*, he thought.

From sadness to disappointment to shock, finally giving way to anger, he found himself wanting to find out more. Feeling like a person who has gone weeks without eating and then filling up on his first meal, making himself ill, he couldn't stop himself from reading more journals. What more did these contain? Everything Gramps had written must be true. Surely, he wouldn't have written lies in his own journal.

He picked up another one. Thumbing through the pages,

he found in the middle of one, where the words seem to leap out:

...the earth melted ....

Later that night after the cousins had left for home, Jesse sat across from his grandfather, silently playing with his dinner.

"Is everything okay? You don't seem well," Gramps said.

Ignoring him, Jesse continued to move the food around his plate.

"Is it your mother? Are you homesick? My lad, what's wrong?"

Throwing his fork down, Jesse looked his grandfather in the eye. "Yeah. Gramps. I don't feel well. My head hurts."

"You should've told me. It's probably the sun. You shouldn't go outdoors without your hat. Let's get you off to bed—"

"No." Jesse shook his head and waved him off. "That's not it!"

"Then what? I'm not sure ..."

His grandfather looked so innocent. It had been so many years ago that he had confided in the journals. How could he let Gramps know that he had discovered what made his dad angry—the reason why his life with Jack was so horrible? But he had no choice; there were too many questions remaining.

"You've convinced me that I should always confront my fears, right?"

"Yes. Of course. What are you concerned with?"

"You told me not to run from them and they'll leave me alone."

"Yes. That's true. But—"

"Have you told me everything about our family?"

Glancing out to the garden the old man noted the scarecrow had fallen over. And there was a hole in the fence. He would remind Hank to repair it tomorrow. Scratching his chin, he became aware how serious Jesse had grown.

"We've talked about many things during this summer. Why do you ask? I don't understand ..."

"This afternoon," Jesse's voice cracked, and he held back his tears, "the girls and I found some letters in the old barn."

"What?"

"Gramps, did Grace ... did Grace really have a daughter that ran away?"

Taking a deep breath, the old man stared sadly toward the porch where his faithful dogs lay, and then looked back at Jesse.

"Who gave you permission to go out there and snoop around?"

"Gramps! Did she?"

Covering his eyes with his hand, Gramps swallowed hard, trying to form the words.

"Yes, she ... we did."

"Why didn't you tell me? Why did you tell me she was Kate's daughter?"

"It's not an easy subject to talk about, even now after these years. It was a hard time for our family, and it changed us in ways that I still regret."

"What do you mean, it changed us?"

Studying the lad, Sam forced a smile. Perhaps he hadn't read too much. He would go out to the barn tomorrow and destroy the damn journals. Writing in them years ago had allowed him to turn from his grieving and attempt to heal. But he should have destroyed them, long ago.

"You mustn't let it bother you. She's dead now. It should have nothing to do with you. Promise me that you won't think about it. And it shouldn't affect you. It happened so many—"

"Gramps? That's not all," Jesse interrupted. "There's something else."

Sam felt a little pain in his chest and grew alarmed.

"Why wouldn't you let Mom and Dad get married? You made her go away. You gave her money to go away. You told her to marry Jack."

The pain began to increase. Sam had not felt one this strong before. The doctor had warned him that they would grow more intense. "No. It's not like that. You don't understand."

"Do you know how bad it is at home? Do you even know how mean Jack is? Some days I wish I were dead, and it's because of you!"

The old man stared straight ahead; beads of sweat began to drench his face. He knew how bad it was. Many times, he wanted to get on the train and meet with Lynn and Jack and try to persuade them to send the lad away to school where he would be safe. He would pay for the tuition.

Several times, he had met with his lawyer to begin proceedings to take Jesse away from them. And then he would stop, deciding he couldn't take Jesse away from his mother. She needed him. He couldn't decide if the pain growing in his chest hurt as much as the ache of watching his grandson's accusing face across from him.

Jumping up, Jesse knocked over the chair. "How could you do that? Why did you lie to me? I trusted you. Why do people lie to me?"

The old man's breathing turned dangerously shallow, but Jesse was too wrapped up in his accusations to notice. Unable to form words, Sam felt as though someone had wrapped a rope around his chest and with each word Jesse spoke, the rope grew tighter. Unable to stop him, the old man watched Jesse bolt out the back door.

.   .   .

Out in the orchard, the thick mud had begun to dry, separating into a thousand puzzle pieces. The sun had sunk below the foothills over an hour ago casting darkness on the trees.

Walking aimlessly, Jesse eventually found himself sitting in front of Daniel Jaeger's stone cross. It was too dark to read now, but his fingers rubbed the stone.

"What else are you hiding from me?" he yelled out.

The "five brothers," roosting in a nearby tree, clucked a little as they settled in for the night.

"I know you're there," he said to the air. "You've been hiding from me this whole time."

But the stone cross with its outstretched arms remained silent.

"Why don't you love me?" he screamed louder. "How could you have let this—"

Suddenly he heard footsteps and was afraid his grandfather had followed him out. Through tears, he faintly made out, over a couple of rows of trees, the glow of a burning cigarette. An eerie feeling climbed up his spine. Paralyzed, he sat watching through the tears, as the small orange glow moved up and down a few times. Then it was flicked away as the dark form disappeared into the darkness.

Sam mustered all the strength he had to follow Jesse. Sucking on the little white pill lessened the pain in his chest. He was beginning to breathe a little easier. Afraid to move but more concerned for Jesse than himself, he pulled himself into the Jeep. Moving more on will than strength, he turned the Jeep down the dirt road toward the orchard.

Not knowing exactly where his grandson had gone, but guessing it was to the stone cross, he stopped the Jeep near the grave. He slouched back in the seat. Fumbling for his pill box, he got another pill under his tongue and waited.

Initially, Jesse was disappointed to see the headlights coming towards him. But he was glad Gramps would be there, especially after having realized someone had been spying on him.

"Come here, my lad!" The old man called out.

Something in his voice didn't seem right. Approaching the Jeep, Jesse noticed his grandfather lying back in the seat. "Gramps. What's wrong? Are you, all right?"

After a moment, his grandfather took a shallow breath. "I've never lied to you, my boy. I've never lied to you."

"Gramps. Are you okay?"

"Yes. Yes. I'm okay. I just need to rest. My chest ..."

"Let's go back to the house. Come on. I'll drive us back," Jesse said.

"Wait. I never meant to hurt you. I had hoped it wasn't necessary. It was so long ago. We can't change what happened, can we?"

Jesse helped him crawl over to the passenger seat. "It's okay, Gramps. I've got to get you back to the house."

"Listen to what I'm telling you!" The old man insisted. "Don't confuse what I've taught you. There's no past or future that matters. It's the present you must face; not the past."

"Gramps, I'm sorry. I didn't mean to hurt you." Jesse drove carefully back to the house.

· · ·

Before bed, Jesse went downstairs to the library to check on his grandfather, who had tried to read for a while. Glancing up, he saw Jesse staring at him.

"Gramps. Do you feel better?"

"Yes, I'm fine. I just forgot I'm not as young as you. I've been riding the horse too much, and the work we did planting trees was too much, that's all."

Jesse stood in front of him. He couldn't move away.

"What is it, my boy?"

"I don't know. I'm just confused, that's all."

"Here. Sit down for a minute." Leaning back in his chair, he closed his book.

"Someday the trees we planted will yield their fruit to others. What do you suppose people will see when they drive by?"

Jesse shook his head. He was too tired to think.

"Depends. They may appreciate the neat rows or be drawn to the shade it provides. But they won't see what happened the day we planted them. How we all came together with joy. How I planned it out and how we all completed it. Including what the lunch was like and the water dousing you gave each other that day. Isn't that a bigger part of the orchard?"

Jesse supposed so and nodded yes.

"It's never a good idea to judge anything based solely on what you see. There's much more to it? Do you understand what I'm saying?"

"I guess so, Gramps. I'm tired."

"I know. Listen. You go up to bed now. I'll explain everything tomorrow."

. . .

Upstairs in bed, the questions rang through his head.

Who was Elizabeth? Why had she run away and had never been heard from again? And why had his parents been forbidden to marry?

Drifting off to sleep, at that precise moment when consciousness is swallowed by sleep, he jolted as the cigarette-smoking, dark figure near Daniel Jaeger's grave lunged for him.

30

Why was this morning so different? Jesse asked himself. Then it dawned on him; he hadn't slept this late before. And remembering the package of yesterday lying at the door of his thoughts, his heart sank. Desperately he wanted to forget what Shay had revealed and what he had discovered.

He wished the chiming clock downstairs would in some way move backwards, taking everything with it. But then that would be as impossible as trying to change the direction of the river or prevent the end of the summer that was quickly approaching.

After getting dressed, he trudged down the back stairs and hesitated at the last step, deciding what he should say to his grandfather. There was so much to be said and yet so little remained. Holding his breath, he jumped from the last step into the kitchen.

"*Hay caramba!*" Stanza's hand went to her chest. "You scare me! *Abuelo* said you still sleep."

"Stanza! I'm sorry." He was glad that it was her and not his grandfather. Scanning the room, he was relieved. "I thought you were Gramps."

Pulling a tissue from her sleeve, she blotted her face. "I no want to wake you. *Bueno*, now you up, I clean upstairs."

Pulling up a chair, Jesse sat at the table and traced designs of the wood. Suddenly he remembered how ill his grandfather was last night. "Where's Gramps? Is he all right?"

"He go out. He said he go to … er … town."

She stopped her scrubbing and stared out the window to the garden, and as though Sam was there, she said, "You know, he no *bueno* this morning. He too stubborn, won't stay in and rest."

The guilt of knowing that he might have caused his grandfather harm was too heavy. Why did he yell at him last night? He suddenly recalled his dream with Moses down at the river. He would never forgive himself if something happened to his grandfather. "Stanza, did he say when he would be back?"

She checked the clock. "No, don't remember. *Tiene hambre* breakfast?"

"No, thanks. I'm not very hungry."

"*Hay caramba*! You no ill too?"

"No, I'm just not hungry, that's all. Maybe I slept too long. I don't know."

She shooed him out of the kitchen. "Go to porch. I bring something there."

On his way to the porch, he glanced into the library, and he felt the house was revealing something about itself. It was as though the house was carved from stone, indestructible and unmovable. His grandfather had built it to last forever. It had its own smell; no matter how many times the night air might be exchanged for the new, the house stubbornly retained this scent. He guessed it was the aroma of the lemon oil that Stanza always used when she scrubbed down the floors and furniture. That, together with the smells of cooking and of musty books and the lilac fragrance that rode the breezes into the house, tinged the air with its own distinctive bouquet.

Out on the porch he threw himself into his grandfather's rocking chair, startling a hummingbird investigating the geranium's blooms.

His fingers rubbed the wood where it had been worn away after years of use. The singing of the reel lawnmower drifted around the corner, announcing that Hank was nearby, perpetually keeping the garden orderly.

In a few minutes, Stanza carried out three mugs of sweet tea and a plate stacked with her homemade Mexican sweet pies. Hank appeared suddenly as though he had the nose of a cat following a mouse.

As she passed a mug of tea and one of the pies to her husband, they exchanged a few words before returning to the porch. Jesse helped himself to her thoughtfulness.

"Stanza? You took care of Dad and Uncle after my grandmother died, right?"

She stirred a second teaspoon of sugar into her tea. "*Si, si.* They *bueno chicos*. Active, *pero bueno*." Looking him over, she seemed to see how he measured up to the two boys she had helped raise.

"Stanza, what was Grace's daughter like?"

Swallowing her tea, she glanced at Hank. "Where you hear about her?"

"The cousins told me that—"

She waved him off impatiently and shook her head, as though she had no interest. "No matter. Only a matter of time. *Conjeturo que es mientras que debe ser.*"

"What?" Jesse asked.

"How you say ... meant to come out."

She examined him as though checking his age. "*Cuantos tiene anos?*"

"I'm fifteen."

"Hmm ... your papa about your age when she left."

She looked Jesse square in the eye. "Been too many *años. Me olvido.* Um ... I no remember much no *mas. Pero* one thing I no forget. Much pain it cause those stay behind. *Su abuelo querido no mereció eso.*"

"What?"

"*Abuelo* no deserve that."

"Stanza, what was she like? Was she—"

She got up abruptly, as though someone inside the house had summoned her. At the screen door, she hesitated, searching for the right words. *"Lo siento* for all pain it made."

The screen door slammed shut after her.

Hank shot Jesse a look of warning as though Jesse had intentionally insulted his wife. Jesse smiled meekly, but Hank disappeared around the corner of the house without saying a word.

It was difficult knowing only so much, and he knew his curiosity wasn't going to let things alone. Slipping out through the garden gate, he left the singing of the lawn mower behind. Wondering where he should go, he found himself staring at Daniel Jaeger's little cottage. Reviewing the events of yesterday, it occurred to him that of all the places on the ranch that he had explored, he had never been inside.

Circling the little house a few times, he tried to peer through the dirty windows. He rubbed a circle in one of them, but years of grime made it impossible to see inside. Guessing the door was probably locked, he rattled the knob anyway.

"Good morning," Gramps said, taking Jesse by surprise.

"*Shi...yoot.* Gramps. You scared me. Stanza said you were in town!"

"I came home earlier. I was over at the stable checking on Bella when I saw you snooping around. You kids never learn, do you?" He glanced from Jesse to the door. "Ever heard the old saying, 'Curiosity killed the cat'?"

Deciding Jesse wasn't going to answer, he asked, "Are you ready to go inside?"

"Why? What's in there?" He was becoming convinced that knowing the past had a price that was dear. And he had mixed feelings about pursuing the completion. "I'm not sure anymore, Gramps. I'm tired of it all." But deep down he knew his curiosity would not curl up and go back to sleep.

His grandfather pulled a skeleton key from his front pocket and jiggled the lock.

"It's too late for that now, Jesse. What has begun must always be finished. The time has come to finish what we've begun this summer."

Pushing the stiff door open, he motioned to Jesse to go in. The musty smell promised many old treasures. Stepping around dusty pieces of furniture and trunks, the old man threw open a window. In a few moments, fresh air forced out the stale.

Brushing off a chair, he sat down, and indicated to Jesse a trunk on which to sit.

"Gramps, are you going to tell me about Dad and Mom?"

"Yes, my lad." Gramps sighed. "But first, one story must finish before another is begun." Taking off his hat, he fanned himself. "I must finish mine first, then perhaps you'll better understand yours. I had hoped this part wouldn't be necessary. But I'm a foolish old man that should've known better."

Jesse felt confused and wished he had not slept so late, thinking this might be the cause of his groggy, tired feeling.

"Taking things out of context is dangerous," Gramps explained.

He took a deep breath. "This old place contains many family things," he said, surveying the familiar interior. "Many of them would have been thrown out if I had not saved them. I believe families need to know what they've been through. Then perhaps lessons learned may be shared, and mistakes made will not be suffered too soon."

Taking a box from a shelf nearby, he opened it, pulled out a neatly folded uniform, and handed it to Jesse. The acrid smell of mothballs burned Jesse's nose.

"This was the uniform I wore in France."

Holding it up to himself, Jesse's grogginess instantly cleared. "What rank were you?"

"I was a sergeant in the 144th Company."

"Was your family proud that you were in the War?"

"I suppose so."

Jesse began toying with the medals pinned to the jacket. "This one," Gramps rubbed one between his fingers, "recognizes the service that I performed on the front lines."

It was the strangest thing to Jesse; it was almost as if the young man in the photograph in the silver frame in the living room sat in front of him. Jesse assumed the light and shadows were playing games in the dusty little cabin.

He handed the uniform back to his grandfather, who carefully folded it and returned it to the box. Turning to one of the trunks, Sam found an old shoebox stuffed with photographs.

Pointing to the top one in the stack, he said, "Look here! This was Elizabeth when she was just a girl. And here's another that shows Grace and Griffen and Polly when they began living in San Francisco, and—" his face took on a shadow, "here's one of Lou and Grace."

"She's beautiful," Jesse exclaimed, pointing to Elizabeth.

Turning to find the spot in the yard, Gramps pointed, "You can see it was taken right over there." He searched the stack for one photograph. When he located it, he passed it to Jesse.

"Why does this look familiar, Gramps?"

"It's of the three sisters' house years ago. It was taken at a party they had marking their brother's birthday. A dreadful day that changed our family forever."

His grandfather pulled a magnifying glass from a box nearby. Carefully, Jesse studied the figures in the picture.

"Gramps, are these the sisters on the front porch?"

"Yes, oldest to youngest, Amanda, Hattie, and Polly."

Knowing that some of the people in the photograph had taken part in his grandfather's story, Jesse wished he could have been there to see them. Hearing so much about their lives, to see what they looked like and how they acted would have made the stories more real.

"If only I could go there. If only I could be there ..." He was unaware of saying aloud what he so wished.

Before he could tell what was happening, the sepia-toned photograph enlarged quickly, seeming to surround him. The walls of the house turned a bright white, and the dark shutters became a rich green, while the shrubs and vines surrounding the house exploded into color, as Daniel Jaeger's little cabin faded away.

His grandfather's fading voice gave way to unfamiliar voices and laughter as the figures in the photograph began to move and speak.

31

Summer 1934

Suddenly, Jesse found himself in the yard of the Three Sisters' Place. But it looked different than the one he had walked by this summer to get to Moses' cabin. The garden was neatly manicured, and the house was cared for, not dark and sinister, at least not in appearance. He climbed the porch stairs, where he took a seat not far from three vacant chairs.

It was strange to be there, and yet he felt no fear or apprehension. Perhaps the reason he wasn't frightened was because this was so much like a dream; if it became too much, he could end it with nothing more than a mere wish, but he couldn't do that with such anticipation.

All heads turned when a Ford touring car turned into the road. Coming to a stop at the garden gate, the driver hopped out to open the door. Amanda, consistent in her prerogative as the eldest in all actions important or not, was the first to emerge. Though no longer a young woman, she was still elegant and slim. She was dressed in a close-fitting gray suit. High cheekbones punctuated her face, with a sharp nose. Her eyes of deep blue set off her hair of light gray.

Brushing past Daisette Westland, who had been exchanging gossip with the mayor's wife, Amanda asked, "Wasn't it a splendid sermon, Daisette?"

"Yes, Amanda. It was. I especially loved what Reverend Petersen said about—"

"We took the time to pay our respects to those unforgotten in the cemetery. It's so nice to have Griffen's friends here to celebrate what would have been his birthday," Amanda said to another neighbor, leaving Daisette to explain to the mayor's wife what part of the sermon was her favorite.

Hattie emerged from the car and silently followed Amanda's path while Polly lagged behind. Though there was no mistaking Hattie for Amanda's sister, she was noticeably less harsh looking, but equally as pretty. Polly, on the other hand, resembled neither one—she was much younger and seemed harmless, though uncomfortable, and not as stiff as the other two.

Just as the sisters made their way through the neighbors and up the porch stairs, a young woman rode in on a beautiful horse. Chills went up Jesse's spine when he recognized Elizabeth, from the photograph his grandfather had just shown him.

She quickly threw the horse's reins around a post and hurried up the stairs where the sisters had positioned themselves.

Strawberry-blond hair pulled back and fastened at the nape of her neck, and striking blue eyes ensured that she resembled her mother. There was something else about her—difficult to identify, and a demarcation from Grace. She seemed more refined, as though she had escaped the often-harsh country life. Maybe it was that she never really belonged on a ranch, working hard, season after season. Yet, like her mother, there was a stubbornness and strong confidence to her walk. She seemed to hold herself well above the Eastside people—perhaps the same characteristic that led her mother away from here.

"My dears, we are so fortunate," Amanda whispered to her sisters with a gleam in her eye, watching Elizabeth come their way. Amanda held out both hands. "I've been looking for you."

Elizabeth kissed all three on their cheeks. Standing up hastily, Amanda took her hand.

"Come, dear. We have so much to catch up on," she said over her shoulder to her sisters, leading Elizabeth inside. "I must have Elizabeth to myself for a minute."

It seemed important, imperative, that Jesse follow them. He realized he was there for a reason. He was not here to be entertained but to bear witness to events that would shortly unfold and would eventually affect him.

Following them down the main hall, he ducked into a room adjoining the room in which they had disappeared. The door between the two was slightly ajar.

Amanda almost pushed Elizabeth down on the sofa. "Sit here, my dear, and tell me all about your wedding plans. Now, who is this lucky young man?"

Instantly a dark cloud seemed to shadow Elizabeth's face.

"Dear, is everything all right?" Amanda asked. "You're happy, aren't you? This is the boy for you?"

"I'm just confused. That's all."

"Confused about what? I'm told that young people become nervous before a wedding. Perhaps that seems normal ..."

Elizabeth played with her engagement ring, twisting it around her finger. "No. It's more than that."

"My dear. What is it? You can trust me."

Tears flooded Elizabeth's eyes. She blurted out, "Grandmother has said some horrible things about Mother."

"What kind of things, my dear?"

Elizabeth shook her head slightly and wiped the tears from her face.

"Now, my dear, you know you can confide in me."

"Grandmother told me I'm not a child any longer, and if I'm to be married I need to know some things. That I need to face the truth. She said that you would bear witness to what she told me."

"Truth, dear? What did she mean?"

"Grandmother said that Mother cruelly used Daddy. She said

that I should be careful in marrying. And to be sure that I'm marrying for the right reasons. She said Mother did Daddy a cruel injustice by marrying him for the worst reasons."

"What did she mean?"

"That Mother married Daddy for his money. And that she only married him to make Sam jealous. Could this really be true?"

From a facing window, Jesse had an excellent prospect of the road and yard, where he watched two more riders arrive. Startled, he recognized Grace, who was in the lead followed by Sam. Once off their horses, his grandfather caught up to Grace and grabbed her arm. Could this really be his grandfather so young? Though their figures appeared distorted through the wavy glass of the window, there was no mistaking his grandfather's gait.

It was all Jesse could do to force himself to stay still and not run out to them. What prevented him was almost an audible voice that convinced him that his presence here was sustained as a delicate feat. Everything he saw had only the substance and thickness of one brittle, old photograph. One abrupt move would cause it all to disintegrate into pieces.

"They said Mother took all of Daddy's money. Is there any truth to this?"

Amanda patted her arm. "Well, dear. There is a lot you don't know about your mother. But now that you've asked —"

"Amanda!" Grace burst into the room; her face flushed with anger. "What have you said?"

"How dare you barge into my house?" Amanda rose quickly and stamped her foot. "You are not welcome here!"

Ignoring her, Grace leapt for her daughter, trying to pull her away. "Elizabeth, you must be reasonable. Please come home and I'll explain. No good can come of anything here."

"Elizabeth, dear, your grandmother failed to tell you the other reason why your father married your mother." She sneered at Grace. "There was a third —"

"Don't listen to this nonsense," Grace pleaded. "She just wants you to herself. Amanda will tell you anything to this end."

"Elizabeth," Amanda persisted, "did your grandparents tell you what killed your father?"

Elizabeth shook herself away from her mother. "Just that when they lost their money in the stock market crash, Daddy had to borrow money to keep up with Mother's spending. He even came to you when I was little, and you loaned them an amount they've never repaid." Her eyes shot daggers at her mother. "In fact, she used it to buy the boardinghouse."

"That's a lie! My mother left that money to me," Grace said. "It had nothing to do with—"

"When Daddy couldn't repay it," Elizabeth interrupted, "he became desperate and turned to gambling. Then he began drinking because of worry. And that's what killed him."

"Tell her it's not true!" Grace pleaded. "You would never give us money. You were only made her guardians because you threatened to tell Elizabeth about Griffen—"

Sam stopped at the doorway to see how this would play out. But when he heard that Grace had slipped, he shook his head in disbelief that she had played right into Amanda's hands.

Elizabeth searched the room as though the house had just gone through a shattering earthquake. She turned pale and stared at her mother. "Cousin Amanda, what about Griffen? What would he have to do with me?"

"Amanda, you have the chance to let this go," Sam said. Then he seemed to change his tack. "Elizabeth, there are things better left alone, unsaid. Some things will only hurt. Your mother is right, let's go. Let the past go."

"We, who have lost our dear brother," Amanda continued, ignoring them, "cannot shrink from telling you the truth, as well."

"What good will come of this?" Grace sounded desperate. "Think, Amanda. Why are you doing this? No one will win. Sam's right. It's years past."

"Because Elizabeth may leave us to be married. I've prayed for this day. It's time she knew the truth. Despite all your selfish actions, you have Sam and two sons. We have no one. Elizabeth is our niece. She's our only blood. She is ours."

"Your niece? What do you mean?" Elizabeth looked as though she couldn't take one more revelation.

But Amanda ignored the question. It was as though she had waited years to say what she would, and she would deal with the steps in her way and time.

"I am sorry to say," she addressed Grace head on, "that we are cousins. We were not raised to be so immoral and cruel. We were raised differently. Your people grew up in the hills away from what was decent. They never attended church."

Completely immersed in listening to the conversation, Jesse did not hear the footsteps coming down the hallway toward the room where he was. Creeping into the room, Polly surprised him. But she gave no indication that she saw him. Taking a place on the sofa next to him, she listened.

"Amanda!" Elizabeth demanded. "What do you mean, I'm your niece? What are you saying?"

She probed her mother's face. Almost hysterical, she began shaking, "What does she mean?"

Grace fell back as though a noxious gust of wind had forced itself through the doorway. All the air seemed to be sucked out of her. She was as pale as the accused listening to the jury deliver the sentence.

Hesitating for a bit, seeming to savor the moment she had waited for, Amanda dropped her bombshell. "Dearest child, there is a third reason why your mother married Lou. Your father is not Lou Landon."

"I don't understand. This doesn't make sense." As though she had barged into a familiar house whose inhabitants had suddenly fled and been replaced with total strangers, she searched the room as though pleading for someone to come forward who would make sense of what was happening.

"Elizabeth, did you hear me? Lou Landon was not your real father," Amanda repeated.

"But he was my daddy." She looked pleadingly at her mother and Sam. Grace could say nothing, and Sam, though furious, was helpless to do anything, standing in front of the truth.

"Your real father was Griffen, my brother," Amanda declared.

"How can this be?"

"When your mother left the Eastside for San Francisco ..." Amanda clasped her hands together and shook her head; her voice climbed with self-righteous anger. "She knew Polly and Griffen were in San Francisco and forced herself upon them.

"And so, they three lived together. She was lonely in San Francisco. Griffen watched over her. Oh, Elizabeth. If you could have known Griffen, your father. He was such a kind, gentle—"

Not taking her eyes off Elizabeth, Grace fought to regain her composure, her life really. And clawing herself to the surface to gulp in precious air to return alive, she gained her voice. "Not exactly as kind as you would have him, Amanda." She took deep breaths. "When I arrived in the city, I was scared and lonely. Different from anything that I'd known. Will had warned me, but I was too stubborn. I was vulnerable, and Griffen was experienced. No, Amanda. You're wrong. He knew exactly what he was doing."

"Bah! Your mother took advantage of Griffen's kindness and trapped him." Amanda walked circles around Elizabeth. "There's no denying that he always had an eye for a beautiful woman. He hadn't a chance. When your mother threw herself at him, he tried to get away. But it was too late."

"Too late?" Elizabeth murmured.

Sam resigned himself to the fact that this news wasn't going away. He was beginning to know how a fly must feel at the center of the spider's elaborately woven web, watching the spider circle its prey, coming closer and closer, preparing to strike.

"Yes, dear. Grace was with child—with you, my dear. Griffen confided to me that he would do the honorable thing. He told me he would marry your mother and asked if he could bring her here to live with us. And of course, I had to agree. What could I say? She was family, and Griffen asked. But, this woman, your mother, who was now, unmarried and with child, she had the impudence to refuse our dear brother."

"What kind of a life would I have had here?" Grace exclaimed. "I couldn't imagine spending the rest of my life with him. He wouldn't have come home. He would've left me here with you while he continued his life in the city. The life he offered was one here with you, Amanda. Could I be blamed? How could I live down the road from Sam when I've always loved him? I was trapped. I had to do something quickly. I couldn't return to Sam, and I couldn't return to the Eastside without a husband."

"See? She admits that she used Lou. What more justification does one need to see through her selfishness?" Amanda pronounced as though she were a lawyer pleading to her jury.

"Why wouldn't you tell me this?" Elizabeth turned on Grace.

"Dear, don't cry." Amanda mustered a kinder tone. "The truth is often painful. Griffen was heartbroken. But he was not the only one who was heartbroken. Polly suffered greatly as well. You see, she was engaged to Lou Landon when Grace came to San Francisco. I didn't care for him, but then of course I didn't approve of Polly leaving the Eastside. Daddy warned us against men like that. They were planning to be married in the spring. So, you see your mother broke another heart by stealing Lou away from Polly."

"It's true, Elizabeth," Grace said. "Lou was engaged to Polly. He admitted that he loved her but didn't think they could be happy. He offered me my first glimmer of hope in the many dark nights I spent alone and frightened about my condition. I thought I found someone who promised to make a good home for me and my unborn child."

At this, Polly slipped into the room.

"Oh, Polly!" Grace looked to her for help. "You were my friend in San Francisco. You've forgiven me. You know that Griffen didn't want to marry me. I wasn't the first. He wanted to get away from Amanda. That's why he left for the war. Griffen didn't die in battle. He died from the pneumonia outbreak even before going into danger."

Amanda ignored Grace and turned to Elizabeth. "Griffen was

beside himself because he wanted to be a father to you. She caused our brother, your own father, to die. And poor Polly has always regretted what Grace did. It was your mother's fault, and you see this is all God's will that she suffer and that you should know the truth. It is as it should be."

"Amanda!" Polly cried out. "It's been so many years now. What does it matter?"

Amanda's lip began to curl into a cruel smile. "Really? What do you mean? It's the truth."

"What you've done is monstrous," Polly uttered before falling into a chair.

Then she reached out towards her niece. "Elizabeth, all that happened years ago. It doesn't matter who was wrong, who was right. Just find forgiveness. It's the only way to make it through now. Don't live with bitterness. Look what it's done to us."

Elizabeth danced past Amanda and ignored Polly's outstretched hand. She dodged her mother and Sam. "I don't know what to believe—what to think."

"You evil woman! Do you even realize what you've done here?" Grace confronted Amanda.

"Amanda, how could you do this?" Polly whispered. "It wasn't yours to tell. Look what you've done to her. You can't keep interfering. It's people's lives you're affecting, hers … mine—"

"Calm down, Polly. You're working yourself up." Amanda then turned on Grace.

"And as for you, I owe you nothing. You can accuse me? You who are the real cause of our brother's death? You've been so selfish that you've ruined several lives. Even your poor sister Mollie might be alive if it wasn't for you. You're the one that deserved the likes of Joseph Hunter. Your life of misery with him would have been justice."

"Here now! That's enough of this!" Sam cried out, taking a step towards Amanda. He almost had to physically restrain himself. He wanted to knock her self-satisfaction out of her, but he had to remind himself she was a woman. He had never felt such fury before.

"Can't you see," she wagged her finger at Grace, "you've made misery wherever you've been? You are finally going to get everything you deserve. You've made us suffer for Griffen's death. We are old women. We have no family left. No one to leave the ranch to. We must have Griffen's child near us."

"But we've all lost now." Grace's form shook. "We've all lost … can't you see that?"

Becoming Jesse's loss as well, the colors and sounds around him faded quickly, leaving only the brittle, thin photograph in his hand.

Summer 1960

Jesse felt so tired, he didn't think he could go on. If his grandfather hadn't pushed him, he would have fallen asleep there in the cabin.

"Jesse. What do you think now?"

"Gramps, no one … no one in Grace's family knew about Griffen?"

"No. Of course not. No one, except perhaps her sister Kate, was ever told the truth."

"And you didn't know?"

"No. I didn't know until their divorce. Over the next few years, she discovered that Lou wasn't as kind and generous as he promised to be. And I must admit he began to treat her worse because of his jealousy. He knew that Grace had always loved me and that I never stopped loving her.

"I didn't realize how cruel he had been. Grace wouldn't let on. She knew if I had discovered that, I would have gone after her. Whenever she came to visit me, she wanted to remain with me and to leave him. But I never really understood. I thought she was just wavering, confused. I thought she wanted both worlds, to a degree, I guess."

"Gramps, why didn't she, if it was so bad?" But then he thought of his mother and how she stayed with Jack.

"Think of it, my boy! The fact that she had a child with her cousin was scandalous enough, but to be unwed as well was unheard of in those days. I know that today, this generation has 'free love' or some such thing—they say it's not such a big deal, but back then, the shame it would have brought on her family would have been unthinkable."

"But, Gramps, she did leave."

"Once her mother and father were both dead, she didn't care any longer. You see, her situation had grown to be as bad as ... well ... as bad as your ...."

"Did Elizabeth like it here?" Jesse asked.

"Like you, she loved to hear about the ranch and what it meant to me. She loved to ride out into the fields by herself. But then after Lou died, she asked to stay with her grandparents in San Francisco more often."

"Why did she want to live with them?"

"Not long after your dad and Colton were born, Elizabeth felt she was no longer the center of her mother's world. We knew Lou had filled her head with what he wanted her to know. We could counteract it to a degree while she was with us. But later, Grace and I had become so busy with farming, raising a family, and growing content in our happiness. I guess we hadn't realized how distant she had grown.

"Then after Lou died, her grandparents wanted to send her to a private school in the city. They said the country wasn't a place for a young girl like Elizabeth. Though Grace allowed Elizabeth to live with the Landons, she was uneasy because she knew that they despised her."

Suddenly Gramps set the photographs on the rocking chair and walked over to the door, where he stood, taking in the smell of the newly mown lawn, focusing on something across the yard.

"And thanks to Amanda," he glanced over his shoulder towards Jesse, "the Landons got their wish when Elizabeth fled to St. Louis where they had returned to live."

"It doesn't make sense. If Amanda hated Grace so much, why did Grace allow Elizabeth to be with the three sisters?" Jesse asked.

"From the time Elizabeth was born, they threatened Grace, convincing her that they would tell Elizabeth and Grace's family who Elizabeth's real father was. They took kindly to the girl, and Elizabeth thought of them as harmless old 'aunts.'"

"But what happened that day after Amanda told her Griffen was her real father?"

"Elizabeth never spoke to us after that day. But Amanda didn't gain, either. You must be careful how you light the stubble of the fields on fire. You don't want to find yourself caught in the middle with no escape. Amanda was burned by the fire she lit. She didn't count on Elizabeth leaving for good.

"Amanda was so desperate for Elizabeth to return that she made her their sole heir if she would return to them. To prove our love, I also left Elizabeth my ranch. But it made no difference."

The old man stopped for a second, taking a deep breath.

"Gramps, Elizabeth never came back to see her mother?"

"No, and this broke Grace's heart. When she was convinced that Elizabeth was really gone and would never return, she no longer spoke of her and forbade anyone else to, as well."

"Gramps, you wrote in your journal that the three sisters worked their evil on Dad. Did they tell him?"

"Yes." He shook his head. "He had many questions. Why had Elizabeth left? What caused his mother such unhappiness and eventually her illness? He persisted in asking until they told him. He discovered that our ranch was going to Elizabeth. And he took it badly. I tried to make him understand about his mother and why I was leaving the ranch to Elizabeth. It was a promise that would always be kept while there was any hope that she might return home."

"Why was Dad so bitter?" Jesse asked. "Why couldn't he understand?"

"He felt he had been cheated twice and then, later, a third time."

"What do you mean twice?"

"He couldn't understand why I would leave the ranch to someone who essentially caused his mother's death. And not only had he been deprived of his mother but had been cheated of his inheritance as well." Gramps sighed.

"Dan never forgave me for my decision. Then, later he found another reason to hate me more. Oh, my boy ... it seemed for his own good. You see—"

"What other reason?" Then he remembered what his grandfather had written about forbidding his parents' marriage.

His grandfather closed his eyes and forced himself to continue. "It was a few years later after Elizabeth left, we heard that she had given birth to a baby boy. Grace had sunk so low into melancholia; she wouldn't do anything. When she realized that she would never see her grandson or daughter, she fell ill and died shortly after."

"Is melancholia like cancer or something?"

"It's a mental darkness, black sadness, so profound, so deep it's difficult to climb back."

"And a person can die from it?"

"I have said quite enough for the day," he whispered.

Astonished to see his grandfather's eyes fill with tears, Jesse sat in silence, daring to say nothing more.

32

Sam regretted that in his quest for wisdom he had never discovered how to stop the earth from turning. If he had, he was sure he would have stopped this day from coming. He could count on one hand the few days he would have ever been tempted to stop. Today was one of those, because this one would result in nothing but emptiness where the boy had been.

Last week, Jesse had received a note from Lynn, enclosing the ticket for his return home. Sam now faced the distressing task of coming to terms that his grandson would soon be gone.

The old man recalled their conversation at the supper table on the night when the boy realized the summer was ending. Except for the dogs' occasional begging on the porch, the silence had grown thick between them like the darkness overtaking the orchard.

. . .

"Gramps, when do you start to harvest the corn?" Jesse broke through the stillness.

"Oh, not long now. A week, maybe."

"You need more help. If I stayed here, I could work alongside Felipe Diego. He'd show me what to do. And you'd save money in wages—you wouldn't have to pay me."

The old man caught a glimpse of the boy from the corner of his eye.

"Now, you know, young man, we've discussed this before. You'll be in school by then, fully immersed in your studies."

His grandfather broke off a piece of bread.

"Gr- Gr- Gramps," Jesse stuttered nervously, "is … there any way I could stay here?"

Couldn't the boy realize this was difficult for him, as well? Couldn't he understand that his place was with his mother now? He must not fight the inevitable. Sam had given the boy everything he could. And he knew, though the boy hadn't realized it yet, the day would come when his grandson would prove the worth of the summer's lessons.

"Your mother is expecting you."

Besides, it wasn't his design that his grandson should escape from his troubles, but to face and master them. His mother would need what the boy now had. She would see that not only was her son safe from Jack, but she would be also. Her life would no doubt change in ways she could not foresee, because of what Jesse had learned here.

"Gramps. Please don't send me …."

Sam studied his grandson. He was just a regular boy, nothing out of the ordinary, really, if one counted talent or uniqueness. He was just a boy, like any other, who looked out onto the world with trusting eyes onto those who, unkind, would betray this trust. What was it about cruel people who preyed on those who were innocent? They were like the man who threw paint at a priceless painting—someone who hadn't the capacity to love great art, so their only response was to leave their mark of hatred.

Proudly, Sam recognized Jesse's hands, large and strong, characteristic of the Hunters. Indeed, if only by his clear blue eyes and his farmer's hands, he was a member of the family.

"She misses you, my boy, and school will be starting very soon. Besides, I'm too old to follow you around! Your place is with her."

Jesse's eyes widened, pleading.

"You needn't be afraid of Jack any longer. Just remember what you've learned."

But the words Sam spoke simply floated on the summer's thick air. He had to push from his mind, that in a few days, he would sit here eating his meals alone, as he had done before Jesse had arrived.

· · ·

And now sitting in the library, on the last day of the boy's stay, he was forced to confront the inevitable.

Glancing at the books and the furniture, he thought how much this room had meant to him over the years. Every detail of the room was familiar. So much had inspired its construction, and so much had happened here. It occurred to him that sometime during his life, as the room existed in the house, so had the house existed solely in his thought. He came to the realization that he didn't really live in this house any longer, but rather the house lived in him. No matter where he was, the house would never leave his thoughts. It was in France where he had first begun to understand this.

After breakfast, knowing he had more to tell his grandson, especially of the boy's story — Jesse had so patiently waited — the old man called his grandson into the library.

His grandfather pulled a leather box from the shelf and carefully laid it on the library table between them. Absentmindedly, he traced the pattern on the top as he reached back to an earlier time.

"As I said earlier, Grace was never the same after Elizabeth left, and she passed away a few years later. One morning, the day of her death, she turned from her illness ..."

Sam's voice grew lower, and Jesse shivered as the room seemed to become dim and shadowy.

Spring 1941

Suddenly Hank rushed into the library. "Mrs. Hunter's calling for you."

Sam dashed from the room and leapt up the stairs.

The scent of lilac rode the breeze, casting aside the lace curtain to infuse the library with its sweetness. Spilling out into the hall, its pungency gave Jesse a feeling he was in another's home. Following the scent, he knew it would lead to Grace.

As he climbed the stairs, convinced all was familiar, still he couldn't shake the feeling that something was very different. Tiptoeing to his grandfather's half-opened bedroom door, Jesse pushed it open to discover Sam sitting on the edge of Grace's bed. In the corner, Stanza whispered her rosary while her fingers danced through her worn beads. Here the gentle scent of lilac rested.

Jesse rubbed his eyes. "What's happening?"

Sam spoke, in a hushed tone but to no one. "She is very ill."

Glancing out the window, Jesse was surprised to see, where minutes before clear blue skies had been, gray clouds were now releasing a gentle rain.

Though he didn't feel particularly sad, he couldn't understand what was happening. The rain's tranquil tempo began to fill his head. If not for the soft drops striking the roof, the sorrow in the room would have become overwhelming. But the gentle rhythm countered the distress with a soothing melody.

Though Grace had suffered her illness for months, the beauty beneath her troubled face remained unmarred. It was true, the illness had gained control over her fight to live, but it could not erase the beauty of her life.

In her pale blue, flowing nightgown, she looked as though she had just then decided to remain in bed and away from her busy days. The air-dried linens protected her from any drafts. To make doubly sure, Stanza had gently tucked a comforter around her. Grace's hair, usually pulled behind her head, lay loose framing her face, just as Sam preferred it. She played with her plain gold wedding band, the only piece of jewelry she owned or ever desired.

A few minutes before, she had called for Colton, talked with him, and sent him to find his brother. And now, Sam sat next to his wife. Callused fingers traced the curves of her face.

She worked up her strength. "I have something to say."

"There is nothing more to say." He patted her shoulder. "Rest."

"No. You must explain to the boys ... the truth." She tried to swallow. "Tell them the truth."

The shadows from her face lifted, and the sunburst lines around her eyes relaxed. She looked as though a veil was being lifted.

"What do you mean, tell them the truth?"

"It's so strange," she said. "It's becoming clearer."

"What's clearer?" His stomach tightened.

"It's difficult to put in words. Do you remember the day I came visiting with Elizabeth and Lou?"

"Yes. I remember. It broke my heart to see you so unhappy."

"You asked me if all my traveling had brought me happiness. How could I answer? The pain it caused me was more than I feel now. The choices I made carried me further away from where I knew I belonged. Why couldn't I realize what I needed?" She reached out to his hand. "But you could see it."

She searched the comforter as though what she needed to say was woven in the colors and textures of its pattern. "It seems so very clear now. So many are like weary travelers, spending entire lives searching for it. And yet it's all in front of them."

She tilted her head, as though listening to a melody. "Can you hear it?" she asked.

The gentle rain falling on the roof echoed its steady song into the room. The air turned a little cooler. Seeming to instantly grow restless, she threw back the comforter.

"Dear, won't you rest now?" He tried to pull the covers back around her.

"I will always be indebted to you."

"You owe me nothing."

"No. You're mistaken." She shook her head slowly. "I owe you everything. You've given me two fine sons and a lovely home. But, of course, it's more than that, Sam; you've given me an unwavering love. You were always here. You never left, but patiently remained, building the house to my wishes, always welcoming me when I visited. You watched me through all my mistakes, and yet you welcomed me back and took me in with Elizabeth and called her your own. Even so far as to leave your precious ranch to her.

"And what have I given in return? My selfishness has caused such pain."

"That's not true ..." He shook his head, wishing he could make her understand otherwise. But knowing it was in vain because she would have him know her mind, especially now.

"And you have remained secure and steadfast." She squeezed his hand. "Your love has sustained me."

Through the window, a large gray cloud caught her eye.

"And will sustain me forever."

"Now, now, my love, we should go, you are tiring yourself," Sam said, sniffling.

But she would not release his hand.

"Please tell the boys the truth. You must tell them about my life. They must know the truth about Elizabeth." Tears trickled down her cheeks. "Oh, Sam. I loved her so much. It was wrong to deny her life. You must explain to Dan. Make him understand why we did what we did. Sam, I can tell he's turning. Don't let him close off."

"What is there to tell?" he said. "What is done is done. We can't go back."

"Teach him what I learned here—that it's all here. No longer will the ranch, the fields, the trees, and river be mine. But no one can take the peace it affords me, now. This will carry me through."

This realization was grand—almost grand enough for them both. He caressed her face gently, before leaving a kiss on her forehead, her chin, then both of her cheeks, adding his tears to blend with hers. Her breathing, though labored at first, now came softly. When the pain sharpened inside her, she held it in until she could no longer. Then crying out, she breathed her last.

Summer 1960

Suddenly, Jesse burst into tears. He felt a gentle pat on the back, and his grandfather smiled kindly. Brushing his cheeks off, Jesse could see they were back in the library. The event was back on the shelf where it would now remain.

"Here, look out the window!" Gramps pointed. "What a welcome shower this is. It will wash everything down." Straining under the weight of the rain, the branches bent low.

"You know, my boy, when the sun dries the rain from the leaves, then the branches no longer are weighted down. So, with what I have given you this summer, will your burden be lightened."

"What about my story? You promised—"

"Yes, I did. And I shall keep my word."

He walked over to the window, as though looking for the right words about the event that happened not too many years ago.

"I was happy to know your mother. Lynn reminded me so much of our Elizabeth. If Grace had lived and known your mother, I'm convinced she would have been comforted because Lynn was so like her daughter. Perhaps then your father wouldn't have remained so bitter, and he and your mother might have had some chance for happiness together.

"But that was not the case, and it troubled me to see them together."

"Gramps, why didn't you let them stay together? Maybe it would've changed."

"No, my lad. I knew that one day your father would've made your mother as miserable as Joe had made Mollie. As miserable as Lou had made Grace. I couldn't allow that to happen again. I was determined that the past mistakes would not be repeated."

"But Mom said that in the beginning they were very happy."

"Your mother told you what she wanted you to believe. What else could she say?"

This was something Jesse did not know. The journals said nothing about this. "How did they meet?"

"In high school. Lynn had just moved here. It was hard for her to fit in, in a small town. I watched her and Dan closely. I was curious to see if your father would change—soften up a bit. But I could tell it wasn't going to happen. Then before I knew it, it was too late." Gramps sighed.

"Change is inevitable, but in a small town, people fight it. What Grace had to face being with child and not married, so did your mother. Lynn's parents and I met one day, and we agreed it would be best in the long run to keep them apart. Her parents moved away and took Lynn with them. And I gave them some money."

The old man shook his head.

"Somehow, hoping against hope, I wanted Dan to fight me and go after your mother. To bring her back and make a good home for you both. But he didn't. He protested at first, but deep down I could see he was relieved when they left. Then he quickly returned to his ways."

"However your father acted, he did insist that we go to the lawyer in town and have a document written up declaring him as your dad and he would be able to see you on a regular basis."

Gramps glanced over his shoulder at Jesse. "Your father has hidden behind excuses, blaming others for his cowardice," he said.

"We say the weld is stronger than the metal it holds together. But in my case, this was not true. As my heart broke in two when Elizabeth left, again it broke in the same place when your mother left. But I prayed to know that what I'd done was right. Somehow, I believed that in the end my decision would be found right.

"Then I heard that Lynn was to marry Jack. She convinced me that Jack promised to take care of you. I thought all was the way it was supposed to be. But I was wrong ..."

Returning to the table, Gramps reached for the box he had taken from the shelf earlier. "I want you to have some things that have been important to me." He placed the container in his lap, closed his eyes, and issued a silent blessing on it.

He handed it to Jesse. "Go ahead and open it."

Jesse hesitated, not sure if this would cause him regret as the journals had.

"Go ahead."

Dried and cracked, the tooled-leather box was disintegrating with age. Removing the top carefully, Jesse found some items loosely wrapped in yellowed newspaper. Gently he unwrapped a gold pocket watch, a photo of his grandfather as a young boy, a small faded American flag, and a twenty-dollar gold piece.

"I want you to take these with you as a reminder of what we've shared this summer," Gramps told him.

Jesse didn't know what to say.

"You asked me one day what I did after Grace died. I'll tell you. I could only go on. I had built the house for her when I didn't yet have her, and then when I lost her, I continued to maintain the ranch and the house and garden to her memory. I had two boys to look after, and they deserved everything I could give them."

Something moving beyond the window seemed to garner his attention. Outside, Hank was busy working, planting the garden in shades of lavender, Grace's favorite color. The end of the summer signaled her birthday, and the old man insisted this be done every year in remembrance.

"It was nearly impossible to carry on without her." He took a deep breath. "But I had our sons. Picking up, I began life anew. You know, I've been the one, the last of a generation." He chuckled. "I've always drawn on the ranch for strength, and sometimes I myself find it difficult to know where the ranch ends, and I begin. We seem so intertwined."

This was what Colton had said to Jesse. Unlike his dad and to some degree his mother, he was beginning to realize that Gramps had not just professed his love for him in empty words or gestures. He had been proving it to him daily, in the most genuine way he knew how. In giving Jesse truth from the breath of his life, with the passing of each day, his grandfather was bestowing a priceless gift.

"No matter what happens, my boy, the ranch will always be here for you. A place of hope. A place of healing. When you feel alone, as you no doubt will at times, turn to what this means."

Gramps studied the library as though he was seeing it for the first time or for the last. "You know, it's a bit like this room full of books, full of ideas. If a book sits on the shelf unread, unexplored, it will never feed the hungry heart, comfort the sad, or enlighten the ignorant. Books can teach how to gain freedom, how to use it, and how to protect it."

"How can a book make someone free? Don't you have to fight for that?" Jesse asked. "Isn't that what you've taught me—to fight?"

"In one sense, yes, but in a higher sense, a different type of fight. Freedom comes from ideas. My daddy, who fought in the Civil War, explained that the slaves couldn't be freed simply by a proclamation or a war."

"They couldn't?"

"No. They were free the minute the idea of freedom began to grow in their hearts. And it was when this idea was fully ripened that the slaves could show others their freedom. The war just enabled it. And, my lad, in the same way, the idea, and the essence of the ranch, is far more powerful than the property specified on a thin sheet of paper." He paused a moment, while Jesse thought carefully about those words.

"When I realized this, I gained the absolute, essential reality of freedom. So many people don't even have a clue about this because they go through life with their eyes closed, bumping into obstacles, when it's as simple as opening their eyes.

"Every event in our lives brings us to a crossroad. We are free to make decisions about what to do. If we fall victim, giving up or running away, then we are defeated and destroyed. But if we meet it head-on, we grow in strength and courage. This is what builds our character, leading us to where we are ready for the next one that will make us even stronger. Often when everything is taken from us is when we can most clearly see all that we have."

The old man studied Jesse's face. He had been explaining something so profound it had taken him a lifetime to understand. The boy in turn would have plenty of time to wrestle with it and make it his own.

"We've spent a lot of time looking back on the past, but that was only to prepare you for what's to come," Gramps said slowly.

"What's to come?"

"I can't tell you about it."

"Can you see my future?" Jesse asked.

"Yes."

"Then please tell me."

"I cannot, my boy."

"Why not?"

"Because it's yours to experience. I can't rob you of that. I interfered with your mother and father. I've learned my lesson. I won't do it again."

His eyes enclosed the boy. His heart reached out to him. A tremendous burden had been lifted. He had held nothing back, now. Though shame tried to make him withhold telling his grandson his part in the story that had gone wrong, he should have known better. He had not the right to withhold what would enable Jesse to grow. Having said all, he could now rest. "Let's go out to the porch."

As though the old man's presence on the porch was a signal, the showers stopped. Just as he had forecasted, the showers had freshened and cleaned the air.

33

L ater that day, his grandfather had warned Jesse it was almost time to leave. Beyond the orchard, Dan drove the tractor preparing the back field for the harvest.

Jesse retraced his steps through the north side of the orchard, where now Felipe Diego and the workers demolished the checks, preparing for the impending walnut harvest. Over in the next field, the corn had ripened, ready for those who would soon begin picking. And he knew his uncle and cousins were at their place preparing for the rice harvest.

Though he now knew his entire story and felt closer to his grandfather than ever before, he still felt an aching sadness. He had never really felt a part of this place, though during the summer he had pretended he had. But now that he was leaving, his pretending would end. The harvest would take place whether he was here or not. He felt like the hawk circling high above, searching for what was elusive but what he needed, and at the same time watching everything happen without him.

At the foot of the stone cross, he pulled out a thick piece of butcher's paper from his pocket, and not exactly sure why this was important, he scooped a handful of soil and let the dirt sift through his fingers onto the paper. Folding the paper twice and tucking the ends in carefully, he stuffed the packet into his pocket.

Before grabbing his things for home, Jesse stopped at the garden, the only place on the ranch he had truly felt was his, because he had worked to earn it. Yet no comfort could be found. The shadow of loneliness followed him, knowing it would always be Grace's garden and not his. He etched every detail to memory. Somehow feeling he would never see it like this again, he made himself swallow gulps of the garden air in his efforts to take it with him.

He noticed that the scarecrow had fallen over. It was unlike his grandfather to let something remain in disrepair, so he set it upright. Finally, fatigued with trying to stop time from moving, knowing that the battle had already been decided, he gave in and let the hour overtake him.

Upstairs, he took a last look around his room. How simple it was; empty of his things, with no mark of him ever being there.

He hauled his duffle bag outside, where his grandfather waited. Searching the backfield, the old man looked for Dan to see if he was on his way in to say goodbye to his son.

By the time they had climbed into the Jeep, ready to leave, Jesse heard the tractor grow closer and, searching the road, saw his father navigating the diesel to the gate—the spot where the cousins had driven through.

Relieved that his dad had come to say goodbye, Jesse ran over to meet him. Straddling the fence, he waited while his dad maneuvered the tractor close by. Punctuating the air with its deafening clamor, the tractor made it perfect— or difficult— for goodbyes, depending on which side of the fence one was on.

"So long, Dad!" Jesse shouted above the noise.

Jumping from the tractor, Dan grabbed Jesse's hand. As he shook it, he seemed to examine his son as though he was sent to judge the quality of a neighbor's livestock. Driving the tractor had left him covered in dust from head to boots. The only place skin was visible was where the rain had left streaks on his face.

Jesse knew that for as long as he lived, he would never forget this image: himself on one side of the fence. His dad on the other, so covered in dust, as to be almost unrecognizable except for the intense blue eyes that could belong to no other.

Then, as though he answered the tractor's command to return to his work, his dad flicked his cigarette away and turned on his heel. "I have work to do," he shouted against the diesel's noise.

Climbing onto the massive machine, he hesitated for a moment and then shouted over. "Take care of yourself, Jesse! I'm sorry. Give your mother my regards."

"What, Dad?" Jesse said. His stomach turned as he grew tense. "Wait! What did you say?"

But the noise of the cruel machine swallowed his words. Looking as though he might repeat himself, his dad waved him off instead. Dan shoved the tractor into gear, then sat back as it jolted forward. Slamming down on the left brake caused the machine to make a sharp turn returning to the orchard where it would take him back to his work beyond the stone cross.

Jesse blinked tears from his eyes.

"Jesse," his grandfather yelled, "we've got to go, or you'll miss the train."

Taking one last look around, he noticed Stanza hurrying from the house to join her husband, who leaned over the garden fence. "You take *bueno* care. We miss you already." Raising her hands, she held them in a blessing, and in a loud voice as if wanting all the Eastside to hear, she pronounced her benediction: "*Puede usted caminar con el valiente y duerme con los angeles, con el Dios en su lado, no teniendo ningun miedo siempre otra vez.*"

After crossing herself, she leaned onto her husband's shoulder.

Climbing into the Jeep, Jesse asked his grandfather what she had said. Gramps told him he had heard her say it to many who would embark on their journey away. "It means, 'May you walk with the brave and sleep with the angels, with God at your side, having no fear ever again.'"

In town, Jesse waited in the Jeep while his grandfather went to the railway office. Returning with a timetable and a couple of root beers, Gramps led the way to the courthouse steps. They sipped their sodas in silence staring at the tracks. Because most everyone was preparing for the harvest, the town seemed deserted. Only the statues on the courthouse steps seemed unaffected by the emptiness.

"How many I've seen leave here." Gramps finally spoke.

"I remember the day Elizabeth left. No one had come to see her off. When she climbed the train's steps, she looked around to see if anyone had come. Though she didn't see me, I was here.

"Then a few years later, I watched your mother leave." He took a sip of soda.

"Departures are never easy," he whispered.

.   .   .

After fifteen minutes, the train's whistle came from behind the grove of cottonwoods at the sunrise edge of Market Street. At first the street vibrated, then a few moments later, the pavement shook as the train stopped at their feet.

Jesse promised himself he would not cry; his face ached for the too many tears already shed. Though it took everything he had, he wanted his grandfather to see him off without any tears.

Jesse shook the rough old hand—rough from a lifetime of giving. Gramps stared straight into the lad's eyes. "You'll do all right because you're a Hunter. Now, be off with you!"

"But, Gramps, I'm going to miss you so—"

"You're not alone," the old man pronounced before turning to leave. But then as though he had almost forgotten the most important, he told Jesse, "Look to Orion. I'll be there."

Jesse promised himself he would not board until Gramps turned around for a final goodbye. But the old man didn't ... he wouldn't; his heart couldn't take it.

Following the conductor, who disappeared inside the Pullman

car, Jesse settled into a seat at the window. He sized up the other passengers, but no one looked his way. Searching the deserted street for his grandfather, he caught just a corner of the Jeep as it slipped around the corner.

As the train gathered speed, he felt that a permanent rift was taking place in the earth—a huge chasm that no bridge would be long or strong enough to span. He on one side, his grandfather, and the ranch on the other.

"Young fella," the conductor said as he punched Jesse's ticket. "If there's anything you need to make your trip more enjoyable, just let me know. OK?"

Astounded to see that the conductor seemed unaware, he wanted to shout out, *Can't you feel it? Can't you see it?*

But he could only bring himself to whisper, "Thanks. I'll be okay."

34

The tipping point for Jesse was the minute the train crossed the county line. It was at this juncture he knew the Pullman car had begun to shrink with each mile it got closer to home. But it was not until the county line he discerned evidence. And as the train continued into town, if he didn't quickly discover a way to escape, he was convinced he'd be crushed.

Instantly, he felt hedged in on all sides. He could even feel it in his chest. Unable to expand his lungs and breathe in, he felt as though his chest had been tightly wrapped.

Jesse knew that coming home would not be easy. Every year proved difficult in severing his ties from the ranch. But this one would be the hardest. He had begun to realize this when his grandfather was in the middle of his story. And safely rooted in the ranch, during the summer, he had pretended there would be no end to those days. As the train pulled into the station, the reality was that he was home and there was nothing he could do about it. He was a felon who had been recaptured after tasting freedom, knowing he could not bring that back with him.

When the train came to a screeching stop, he resolved to accept

339

his fate and be kind to his mother and try to get along with Jack. He grabbed his duffle bag, jumped down the steps, and trudged towards his mother's car. But feeling the emptiness already, he wondered if he could keep his resolution.

Catching sight of Jesse, Lynn waved and then blew her nose. Surveying the parking lot for his stepfather, he smiled. What was he thinking? Jack had never met him at the station. He still had the ride home with his mother before meeting his jailer, who would lock the cell door behind him.

How could two worlds be so different from each other? Or how could one person conceive of two worlds at the same time? He knew it was impossible to think two thoughts at the same time. And that's what caused him the most concern. How could he bring here what he had learned?

Maybe what his grandfather had taught him only made sense on the Eastside and was worthless here. Jesse had known a degree of freedom living on the ranch with his grandfather. And yet he thought that in a sense, the summer of his fifteenth year was not spent in true freedom, but in learning what it felt like and how to attain it.

To be free, he must fight his own fight and make it his own, as Gramps had warned. How could he fight Jack and his mother? He couldn't strike out on his own. He had no money or place to go.

. . .

In the first few days at home, he tried to adjust but found it nearly impossible to reconcile the two worlds. And yet, he found if he pushed the ranch and his grandfather out of his mind, it was almost bearable. He spoke to no one of it, and his silence was interpreted as what his mother called his "post-summer brooding."

How could they understand what he had experienced, seen, felt? How could he make them understand he had circled the earth while they remained below, stuck in and unaware of their one-dimensional lives, aware of nothing above?

Remembering the suppers when he and his grandfather had

discussed many things that summer, he found it foreign to sit across from Jack at the dinner table. Those pale hands, holding up the newspaper against his mother and him every night at the table, made any discussion impossible.

It wasn't that Jesse faulted Jack for working indoors in an office, his skin untouched by the sun. It wasn't even because his slicked-back hair had never felt the weight of a hat or that he had never ridden a horse. No. This wasn't it. It was that his mother and Jack possessed no real life. His mother existed in a world where the papers she moved from one department to another were the visible end result of her day. And Jack seemed to be in perpetual conflict with everyone he met—from juvenile delinquents to the "moronic" judges determining his cases. They seemed to move lifelessly through the motions, measured by the clocks on the walls of their everyday schedules.

This was so unlike the farmers who worked from sunup to sundown, at one with their work. Farming was a life, not an occupation detailed in a job description, paid bi-monthly with two weeks' vacation. Did Jack even know that fruit fresh from the tree tastes distinctly different from those that sit chilled in the grocery store bins? Did he even know there was such a thing as a blood orange?

In the country, the farmers were honest because the land was honest. They wasted no time in fooling themselves or others, and if they tried, they would be quickly found out. Time was precious and there was nothing to be gained from throwing it away on activities where there was no movement towards their goals. Their days were full of hard work and an unwavering faith in what they were doing and what nature had given them to do.

Working solitary most of the time, the farmers were compelled to spend many hours in contemplation. They could not run from, but were forced to confront, what they were thinking. An open field provides no place in which to hide. And the sun will illuminate a shadowed orchard.

Exactly two weeks after Jesse left the ranch, he was sitting at the dinner table, picking at his TV dinner, when the phone rang.

He reached for it, as the voice behind the newspaper warned, "Don't answer it!"

"Hello?" Jesse said.

"Goddammit. I said not to pick it up!" Jack growled through his paper. "No phone calls during dinner!"

Jesse plugged his other ear and turned away.

"Jesse?" the voice on the phone asked.

"Yes? Uncle Colton! It's you! I miss you guys—"

"What's wrong?" his uncle asked. "Who's yelling in the background?"

Jack threw down his paper and began howling at Lynn, who raised her hands in a futile effort, begging him to stop.

Jesse cupped his hand around the transmitter. "Oh. That? Uh … it's nothing. It's the nightly news. There was a murder somewhere in town."

"Listen, my boy. I have some bad news."

"Bad news?"

"Jesse. I can't think of an easy way to say this. Your grandfather died last night."

Jesse knew he hadn't heard correctly. But somehow, he had lost his voice to tell his uncle they had a bad connection, and he should try again.

"Stanza found him just before she left for the night. She had finished cleaning up the supper dishes and went out to tell Dad goodnight. But he … was … gone. She found him sitting in his chair under the oak. There was an old drawing of the farmhouse on his lap. He was so peaceful, she said. She thought he had fallen asleep. Brownie and Tex were at his feet."

It was a strange position in which Jesse found himself, standing precisely at the point between two worlds—between darkness and light. The two cannot exist at the same time in the same place. He knew that when his uncle hung up, the light would disappear, and the darkness would overtake him.

He shook himself. "He couldn't die!"

"You know," his uncle continued, "I knew he wasn't feeling well. I could tell he had been slowing down this summer. The doctors said his heart had been failing."

There it was again, drawing tighter and tighter, that feeling in his chest. He could not breathe. The room began to shrink, and he broke out in sweat. He wanted to shout out anything to convince his uncle there had been a mistake. Stanza was wrong. His grandfather was only asleep. He could picture him finishing his chores. Why couldn't they see it? He couldn't be dead. It was impossible to conceive.

"He just wore out, son," his uncle continued. "He had a full life. A good life. I'm so glad that you got to be with him this summer."

Jesse thought about the birds flying wild before he opened the grain barn doors. A thousand random thoughts flew at him. So many seemed unimportant and silly. He couldn't put them in any order.

"Uncle Colton, what about the little cottage—the Jaeger house? There were some pictures and a World War I uniform—"

"Oh, son, I'm sorry to have to tell you. Just a few days ago, that and everything in it was destroyed by a fire. Dad was heartbroken."

Jesse was stunned.

"Are you okay, son?" Colton asked. "I know this news is a shock. But you know your grandfather thought the world of you. In fact, you know ... well, you knew that your aunt was in St. Louis this summer. Mother had a daughter from a previous marriage, named Elizabeth. I guess the girls told you already. Anyway, Lil discovered that Elizabeth had died years before."

Colton added quickly, "It's very involved, so I won't trouble you with the particulars now, but when your grandfather learned this, he decided to leave the ranch to you."

"The ranch, mine?" Jesse whispered. Turning his back to his mother and Jack, he asked, "Uncle Colton, Is there a funeral or something? I mean ... can I come up?"

"No. Pal, Dad didn't want any. After Mother died, he made us promise that we wouldn't have any services. I'm sorry.

"What's that?" Colton said speaking to someone in the background. "Oh, Jesse, Lil and the girls send their love. I'd better go for now. I'll call you in a few weeks. I hope you'll be okay. Give your mother my regards. Take care, nephew!"

When he hung up the phone, true enough, he found himself in a room of darkness, very much alone. He was desperate to connect with his grandfather. How could he accept that he would never see him again?

Lynn knew that somehow her son had changed this summer. He seemed much older than his fifteen years. The little characteristics he brought back with him, which usually disappeared after a few days of being home, did not go away this time. As she had done every year when Jesse returned, she had inventoried the usual changes, tanner, taller, blonder hair. But there was something additional this year.

Over the years, she had harbored the fear that he might turn out like Dan. But she could now see her fears were unnecessary. She could discern a depth of understanding clear in his speech and bearing, something she had admired in the boy's grandfather but never found in the boy's father.

Jesse stood motionless after hanging up the phone. It was almost déjà vu to Lynn. It reminded her of the time when he was about six or seven and she was supposed to pick him up at the train station. She was in the middle of something and had lost track of time. Rounding the corner, she caught a glimpse of him, alone. Her heart almost broke to see him standing there, not moving, not sure what to do. And yet, there was an almost tangible feeling that he was working something out in his mind, trying to resolve whatever it was. This is what he looked like at this moment.

"Jesse, what's the matter? Why did your uncle call?"

"Gramps died," he blurted out.

"Oh. My God!" Her hand flew to her mouth.

Jack, who was in the middle of deciding whether he should put his paper down, peeked over the edge.

"I'm ... sorry..." Clearly, he was stumbling for something appropriate. "But he was just an old man. I guess it was his time."

"Did your uncle give you any details?" his mother asked. "How did he die? When—"

"Mom, I can't talk right now."

"But, honey, you should talk about—"

"I don't want to talk about it now!"

Jack threw back his chair and jumped up. His face began to transform into that sour look that materialized when he began to work himself up. "Listen here. I don't like your tone. No punk is going to talk to his mother—"

"Jack!" Lynn pleaded.

"I won't have it." He turned to her. "I don't care what's happened."

Another night of fighting. Why did it have to start tonight?

"Stop it!" Jesse yelled out.

Jack's face twisted up in his ugly way.

Who was this person? Jesse wondered. Why had he been afraid of him all these years? He was nobody. He had no power. What could he possibly do to him now?

"Don't even mention my grandfather. You're not even good enough to say his name."

"Jesse!" Lynn yelled.

"You little punk!" Jack's face turned almost purple. "No son of mine will speak to me like that!"

"Your son? Don't ever say that word to me. I'm nothing to you. You're nothing to me."

Anticipating Jack's lunge toward Jesse, Lynn jumped in his path, trying to grab his arm. But he shook her off and shoved her out of the way. She fell back against the table.

"Jack. No!" she pleaded. "Please, Jack. Not tonight!"

"Don't talk to me like that, you little sniveling creep," Jack yelled at Jesse. "I deal with your type in juvenile hall all day long."

"I'm not afraid of you anymore. You're nothing! You don't even exist!"

Lunging towards him again, Jack crouched into a boxer's stance. "You want a piece of me? Come on, you little creep. Just try!" He clenched his fists in front of his face, hungering for a jab at Jesse.

Jack looked ludicrous, and the scene was ridiculous. This wasn't supposed to be real.

Impatient with Jesse's hesitation, Jack jumped towards him with his left fist lunging for Jesse's face. Though Jesse didn't feel any fear, he still couldn't imagine slugging Jack. Without really thinking about what he would do, he ended up kicking Jack in the inside of his thigh.

Losing his balance, the man fell headfirst into the door jamb and then bounced back, stunned. He landed on the floor next to Lynn, gasping for air like a guppy out of water.

Jesse dashed into his room, slammed the door shut, and wedged a chair under the doorknob.

"You little shit!" Jack coughed and sputtered.

Footsteps pounded down the hall. "Let me in right now!" Jack began kicking at the door. "I'll bust the goddamn thing in if you don't! You know I will!"

Stuffing some things into a duffle bag, Jesse heard his mother pleading with Jack from the kitchen. He popped the screen from the window and jumped out, leaving Jack kicking at the door behind him.

. . .

Halfway down the block, Jesse jumped in the street. A car narrowly missed him; the driver laid on the horn. His head felt as though it would burst. "It's all right. It's all right," he told himself. "Oh, Gramps! I need you!"

Running down the other side of the street, he checked over his shoulder, before reaching the park. At the far edge of the park stood an ancient oak tree that he threw himself against.

If only he could get back to the ranch, where he could find peace. If he could only see the river. But how could he get back? There was no going back now. No, it would be worse, knowing that his grandfather was no longer there. There was no escape. He was hopelessly trapped.

The loop of the tape of the scene at home kept replaying. How typical it was. It was not something new. But why was this night different? Ah, he had stood up to Jack for the first time. He had decided not to wake up from the nightmare but to confront it head-on. That was what was new.

What made him do it? He had never been able to before. He recalled his uncle had told him that sometimes when you stop running from what you fear the most, to face it, it stops running after you. And his grandfather had spent the entire summer encouraging and teaching him just how to do this. He knew he would never be afraid of Jack again.

He must have had a premonition this night might happen. Returning home from the ranch, he had hidden his duffle bag under his bed, thinking he would be prepared for a quick escape. He had thrown some clean clothes from his closet into the laundry, so his mother wouldn't be suspicious.

From that bag, Jesse now pulled out the old leather box that his grandfather gave him the day in the library. Carefully he pulled the objects from their wrapping of newspaper. Vividly, he recalled the afternoon in the library with his grandfather.

"I know that when you return home, you may not remember all that I've told you this summer. But I want you to have these to remind you of my words.

"The twenty-dollar gold piece minted the year I left for France—my mother thrust into my hand the day I climbed aboard the train to go to the war. She whispered to me that the gold signified the protection of her golden love.

"As gold is the most precious metal on earth, so is love the most priceless in heaven," the strong voice went on. "Alchemists throughout the centuries have tried to find a way to change base metals into the most precious and priceless. They were working from the wrong basis. It can be done. But it's love that will change anything into something priceless. Love is, indeed, what will protect you and carry you through."

Carefully returning the coin to its place, Jesse unwrapped the next bundle where the detailed work of his grandfather's gold pocket watch struck him once again.

"My family brought this watch from Scotland. Though time is important and seemingly necessary in this world, it pales in significance to the gold, value of eternity which transcends the limitations of this world.

"Time is an imposter. There is an old saying my father used to say when we would fret about the lack of time, '*Tempus concedeo adeo aeterneum nunc.*' It's Latin for 'Time concedes to the eternal now.' Now is the only time to be concerned with. We cannot live in the past, though we may have to correct or reconcile ourselves with it, but we can't 'live' it. And the future is not somewhere we can escape. Now is where we always are and now the only place we can ever live."

Returning the watch next to the coin with care, Jesse took out the photograph of a small boy in a sailor outfit—his grandfather.

"Unless you approach life with childlike innocence, trust, and faith," the old man explained, "you'll miss all the value of life around you. Most people think innocence is weakness or vulnerability. But innocence is power. When you remain innocent, you are not guilty of anything. If not guilty of wrongdoing, you are not captive, and with freedom, you possess power. You have the power and strength to do whatever you will need to do. But it is not enough to know this; you must claim it."

The last object Jesse removed was a faded remnant of an American flag. In the shape of a star, attached in the middle, was a photograph of his grandfather taken at the time he had gone off to war.

Gramps had told him about people putting these in their windows during the war to show their family's contribution to their country. Their willingness to fight and risk their lives for the good of others. "Sacrifice is necessary and important if it contributes to the good of all," as Gramps had put it.

"The greatest happiness I have ever known was in doing something for others. I had gone off to war for my country. I built the farmhouse for Grace. I maintained the garden to her memory. I was a farmer because the fruits of my labor were necessary and enjoyed by others. I gave my sons the benefit of this learning, and I had bequeathed the ranch to my wife's daughter, proving my sincerity in the face of deception and hatred. Over the years, this unselfishness has brought me such joy."

The voice of his grandfather faded into the sound of Jesse's sobbing.

Gently folding the flag, he returned it with the other keepsakes to the box. He tasted the warm salt water on his lips. His were not only tears of grief but also tears of change. Things would never be the same. Wiping the tears from his eyes with his young farmer's hands, he laced his fingers behind his head and lay back to watch the squirrel scramble up the branches.

And the familiar voice returned.

> *"I and many others around me have weathered many storms in our lives. But I always came back to the peace and security the ranch offered. This is what gave me the strength to endure life's many lessons."*

. . .

As the sun fell below the horizon and darkness enveloped him, Jesse felt as though the whole world was very quiet. Searching the night sky above the oak, he found the North Star and followed the line of stars until he came to Ursa Major, where he saw his grandfather's star, shining as brightly as Grace's. Orion the hunter was up in the sky and would never be far away from him again.

How strange, he felt, he hadn't thought about this in a long time. Yet it was very much like his feeling on the ranch when he studied the night sky that night. The realization that he was a part of this vast forever—he did belong. And yet it was even more profound—it was that this vast forever wasn't out there, but in him. He couldn't lose it because it was him.

There was a time when he could not have been more than five years old, he and his mother had been out walking alone in the dark. Apparently after a fight with Jack, she was sobbing about having no place to go and how scared she was. Though it was dark, he knew she was wrong. There was no reason to be scared, because holding her hand tightly, he wasn't scared.

And he recalled trying to think of something to say to make her feel better. Searching the sky, it seemed to him that the sparkling array of stars kept them company and safe. He wondered what the stars were made of and how they stayed up there. Then it dawned on him with a great profundity that only a five-year-old can have. He wondered why no one had ever told him before. What looked to be stars were simply small pinprick holes in the dark fabric of the sky. What made them sparkle, and the source of their brightness was only one powerful light shining behind.

He remembered telling his mother that somehow, if he could just reach high enough, he would grab the sky and pull it down. And there, he believed, the amazing light would surround them, leaving them warm and forever safe.

Now, resting on his duffle bag, staring at the sky, he felt safe and somewhat content, as though he needed nothing but to be here forever. He realized his grandfather was still happy. He imagined the reunion the old man might have with Grace and Will in their chairs around the oak tree. He knew if that were true, they had a lifetime of memories to catch up on. Jesse felt a peace draw over him. It was all as it was supposed to be.

"Gramps," he said out loud to his star, "one day, I'm going to pull down the sky. Then we'll be together again."

35

Summer 1980

J esse enjoyed the prospect of the lush lawn dotted by different shapes of gravestones and host to the many trees. Serene and majestic stood the eucalyptus, oak, weeping willow, and black walnut trees. Swimming ducks with their wiggling rears broke the surface of a small pond reflecting the cloudless sky. He had to admit, though it was a graveyard, it was a beautiful park.

His three children were still immersed in their games, darting among the granite and marble markers, their voices carried from the older part, where they were captivated with the larger, carved stones. Trading the dates gathered from each stone, they shouted to one another. The hopeful winner was looking for the oldest dates. With some difficulty, they made out some of those nearly faded from the weathered marble.

Under the canopy, Alix sat by the mound of flowers that hid his father's grave. She searched her pockets for a handkerchief. He was touched but knew that all things requiring resolution affected her like this. She sometimes lingered too long on the surface of a problem, even if this meant that she suffered more than she needed to.

351

Feeling an immediate need, he went to her. Taking her hand, he gently squeezed it and said, "Anything."

For the family had a signal among themselves. Sometimes when holding hands with the children, they would convey their silent message by a gentle squeeze. This meant, "I love you more than ..." followed by a word. It was just a simple gesture that was meaningful when offered at the right time.

Squeezing his hand in return, she smiled, then began to laugh between her tears.

"Why did your dad contest your grandfather's will and take the ranch from you?"

"I suppose he felt he had worked for it, and it belonged to him."

"Do you regret not having it?"

"In the beginning, certainly I did. I was very angry. But not anymore. It's been right here. "He pointed to his chest. "All these years. That can never be taken away."

"What a waste," she said. "He denied himself the joy of his son and three grandchildren. Why did he keep himself so far from the joy life affords?"

He shook his head in wonder. "Instead, he lived in only its disappointments. I don't know why. I ask myself that a lot."

"I'm sorry." She dabbed her eyes. "I'm being silly. You should be the one with tears. I never knew the man."

"It's okay. Neither did I."

"Should we go?" she asked.

Jesse recognized a gathering of lilac blooms at the grave. Someone must have brought them from the ranch's garden.

"Yes, in a minute. I've got one last thing to do."

She nodded and left to join the children.

Wondering what to say or think now, he had already said goodbye to this man, years before. But he had brought something that he had kept over the years, deciding to offer it here. Reaching deep into his pocket, he pulled out a plastic bag. Inside was a yellowed piece of butcher paper wrapped around a boy's handful of soil. How many years ago had he gathered this from one grave, now to be left at another?

Standing directly over the flowers, he whispered, "I have much to do. Take care of yourself, Dad! Give Gramps my regards."

Then he emptied the packet onto his palm and watched as the soil, like the sand in an hourglass, fell slowly from his farmer's hands around the flowers to the grave below.

He stepped into the warm sun and went towards his family.

Alix asked, "When you were resting on the stone bench, what were you thinking? Were you thinking about your grandfather and his ranch?"

"Yes, I thought about it all."

The children yelled out familiar names read from the stones to him. Grabbing his hand, Tyler led him to a place he wanted him to see. Stopping in front of a massive cross, the boy pointed to a large carved angel resting on top.

"Look, Daddy. Look. An angel. What do the words say?"

Jesse read aloud: *"Blessed are they that have not seen, and yet have believed."*

"Dad." His daughters were interested in what had captivated Tyler. "What does that mean? Seen what?" Clare asked.

"How can you believe something if you don't see it?" Jordan chimed in.

"I guess it means that some things that are very valuable cannot be seen. We just must know they're there."

Though it was too early to see the constellation of Orion and pick out his grandfather's star, he knew the old man was there. "Thank you, Gramps," he whispered.

Acknowledgments

Everyone must realize that a book doesn't just happen without a lot of support and input. I'd like to express my appreciation and gratitude to some specific people who were so helpful in getting this novel out in a published form.

- Emily Carmain at Editor Noteworthy Editing. Thank you, Emily, for being persistent and encouraging, and paring this novel down to a manageable form without risk to the story.
- David Gerhard, Illustrator of Oak Tree. Thank you to my son-in-law for his artistic interpretation of the meaningful Oak Tree.
- Thank you to my three amazing children, Whitney, Lindsay, and Zachary, who inspired me to write up some stories to share with them while they were growing up, which later grew into this novel.
- Donna, my patient wife who not only read the first iteration of the novel, but after years of my doubting, encouraged me to bring it to fruition.

About the Author

David D. Boggs is an avid reader and book collector. In his library of over six thousand books, he has collected many of his favorites on philosophy, political science, world and ancient history, classic literature, biographies, and religious studies. After many years as an executive in California, and now retired, he has the time to devote himself to his many construction projects, traveling, gardening, teaching Sunday school, and holding church services at the local military facility in South Carolina where David and his wife live. Growing up, he was very grateful to have spent many summers with his grandfather on his ranch. This novel is the result of these meaningful memories.

www.ingramcontent.com/pod-product-compliance
Lightning Source LLC
Chambersburg PA
CBHW021344130726
47899CB00018B/2947